The Measure of Manliness

Corporealities: Discourses of Disability

Points of Contact: Disability, Art, and Culture
    edited by Susan Crutchfield and Marcy Epstein
A History of Disability
    by Henri-Jacques Stiker
Narrative Prosthesis: Disability and the Dependencies of Discourse
    by David T. Mitchell and Sharon L. Snyder
Backlash Against the ADA: Reinterpreting Disability Rights
    edited by Linda Hamilton Krieger
The Staff of Oedipus: Transforming Disability in Ancient Greece
    by Martha L. Rose
Fictions of Affliction: Physical Disability in Victorian Culture
    by Martha Stoddard Holmes
Foucault and the Government of Disability
    edited by Shelley Tremain
Bodies in Commotion: Disability and Performance
    edited by Carrie Sandahl and Philip Auslander
Moving Beyond Prozac, DSM, *and the New Psychiatry: The Birth of Postpsychiatry*
    by Bradley Lewis
Disability in Twentieth-Century German Culture
    by Carol Poore
Concerto for the Left Hand: Disability and the Defamiliar Body
    by Michael Davidson
Disability Theory
    by Tobin Siebers
The Songs of Blind Folk: African American Musicians and the Cultures of Blindness
    by Terry Rowden
Signifying Bodies: Disability in Contemporary Life Writing
    by G. Thomas Couser
Disability Aesthetics
    by Tobin Siebers
Stumbling Blocks Before the Blind: Medieval Constructions of a Disability
    by Edward Wheatley
Mad at School: Rhetorics of Mental Disability and Academic Life
    by Margaret Price
The Metanarrative of Blindness: A Re-reading of Twentieth-Century Anglophone Writing
    by David Bolt
Shakin' All Over: Popular Music and Disability
    by George McKay
American Lobotomy: A Rhetorical History
    by Jenell Johnson
The Measure of Manliness: Disability and Masculinity in the Mid-Victorian Novel
    by Karen Bourrier

The Measure of Manliness

*Disability and Masculinity
in the Mid-Victorian Novel*

KAREN BOURRIER

University of Michigan Press
Ann Arbor

Copyright © by Karen Bourrier 2015
All rights reserved

This book may not be reproduced, in whole or in part, including illustrations, in any form (beyond that copying permitted by Sections 107 and 108 of the U.S. Copyright Law and except by reviewers for the public press), without written permission from the publisher.

Published in the United States of America by the
University of Michigan Press
Manufactured in the United States of America
♾ Printed on acid-free paper

2018 2017 2016 2015   4 3 2 1

A CIP catalog record for this book is available from the British Library.

ISBN 978-0-472-07248-4 (hardcover)
ISBN 978-0-472-05248-6 (paperback)
ISBN 978-0-472-12083-3 (e-book)

Acknowledgments

I am grateful to many people and institutions for their support of this book. The Social Science and Humanities Research Council of Canada (SSHRC) provided a doctoral grant at the very beginning of this project, and then a timely postdoctoral grant that allowed me to complete the manuscript. A James and Sylvia Thayer Research grant enabled me to consult the Mulock Family Papers, which made their way into chapter 2. Audiences at the North American Victorian Studies Association conferences at Purdue and Yale universities, the City University of New York's Victorian studies conference on "Victorian Boyhoods," the Centre for the Humanities and Health at King's College London, and the Harvard Victorian Studies Colloquium provided valuable feedback on this project at various stages. I'd like to thank two journals for permission to reproduce parts of this project that appeared earlier. Part of the introduction appeared in different form in *Nineteenth-Century Contexts* 36.1 (2014) as "Orthopaedic Disability and the Nineteenth-Century Novel." Part of chapter 1 appeared in earlier form in the *Victorian Review* 35.2 (2009) as "'The Spirit of a Man and the Limbs of a Cripple': Disability, Masculinity, and Sentimentality in Charlotte Yonge's *The Heir of Redclyffe*." I am grateful to my editor, LeAnn Fields, and to everyone at the University of Michigan Press, who treated the manuscript with tremendous consideration. I would like to thank Clinton Machann and two anonymous peer reviewers for their helpful reports. Thanks to David Mitchell and Sharon Snyder, the editors of the University of Michigan Press's series in disability studies, of which I am very pleased to be a part.

At Cornell University, where this project began as a doctoral dissertation, Shirley Samuels, Paul Sawyer, Harry Shaw, and especially my chair, James Eli Adams, supported this project through its early stages and beyond. My writing group at Cornell, Ashly Bennett, Peter A. A. Bailey, and David Coombs, read early drafts of this work with enthusiasm; their comments were crucial in shaping the direction of the project, and their friendship continues to sustain me.

I was fortunate as a junior scholar to land in the Boston area, where I found a convivial and helpful group of Victorianists. I am grateful to many people, including Mary Wilson Carpenter, Laura Green, Kelly Hager, Anna Henchman, Sebastian Lecourt, Maia McAleavey, John Plotz, Matthew Rubery, David Russell, and especially Martha Vicinus, organizer of the Boston Reading Group, for their helpful suggestions and companionship in all things Victorian. At Boston University, I am grateful to Joseph Bizup, Aaron Garrett, Christopher Walsh, and my colleagues in the College of Arts and Sciences Writing Program, who supported me at a crucial stage in the development of this book, and to the students in my seminar Disability in Contemporary American Culture for their lively discussions of disability today. I am also grateful to the faculty writing group at BU, especially Ivan Eubanks, Gwen Kordonowy, and Diane Greco Josefowicz for their support and helpful comments on the manuscript.

A SSHRC postdoctoral fellowship at Western University came at the perfect time to enable me to complete the manuscript. At Western, Christopher Keep has been a source of support from my early graduate school days to the present. I am grateful to the contributors to *Nineteenth-Century Disability: Cultures and Contexts*, www.nineteenthcenturydisability.org, which began at Western, for keeping nineteenth-century disability studies fresh and exciting and for sharing their research with the public online. Thanks are due to my new colleagues at the University of Calgary for their enthusiasm for this project. I have also benefited more than I can say from the mentorship and friendship of Alice Eardley, Jennifer Esmail, Christine Ferguson, Sally Mitchell, Talia Schaffer, Martha Stoddard Holmes, and Vanessa Warne.

Last but not least, I would like to thank my family. Jackie, Michelle, Greg, Larry, Lori, Carol, and Emma kept me grounded. To my Mémère, who reread *The Mill on the Floss* and agreed with me that Maggie Tulliver should have married Philip Wakem. And to my parents, Richard and Louise, who encouraged my love of reading and writing from the start.

Finally, for Dave, who has lived with this project as long as I have. This book is for him.

Contents

Introduction: Men of Feeling 1

1. Charles Kingsley's and Charlotte Yonge's Christian Chivalry 26
2. Invalidism and Industry in Dinah Mulock Craik's *John Halifax, Gentleman* 52
3. Tom Tulliver's Schooldays 76
4. The Portrait of Two Gentlemen: Henry James's Invalids and Self-Made Men 103

Conclusion: Modern Men 123

NOTES 137

BIBLIOGRAPHY 157

INDEX 169

Introduction

Men of Feeling

[W]e think the lavish mutilation of heroes' bodies, which has become the habit of novelists, while it happily does not represent probabilities in the present state of things, weakens instead of strengthening tragic effect.
—George Eliot, Review of *Westward Ho!*

We have had for heroes the consumptive, the insane, the inane, the hunchbacked, the lame, and the blind.
—Justin McCarthy, *Paul Massie*

George Eliot and Justin McCarthy, writing in 1854 and 1866, respectively, are responding to a vogue for disabled men in the novels of the mid–nineteenth century. Both writers are skeptical of the proliferation of disability in the novel. Eliot finds it fortunate that heroes in real life are not as likely as Rochester, Romney Leigh, and Amyas Leigh to end up maimed, while McCarthy complains that disabled protagonists have become so commonplace that one has no choice but to endow one's hero with a clubfoot or a consumption. The fact that Eliot and McCarthy feel compelled to comment on this trope attests to how widespread the figure of the disabled man had become in the mid-nineteenth-century novel. Novelists who gained reputations for writing about characters with disabilities include Charlotte Yonge and Dinah Mulock Craik, who remain known for their portraits of invalids, but authors, including

Charles Kingsley, Thomas Hughes, Henry James, and George Eliot, to name but a few, all wrote about weak and disabled men as emotionally compelling characters.

Why was there a proliferation of masculine weakness and disability in the mid-nineteenth-century novel? Even in novels by muscular Christian writers like Charles Kingsley and Thomas Hughes, which praise a muscular manhood as best fitted to take on the tasks of modern life, masculine disability and weakness remain a persistent presence. This unexpected interest in masculine weakness and disability seemed to be a response to the rise of a new Victorian culture of industry and vitality, and its corollary emphasis on a hardy, active manhood. The muscular Christian hero of the 1850s was a broad church man who was more interested in rowing than debating the finer points of theology, and whose worship was all the healthier for it. Related to the muscular Christian was the self-made man, a captain of industry championed by midcentury thinkers like Thomas Carlyle, whose masculine virility translated into the healthy work ethic, and whose business decisions were most often made by instinct rather than intellect. It was difficult to describe the muscular Christian hero or the self-made man precisely because he had few distinguishing features. At the end of the century, Margaret Oliphant described this "ideal young man of Victorian romance" as a "fine athlete, moderately good scholar, and honest, frank, muscular, and humble-minded gentleman" (493). By contrast to this strong hero, who is mainly distinguished by his athletic prowess, the weak or disabled man was physically distinct and able to articulate his feelings, as well as narrating those of his stronger friend. In his memoirs, Walter Scott connected the experience of being lamed as an infant to his storytelling abilities. "My lameness and my solitary habits had made me a tolerable reader," he writes, "and my hours of leisure were usually spent in reading aloud to my mother" (Lockhart 36). The figure of the voluble weak man was a necessary narrative complement to the silent strong man. The crippled male embodied traditionally feminine virtues, softening the taciturn strong man and eliciting emotional depths from his seemingly coarse, muscular frame. Yet the weak man was able to follow the strong man where female characters could not, to all-male arenas such as the warehouse and the public school. This pairing led to a formal innovation in literature: the focalization or narration of the novel through the perspective of a weak or disabled man. This narrative innovation demonstrates how, far from being marginalized in a culture that prized health and industry, weakness and disability came to serve an integral role in shaping narrative form, and ideals of what it meant to be a man in the Victorian era and beyond.

The weak or disabled man thus often appeared as a friend or rival of the strong protagonist and took on the affective and narrative burdens that would undermine the hero's strength. Male invalidism and disability persisted as an alternative and complementary Victorian mode of masculinity, supplementing masculine strength, which might otherwise appear coarse and unfeeling, with loquaciousness and susceptibility. Within a disability studies framework, the pairing of the strong man and the weak man is part of a system of characterization in which the otherwise illegible contours of the protagonist's normalcy are filled out by the oddities of disabled supporting characters. Lennard Davis suggests that deviance is at the core of normalcy, writing that "to understand the disabled body, one must return to the concept of the norm, the normal body" (*Enforcing Normalcy* 23). A key tenet of disability studies is that "seemingly neutral norms" exist only in contrast to forms of deviance (Garland-Thomson 6). The pairing of the strong man and the weak man enacts the construction of these masculine norms, and also serves a structural purpose as the ascendancy of the strong man is often narrated or focalized through the point of view of the weak man.

Theories of Emotion and Disability in Literature and Medicine

Weak or disabled characters were cast in this role as narrator figures because of the emotional depth that was increasingly presumed to accompany the experience of physical disability. As disability studies scholar Martha Stoddard Holmes has argued in *Fictions of Affliction*, the Victorians constructed "physical disability as primarily a *feeling* state" (29). The assumption that a physical disability would engender mental suffering, both for the person with a disability and for the onlookers who sympathized with him, gave rise to the idea that the disabled body was a feeling body. Stoddard Holmes writes, "Nineteenth-century literature recurrently and problematically represented disability as primarily an emotional state—in that it evoked sympathy and pity in onlookers, and feelings of isolation and despair in the disabled—rather than a social or medical problem" (3–4). This mode of viewing disability tends to shift the focus on disability as a problem with the individual rather than a broader social problem. Stoddard Holmes writes that "constructing physical disability primarily as a *feeling* state" minimizes "the importance of the material circumstances that surround all disabilities" and maximizes "the importance of personal agency while minimizing the need for social change" (28–29, emphasis original).

This theory of the feeling disabled man was anchored in nineteenth-century medical literature as well as in the novel. Midcentury surgical treatises on orthopedic surgery speculated about the psychological effect a highly visible deformity might have on a man as part of the justification for operating.[1] In 1846 surgeon R. W. Tamplin defined orthopedic deformity as "any and every deviation from the recognised symmetrical proportions of the human frame" (*Lectures on the Nature and Treatment of Deformities* 2). By the mid–nineteenth century, orthopedic surgery was fast becoming, to quote the surgeon William Adams, "what is called a specialty, or special branch of Surgery," which treated a wide assortment of "deformities" from hunchback, to "club-foot, contracted knee, wry-neck, contracted fingers, &c." (*Curvature of the Spine* 9). The Royal Orthopaedic Hospital of London, which began as a small institution in Bloomsbury Square in 1838, had moved to Oxford Street by 1865 and treated over sixteen hundred cases of "deformity of all kinds" annually (9).

In their lectures on deformity, surgeons often elaborated on the emotional impact of disability as a spur to developing new surgical techniques. In his *Lectures on the Nature and Treatment of Deformities*, Tamplin speculated about the moral effects on "the deformed," who "have been regarded as loathsome in body, and depraved in mind" and consequently "have often isolated themselves from their fellow creatures."

> Possessing all the feelings, and susceptible of all the impulses which animate the breast of man, frequently morbidly sensitive from the consciousness of their deformity, adorned with genius, gifted with wit, graced by fortune and birth, crowned with learning,—still is the deformed man exposed to the derision of the heartless, and is shut out from the world simply because nature has played some freak by which he differs from his fellow mortals. (3)

The notion that a disabled body was a feeling, suffering body primed it for narrative, since the disabled character was now seen as a man who could both elicit emotions from others and feel for others, having suffered so much himself.

Tamplin was not alone in his assessment of the potential emotional consequences of highly visible disabilities. William John Little similarly wrote in 1853 that "The effect of distortion on the physical and moral condition of the individual is one of deep interest. It is undeniable that the consciousness of an infirmity of this nature has displayed itself in a most marked manner in many individuals who have been thus affected. Historians have described the influence of deformity in alternately stimulating the cultivation of the worst and of the best passions and instincts" (18). William Adams, describing Byron, outlined a pattern of the psychological sensitivity stemming from deformity.

> It has generally been supposed that the existence of congenital *talipes varus* exerted an unfavourable influence on the highly susceptible mind of Lord Byron. In more than one instance I have myself witnessed some of the worst of these moral effects, in individuals who have on account of their deformity withdrawn themselves from the society in which, by birth and education, they were intended to move, and by their accomplishments they would have adorned.

He continued to argue "Such ill effects, however, do not always result from the influence of deformity, but, on the contrary, sometimes it appears to stimulate the cultivation of the highest qualities of the mind, of which many instances could be adduced to statesmen and artists, who are known to have been deformed" (*Club-Foot* 129). It makes sense, then, that the mid-nineteenth century saw a proliferation of masculine weakness and disability in fiction at a time when the culture of masculine industry, self-help, and self-restraint was gaining force.

The idea that highly visible orthopedic deformities engendered so much suffering that they could lead to a rich interiority became so widespread that it could be used as a shorthand for suffering in the novel. In *Daniel Deronda* (1876), George Eliot makes an unlikely comparison between bastardy and Byron's clubfoot. She likens "the silent consciousness of a grief within" that her hero feels when he begins to suspect that he is Sir Hugo's illegitimate son and the poet's "susceptibility about his deformed foot" (147). "The sense of an entailed disadvantage—the deformed foot doubtfully hidden by the shoe, makes a restlessly active spiritual yeast, and easily turns a self-centered, unloving nature into an Ishmaelite," writes Eliot. Yet she points to another possibility, that the mental suffering engendered by one's feeling set apart from other men will bring one closer to one's fellow men. She writes that "in the rarer sort, who presently see their own frustrated claim as one among a myriad, the inexorable sorrow takes the form of fellowship and makes the imagination tender" (148–49). Byron's clubfoot is a likely analogue for Eliot's discussion of illegitimacy because of the relatively new idea that a physical deformity was a deeply individual mark that could cause as much psychological suffering as it did physical.[2] Eliot frequently uses disability as way to think about how people can be made to feel uncomfortable and isolated. In *The Mill on The Floss*, when Tom Tulliver struggles with his lessons at school, she writes, "A boy born with a deficient power of apprehending signs and abstractions must suffer the penalty of his congenital deficiency, just as if he had been born with one leg shorter than the other" (178).

Typing the Strong Man

The Measure of Manliness: Disability and Masculinity in the Mid-Victorian Novel is an exploration of this unexpected proliferation of weak and disabled men in the novel, who appeared just at the moment when the new muscular hero of the 1850s gained force. Building on the idea that weakness and disability could occasion intense psychological suffering leading to tenderness for others, some midcentury novelists thought this suffering could instill a capacity for sympathy. Novelists like Dinah Mulock Craik and Charlotte Yonge gained reputations for writing about the morally improving trials of disabled characters. A critic for the *Saturday Review* saw the didactic use of disability as a positive trait in women's fiction of the 1850s. He regretted that a certain character had lately dropped out of fiction, an "angelic being with a weak spine, who, from her sofa, directed with mild wisdom the affairs of the family or the parish" (Anon., "Novels, Past and Present" 438). "The perfecting of strength out of weakness, in the person of a disabled aunt or invalid sister, was a fascinating theme to such writers as Miss Yonge or Miss Sewell," writes the critic. "They were fond of exhibiting moral influence in combination with physical infirmity, which gave a piquancy to their domestic hero-worship" (438).

"The perfecting of strength out of weakness" is also an apt phrase with which to describe the narrative function of the pairing of the strong man and the weak man, where the weak man humanizes the strong hero, in both men's and women's fiction of the same time period. In the mid–nineteenth century, the pairing of the strong man and the weak man became a widespread trope similar to the fortunate fair-haired woman and the unhappy dark-haired woman of Walter Scott's novels. In *The Mill on The Floss* (1860), when the dark-haired Maggie Tulliver complains to

Philip Wakem, "I'm determined to read no more books where the blond-haired women carry away all the happiness" (345); Philip may well have responded that he, too, is tired of reading books in which the disabled man is an adjunct to the strong man, with little hope of winning the heroine of the novel, regardless of whether she is fair or dark.

The pairing of the strong man and the weak man is distinguished by physical features almost as distinct as those of the fair and the dark woman. Typically, the strong man is a fair Saxon type with blond, chestnut, or light brown hair, blue or gray eyes, and a stature of near six feet tall, while the weak or disabled man (whose illness might range from a vague sort of invalidism to a highly visible orthopedic disability) is often a Celtic type who is darker than his companion. Adam Bede and his brother Seth typify this physical pairing, with the exception that both brothers are dark, which Eliot notes as a deviation from the norm in Adam. Eliot describes Adam's "strong baritone" as he sings in the workshop as the first indication of his exceptional physical features.

> Such a voice could only come from a broad chest, and the broad chest belonged to a large-boned, muscular man nearly six feet high, with a back so flat and a head so well poised that when he drew himself up to take a more distant survey of his work, he had the air of a soldier standing at ease. The sleeve rolled up above the elbow showed an arm that was likely to win the prize for feats of strength; yet the long supple hand, with its broad finger-tips, looked ready for works of skill. In his tall stalwartness Adam Bede was a Saxon, and justified his name; but the jet-black hair, made the more noticeable by its contrast with the light paper cap, and the keen glance of the dark eyes that shone from under strongly marked, prominent and mobile eyebrows, indicated a mixture of Celtic blood. The face was large and roughly hewn, and when in repose had no other beauty than such as belongs to an expression of good-humoured honest intelligence. (*Adam Bede* 7–8)

By contrast, although he has the same Celtic complexion and "type of features" as his brother and is even "nearly as tall," in Seth Bede "the strength of the family likeness seems only to render more conspicuous the remarkable difference of expression both in form and face. Seth's broad shoulders have a slight stoop; his eyes are grey; his eyebrows have less prominence and more repose than his brother's; and his glance, instead of being keen, is confiding and benignant" (8). Furthermore, his hair is "thin and wavy," unlike Adam's "thick and straight" jet-black mane (8).

Physical descriptions of the strong man, such as the one that Eliot offers of Adam Bede, tend to concentrate on his coloring and upper body. The strong man is fair, deep-chested, broad-shouldered, symmetrical, and straight, with hands skilled in workmanship; presumably he has the legs to match this upper half, although we hear about them less often. Kingsley's Tom Thurnall in *Two Years Ago* is "sturdy, and yet not coarse; middle-sized, deep-chested, broad-shouldered" (3); Dinah Mulock Craik's John Halifax is blessed with "muscular limbs" and "square, broad shoulders" (*John Halifax, Gentleman* 32); and Eliot's Tom Tulliver is "gentlemanly as well as tall and straight" (368). Even Henry James follows suit in his strong men. In *The Portrait of a Lady* Lord Warburton is a "remarkably well-made man of five-and thirty" with fair features and gray eyes (21–22); blue-eyed Caspar Goodwood is "tall, strong and somewhat stiff; he was also lean and brown" (52). The author of an article on rowing emphasizes deep-chested university oarsmen as models of health: "Certainly, if I wished to produce models of health and strength, I should take some old University oarsmen; sturdy, square-shouldered, deep-chested men, who seem to have been put together of the best materials regardless of expense" ("On Rowing" 251). The typing of the strong man and the weak man even extends as far as the naming of the pair. The strong man is most often named Tom, a good generic English name that indicates the hero's generic nature, or sometimes Guy, which points to his chivalry, while the weak man is often named Frank or Philip.[3] In her *History of Christian Names*, Charlotte Yonge calls Thomas a "deeply-rooted national name," noting that several common English surnames are related to the Christian name, including Thompson, Tomkins, and Tomlinson (I.65).

The moral characteristics of the strong man are intimately related to his physical prowess, which is kept in check at all times. The able-bodied man is defined above all by his ability to practice self-restraint. He is chaste, continent, and devout; an ideal strong man like Craik's John Halifax could live on a crust of bread while doing hard physical labor all day and studying at night. To be able-bodied is to be able to endure privation and suffering almost to the point of asceticism, all while maintaining good health. Charles Kingsley saw the healthy bodies of the Greeks as a new ideal for all, suggesting that able-bodiedness was marked by strength, symmetry, and chastity or continence generally: "I would make men and women discontented, with the divine and wholesome discontent, at their own physical frame, and at that of their children. I would accustom their eyes to those precious heirlooms of the human race, the statues of the old Greeks; to their tender grandeur, their chaste healthfulness, their unconscious, because perfect, might" (*Health and Education* 22). Here Kingsley links tenderness and strength, a link that he was to build on in his own fictionalizations of the pairing of the strong man and the weak man.

An emblematic yoking together of the strong man and the weak man occurs repeatedly in the novels of the mid–nineteenth century when the strong man takes the weak man's hand in his own, only to recognize the physical contrast of the two. In Eliot's *The Mill on the Floss*, after ascertaining that Tom will recover from the lameness caused by a swording accident, Philip tells him the good news and puts out "his small delicate hand, which Tom clasped immediately in his more substantial fingers" (191). In Hughes's *Tom Brown's Schooldays* (1857), at the moment when Tom promises Arthur to give up his vulgus and learn his lessons in earnest, the two clasp hands. Hughes writes, "Arthur laid his thin white hand, on which the blue veins stood out so plainly, on Tom's great brown fist, and smiled at him" (308). In *John Halifax, Gentleman* (1856), Phineas Fletcher makes the moral lesson of the physical difference clear when he grasps the eponymous hero and exclaims, "I put my hand on his wrist . . . his strong brawny wrist. Perhaps the contrast involuntarily struck us both with the truth—good for both to learn—that Heaven's ways are not so unequal as we sometimes fancy they seem" (54). In Kingsley's *Westward Ho!* (1855), Frank lays his "bloodless, all but transparent" and "delicate fingers" on his brother's hand, which is "hard and massive as a smith's" (303). The clasping of hands, a gesture of friendship between two boys, is one of the most significant tropes in representations of midcentury relationships between men. The moment when the two friends clasp hands and recognize their physical differences encapsulates the moral education of male friendship: each learns the value of strength and sensitivity, and of the power of sympathy to bridge physical differences. The clasping of hands is an acknowledgment of the value of both their friendship and their differences.[4]

In the chapters that follow, I argue that in order to represent this new muscular yet silent hero Victorian novelists drew on what had become a naturalized connection between the weak, nervous body and the body that speaks. The weak man and the strong man embodied larger cultural impulses toward industry, on the one hand, and invalidism and idleness on the other. As Miriam Bailin has noted, it is not surprising that in the work-obsessed culture that followed in the wake of the Industrial Revolution, the cult of the invalid developed alongside the "coexistent imperatives of self-discipline, will-power and industriousness" (12).

Maria Frawley has similarly argued that "invalids embodied inertia," or stasis in an age of progress, and speculates that invalidism was perhaps "symptomatic of its epoch, as a response of nineteenth-century Britain to the gradual encroachment of modernity" (252). She further observes that masculinity proved to be "the component of identity most crucial to understanding how invalidism was experienced and represented" in the narratives she analyzes.

> While domestic ideology, medical understanding, and the iconography of the period ensured that most middle-class women in the nineteenth century would not have associated being bedridden and confined to the home as compromising their femininity, the men who sought to represent the experience of being "confined" by sickness were very much preoccupied with their masculinity. (7–8)

This tension between norms of healthy masculinity and invalidism had provocative consequences for the novel. In this study, I explore these twin impulses of industry and invalidism, arguing that these impulses were embodied in strong and weak characters that structured the novel's form.

In the nineteenth century, orthopedic deformities like clubfoot were increasingly represented with sympathy in literature, a shift from eighteenth-century models, which sometimes saw disabilities as humorous, or other nineteenth-century models that used deformity to visually mark a villain.[5] Recent research suggests that in the eighteenth century visible physical disabilities were often treated as risible. Roger Lund argues that the eighteenth century was gripped with a "powerful persuasion that deformity was implicitly ridiculous, that one could no more help laughing at cripples than one could help smiling at a beautiful face" (104). Similarly, Simon Dickie writes in his research on jest books, "In mid-eighteenth-century England, it would seem, any deformity or incapacity was infallibly, almost instinctively, amusing" (16). This is not to say that the eighteenth century was wholly unsympathetic to physical disability; David M. Turner suggests that sympathetic approaches to disability came to the fore as Georgian London "emerged as a centre of polite sociability" (103). Yet, Turner notes, "Laughter at the comic spectacle of disability or deformity was not necessarily deemed inconsistent with a more compassionate approach to disability in social life. Humour may have provided a safety valve which allowed people to laugh at subjects no longer deemed acceptable in polite society" (64).

In contrast to visible physical disabilities, masculine weakness, as embodied by the man of feeling, was in some ways desirable in the eighteenth century. Indeed, one progenitor of the weak or disabled man of the midcentury novel was the eighteenth-century man of feeling.[6] Histories of masculinity have emphasized the move away from effeminate, feeling masculine bodies as an ideal in literature. In her study of Victorian nerves, Janet Oppenheim has shown how in the mid–nineteenth century the man of feeling was yielding to the self-made man, whose physical prowess on the rugby pitch was only equaled by his business acumen in the workplace (145–47). This susceptible body with the power to feel of the eighteenth-century hero stands in stark contrast to the more vital, self-contained body of the strong man of the mid–nineteenth century. Work in Victorian masculinity studies, starting with that of David Newsome, has similarly emphasized the shift from a gentle, pious mode of "Christian gentlemanliness," akin to the eighteenth-century man of feeling, to the muscular mode of masculinity that characterized the mid–nineteenth century. Building on this work, James Eli Adams and Herbert Sussman have emphasized the mid-Victorian need for manly emotional and sexual restraint. Adams sees an "elaborately articulated program of self-discipline" as a key quality of several types of the Victorian man, including the gentleman, the prophet, the dandy, and the soldier (2). Sussman focuses on monasticism as an emblem of the relationship between masculine sexuality and artistic potency. "As celibate male," he writes "the monk becomes the extreme or limit case of the central problematic in the Victorian practice of masculinity, the proper regulation of an innate male energy" (3).

Yet, within this well-documented shift from sentimental gentlemanliness to a restrained, manly muscularity, masculine weakness and loquaciousness continued to play an important if often undertheorized role. In the nineteenth century, norms of masculinity came under increasing pressure, bifurcating the strong hero and his weak companion. Industrialization and developments in medicine and technology meant that the male body came to seem both perfectible and newly susceptible to damage. The factory and labor debates of the 1830s and 1840s underscored the fragility of men's bodies in a world where heavy machinery could cause the loss of a limb.[7] Even without the misfortune of an accidental disability, factory workers were held to be stunted in manliness; Elizabeth Gaskell's John Barton in *Mary Barton*, for example, is a "typical Manchester man" and has "almost a stunted look about him; and his wan, colourless face, gave you the idea, that in childhood he had suffered from the scanty living consequent upon bad times, and improvident habits" (7). In the 1850s in the Crimea, men's bodies froze in the cold and were ravaged by war; these soldiers were depicted on duty in Lady Butler's iconic *The Roll Call* (1874) and as aged and infirm veterans in Hubert von Herkomer's *The Last Muster, Sunday at the Royal Hospital, Chelsea* (1875). While the soldiers who came home were often maimed and depicted on crutches in paintings, they also popularized a rugged, bearded masculinity.[8]

On the home front, innovations in public school education emphasized sport and an active, hardy boyhood as preparation for fighting for England abroad. The historian J. A. Mangan writes of organized games in the public school, "It was a genuinely and extensively held belief that they inspired virtue; they developed manliness; they formed character" (9). Surgeons advancing new technologies in orthopedic medicine and crusaders for sanitation reform felt that the moral fiber of the nation could be improved if men's bodies were improved.[9] The surgeon William John Little embodied the feeling of confidence in the perfectibility of the human body when he wrote in 1853, "Without exaggeration, it may be stated, that at the present moment many of the most unsightly deformities can be cured with less inconvenience than any other class of afflictions at all comparable with deformities in the bodily and mental suffering they occasion" (5). Within the Anglican Church, muscular Christian writers popularized the view that a man with a healthy body free of morbid thoughts was best able to worship with a clear conscience and worried that high church acolytes were popularizing a mode of masculinity that was high strung and effeminate.[10] As Bruce Haley puts it, "No topic more occupied the Victorian mind than Health—not religion, or politics, or Improvement, or Darwinism. In the name of Health, Victorians flocked to the seaside, tramped about in the Alps or Cotswolds, dieted, took pills, sweated themselves in Turkish baths, adopted this 'system' of medicine or that" and "invented, revived, or imported from abroad a multitude of athletic recreations" (3).

This pairing of masculine strength and weakness—with its emphasis on the erotic tension between the two men and its potential to structure the plot of the novel—has much in common with Eve Kosofsky Sedgwick's influential theory of the love triangle, which she argues is really more about the homosocial bond between men than the woman at its apex. Sedgwick describes the emerging patterns of "male friendship, mentorship, entitlement, rivalry, and hetero- and homosexuality" in the mid–nineteenth century as primarily organized around class differences (*Between Men* 1). While Sedgwick concentrates on class affiliation as structuring the difference between the two men in the love triangle, the pairing of the strong man and the weak man is structured around an eroticized physical difference. This contrasting of men based on physical difference is latent even in a poem like Tennyson's *Enoch Arden*, where the difference between "Philip Ray the miller's only son, / And Enoch Arden, a rough sailor's lad" (13–14), is not only in the financial comfort that Philip can offer Annie, the woman they both love, but also in their relative strength. When they quarrel over Annie as children, Enoch as the "stronger-made" is "master" and reduces Philip with his "blue eyes / All flooded with the helpless wrath of tears" (30–32). In a further departure from the Sedgwickian triangle, this dyad is often self-sufficient, as the two men experience an intense friendship or rivalry unmediated by a female character. Varieties of this pattern—which could be accounted for not only by homosociality but also by new ideals of physical masculinity and men's work—showed up in a wide range of novels.

In the chapters that follow, I show how the pairing of the strong man and the weak man set up a number of dualisms. The focus of the strong man is on the surface, on his outward calm, while the weak man's focus is on depth and his inward-looking passion. The strong man is unreflective and knows what is right without thinking about it, while the weak man overthinks and overtalks everything. Yet the weak man is necessary because he is equipped to tell the strong man's story, which would be opaque without his ability to read the strong man's muscular body. The physical imbalance between the two men heightens the novel's emotional register. While the strong man is seemingly complete in himself, part of his companion's weakness is a longing for intimacy. The weak man is coded as feminine in his susceptibility to feeling and ability to understand and express his stronger friend's inner life. He elicits unexpected moral capacities from the strong. While the strong man might seem self-absorbed in his physicality, as well as complacent and potentially even brutal, the weak man shows himself otherwise by giving his friend an opportunity to demonstrate his tenderness and sympathy, showing that the strong man, too, has feelings that his stoicism tends to disguise. The strong body is not callous but has the ability to feel mental and physical anguish. Suffering thus serves as a threshold to a new moral awareness for the strong man, showing his openness to character development and moral progress—without which there would be no plot. Seen in this context, the strong man and the weak man are mutually dependent: while the strong man provides physical support to the weak, the weak man is more unexpectedly an emotional support for the strong.

There was always potential for the strong man to collapse or suffer injury and become a weak man himself. Although any injury or collapse might prove that the strong man shares some of his weak friend's sensitivity, it does not result in him becoming a weak narrator figure himself. The weak man's illness is typically congenital or at least has some hazy origins in his infancy or early childhood. George Eliot is more specific than most authors when she tells us that Philip's humpback is not congenital but rather "the result of an accident in infancy" (170). The congenital, or at least long-standing, nature of the weak man's illness has two effects: first, it is seen as a permanent part of his character; and, second, it is something that he is not to be blamed for, but rather an affliction that garners him sympathy. As William John Little put it, "Popular emotion has at all times been powerfully excited by the view of congenital deformities, and they have been speedily brought to the notice of professional men; this affords an additional explanation why more frequent attempts at restoration have been made of these than of acquired distortion" (7–8). In other words, people with congenital deformities gave rise to more powerful emotions than those with acquired disabilities and prompted surgeons like Little to devote more attention to the cure of their deformities.[11] Dinah Mulock Craik offers a Christian explanation for her narrator's lack of responsibility for his own illness. Phineas Fletcher explains, "The physical weakness—which, however humiliating to myself, and doubtless contemptible in most men's eyes—was yet dealt by the hand of Heaven, and, as such, regarded by John," and hopefully also by Craik's reader, "only with compassion" (92). The weak man is not culpable for his illness—he has not been injured through a show of reckless bravado in a horse-riding accident or a wrestling match, and thus he bears no responsibility for it. Furthermore, his illness or disability is incurable—although it may cause him some degree of physical pain or incapacitate him to some extent at crucial plot points, it is understood that he will always be ill. His disability is thus seen as a permanent part of his character. His sympathetic nature as a narrator figure is permanently ingrained in his constitution.

Disabling Men

My methodology bridges recent work in disability studies with the work on the culture of invalidism and illness that has long been a staple of Victorian studies.[12] I use this focus on disability to analyze Victorian masculinity, examining how cultural notions of masculine weakness inflected norms of healthy, red-blooded manliness. As I have presented parts of this work, at conferences and in conversation, to scholars working in Victorian studies but not necessarily familiar with disability studies, I have often been asked about what counts as a disability. It seems clear that Philip Wakem as a hunchback is disabled, but how, for example, does Ralph Touchett, as an invalid, fit into a work on disability and masculinity?[13] Both characters, I would suggest, are marked as physically different in similar ways, and both function as narrator figures because their marginal positions have sharpened their observational abilities. Philip's hunchback is a dramatic visual difference, but the main physical impairments attendant on his disability are fatigue and immobilizing nervous headaches. Ralph's tuberculosis may be less visible, especially early in the novel, but he, too, suffers from fatigue and a lack of mobility. The figure of the invalid has received much more critical attention in Victorian studies than the figure of the disabled man, yet both have an important narrative function.[14] By bringing these two figures together I hope to show how widespread these tropes of weakness and disability were in Victorian thinking about masculine norms.

My analysis of the pairing of disabled men in the Victorian novel contributes to disability studies by offering a focus on one way in which the trope of disability was deployed in the mid–nineteenth century. The first monographs in disability studies offer a broader view of physical difference in the nineteenth century. Lennard Davis argues that, broadly speaking, "the social process of disabling arrived with industrialization and with the set of practices and discourses that are linked to late eighteenth- and nineteenth-century notions of nationality, race, gender, criminality, sexual orientation and so on" (24). Martha Stoddard Holmes concentrates on affect and disability, arguing that "Victorian discourses of disability, and the texts that convey them, are overwhelmingly 'melodramatic,'" both in terms of the presentation of characters with disabilities in terms of the formal tropes of theatrical melodrama and in the association of disability with emotional excess (*Fictions of Affliction* 4). David Mitchell and Sharon Snyder critique the use of disability in literature as a means of soliciting an emotional response from the reader, a tactic, they suggest, that authors often use without paying sufficient attention to the material conditions of disability or even the possibility that disability may not be emotionally damaging. Snyder and Mitchell write that disability is often "a deterministic vehicle of characterization" (50) in literature, which "borrows the potency of the lure of difference that a socially stigmatized condition provides" (55). The Victorian view of disability, I suggest, was not as stigmatizing as our contemporary view, although the Victorians did see disability as emotionally compelling. I take it as a task of this book to flesh out some of the larger claims of the first monographs in disability studies by focusing on one particularly compelling form that disability took in the mid-nineteenth-century novel, and by interrogating ideals of masculine strength as well as disability. I follow Stoddard Holmes's work in particular by concentrating on the affective pairing of masculine strength and disability and the impact it has on the narrative form of midcentury novels.

A disability studies perspective can also help move work in Victorian studies, and particularly work on Victorian invalidism, forward. Work in Victorian studies aims to show how culturally diffuse the cult of the invalid was, permeating many aspects of life in the nineteenth century.[15] Yet these studies tend to focus on sickroom scenes or characters that suffer from illnesses such as tuberculosis, and to overlook other forms of bodily "affliction" such as orthopedic deformities like hunchback or clubfoot. The Victorians would not have drawn such a sharp line between illness and what we now call "disabilities"; nor did they use the term *disabled* to indicate a physical or mental impairment as we do today. As Jennifer Esmail and Christopher Keep note, "When various groups that might now be understood as disabled were grouped together, it was typically through the lens of the pathologizing notion of 'fitness'—whether fit to work, to be educated, to have legal rights and responsibilities, or to reproduce" (46). The lack of a distinction in Victorian culture between illness and disability would seem to suggest the appropriateness of looking at representations of, for example, a clubfoot and a tubercular knee together, since the Victorians themselves would have done so. Disability and illness were part of the fabric of daily life in the nineteenth century. As Martha Stoddard Holmes points out, "It was very common to know someone with a mobility impairment or a chronic illness, or to have a relative who was deaf or blind" (*Fictions of Affliction* 14).

The Victorians thus arguably anticipate contemporary arguments that sickness and disability are not fixed biological states but part of a culturally constructed continuum of ideas about the fit body. What happens when the invalid leaves his couch for a quiet seat underneath a tree in the orchard? In the novels I consider, characters suffer relapses and recoveries, whether it is from an opium addiction or tuberculosis. At these points, illness is not a crisis at the center of the story but rather a chronic condition that permeates the narrative. In such cases, thinking about patterns of illness and recovery can help us appreciate the subtleties of narrative form. For example, instead of narrating John Halifax's relentless rise to power in detail, Dinah Mulock Craik will often speed through months of her narrative with Phineas's assertion that he was painfully ill during this time. A disability studies perspective offers a more open understanding of the dynamics of health and illness, which may actually have seemed more familiar to the Victorians, who lived in much closer proximity to illness and death than many of us do today, and who would have understood the vulnerability of the body to debility and disease through more intimate experience with it.

I thus take two main insights from disability studies: one, that illness and disability are fluid states rather than fixed identities; and, two, that ideas of normalcy and health are defined relationally against ideas of illness and disability. Masculinity studies has explored ideas of normative masculinity, but this picture of Victorian manly ideals becomes more complete when one considers the normative function of illness, invalidism, and disability. This perspective results in a more dynamic understanding of how characters, who can be more or less weak or healthy at any given point in the narrative, structure that narrative when, for example, it comes to seem natural that a weak man should take up the position of narrator figure, and also how weakness and oddness can come to define strength and normalcy. Stoddard Holmes suggests that disability is a relational state in two ways: first, the sight of a physically "afflicted" character can rouse sympathy and pity in both other characters and readers, so it connects the two emotionally; and, second, the able-bodied and the disabled are defined against each other. Stoddard Holmes writes that many novels "posit an emotional exchange system in which currents of feeling, stimulated by the presence of a corporeally 'different' body, connect people who are not disabled and people who are; disability is thus as relational a category as emotion itself" (*Fictions of Affliction* 29).[16] The dyad of the disabled man and the strong man also emphasizes the value of interdependence. As Stoddard Holmes argues in her exploration of (mainly female) dyads of caregivers and the cared for, the "most common Victorian fictions of interdependence feature two characters in a caring relationship characterized by an emotional parity that subsumes their asymmetry as physical or social agents." These plots thus "normalize and valorize relationships built on vulnerability and need" ("Victorian Fictions" 2).

The idea that disability is a relational category and that weak and strong characters exist together in a system of characterization gives us insight into the way in which Victorian novelists drew on contemporary ideas about health and illness to structure their novels. The pairing of the strong man and the weak man fleshes out characterization in the novel form in particular. Alex Woloch's recent work on such "systems of characterization" in the nineteenth-century novel, in which "the space of a particular character emerges only vis-à-vis the other characters who crowd him out or potentially revolve around him," is germane here (18). Woloch's insight that eccentric minor characters in nineteenth-century fiction often pull the narrative attention away from the focal character, who seems ordinary if not bland by contrast (125–33), can be read as having a normative function when one considers that minor characters are often marked as odd with a disability. Dickensian minor characters are often comically grotesque or eccentric, a distortion that can make the hero or heroine seem normal by force of contrast. In fact many of Dickens's minor characters are disabled—well-known examples include Jenny Wren and Silas Wegg. I would suggest that their physical and mental differences also have a normative function that throws the protagonist's normalcy into relief. As Mitchell and Snyder argue, disability "lends a distinctive idiosyncrasy to any character that differentiates that character from the anonymous background of the 'norm'" (47).

This insight into the function of systems of characterization helps to explain the predominance of the pairing of the strong man and the weak man in the novel as a genre. Several canonical Victorian poems offer fascinating portraits of disabled, weak, or aging masculinity, including Tennyson's "Tithonus," "St. Simeon Stylites," and "Ulysses" or Robert Browning's "Caliban upon Setebos," which concentrates on cognitive, as well as physical, difference. Rather than developing the interiority of a stronger, masculine character through the narrative pairing of the strong man and the weak man, however, these dramatic monologues reveal the speaker's character through his own words. The focus, then, is on a single interiority rather than on character development through the juxtaposition of two interiorities. Longer narrative poems, such as Elizabeth Barrett Browning's *Aurora Leigh*, Tennyson's *The Princess* or *Idylls of the King*, or Arthur Clough's *The Bothie of Tober-na-Vuolich*, offer more sustained portraits of the relationship between masculine strength and weakness. In Tennyson's *The Princess* and Elizabeth Barrett Browning's *Aurora Leigh*, the male heroes are only acceptable marriage partners once they are injured and invalided in contrast to their previous strong states. Clough's *Bothie* prizes masculine strength over learning much as midcentury schoolboy stories do, as I will discuss briefly in chapter 4. In Tennyson's *Idylls of the King*, a strong masculinity bleeds easily into brutality in the characters of King Mark and Balin and Balan, and it is not subdued through the presence of masculine disability or weakness. As Clinton Machann has argued, these long narrative poems offer compelling portraits of the tension between a civilized masculinity and a masculine propensity for violence, which can sometimes end in disability.[17] However, none of these narrative poems makes the pairing of the strong man and the weak man a central feature as the midcentury novel does.

The pairing of the strong man and the weak man is most prominent in the domestic novel as a genre. Perhaps this is because, as Martha Stoddard Holmes notes, while female characters with disabilities are habitually excluded from domestic plots of marriage and child rearing, "The disabled man's difference, correspondingly, is that he is either tied to the domestic sphere or else roams the streets without a regular workplace" (*Fictions of Affliction* 94). She discusses images of the beggar in Dickens and Mayhew in her work on disabled masculinity. I turn instead to images of the disabled man in the home as a defining feature of the domestic novel. This choice of genre directs the focus of my argument to middle-class masculinities, although there would certainly be ample material for another study of working-class masculinity and disability in looking at the Condition of England debates of the 1840s, with the reality of disability through injury in the workplace, or at the fear of the degeneration of working-class men of the fin de siècle.[18]

The Measure of Manliness

Once one starts looking for pairings of masculine strength and weakness in the nineteenth-century novel, examples crop up everywhere. In *Wuthering Heights* (1847) the invalid bachelor Lockwood narrates the story of the brutishly strong Heathcliff, a self-made man who is also paired with the effeminate and more aristocratic Edgar Linton. In the next generation, Lockwood observes another strong man and weak man, Hareton and the invalid Linton, compete over the second Cathy. In Dickens, David Copperfield, the effeminate domesticated writer, is paired in erotic friendship with the rakish Steerforth, and Nicholas Nickleby protects the damaged Smike. George Eliot's novels engage this trope repeatedly, pairing the well-built, Saxon-featured Adam Bede with his Celtic-featured, dissenting brother Seth, the unctuous foreign Harold Transome with the stolid Felix Holt, Daniel Deronda with the consumptive Mordecai, and, most important, the hunchbacked Philip Wakem with the red-blooded

Tom Tulliver. Not all of these examples of the pairing of masculine strength and weakness result in the weak man articulating or filling out the consciousness of the strong man. The schoolboy friendship between David Copperfield and Steerforth, for example, seems primarily erotic, and David, far from reading Steerforth's mind and softening his hard edges, is unable to anticipate his seduction of Emily. Similarly, neither Lockwood nor Linton is the recipient of tender care from the strong Heathcliff.

One would be hard-pressed to choose among such rich examples in canonical texts, and, as I suggest in the conclusion, the trope of the pairing of masculine strength and weakness extends well into twentieth- and twenty-first-century literature and film. Yet the examples I have been drawn to are those that served a normative function at this crucial juncture in the history of masculinity, when it seemed difficult to represent the new taciturn hero. Some of the novelists I analyze, in particular Charles Kingsley, Thomas Hughes, and Dinah Mulock Craik, are interested in promoting the strong mode of masculinity by using the character of the weak man as both a supplement and a foil. These novels are remarkable not just for their pairing of masculine strength and weakness but for their attempt to forward an exemplary masculinity through the use of a disabled man as a foil and narrator figure. Other novelists, like George Eliot, interrogated the value of both the strong mode of masculinity and the weak mode, while continuing to utilize the pairing of the strong man and the weak man.

I begin, in chapter 1, by reading Charles Kingsley's two novels of the Crimea, *Westward Ho!* (1855) and *Two Years Ago* (1857), alongside Charlotte Yonge's popular domestic family drama, *The Heir of Redclyffe* (1853), which was incidentally the favorite reading of soldiers in the Crimea. Yonge's high church masculinity, which was often associated with effeminate, high-strung men, might seem antithetical to Kingsley's muscular Christianity, with its emphasis on physical health as an indicator of spiritual health. Yet reading the two novelists together renders the dependence of Kingsley's strong heroes on weak or disabled companions newly apparent. Spectacles of masculine suffering are central to both novelists in developing the hero's sense of Christian duty. This theory of Christian chivalry is refined through sickroom scenes and the care of an invalid friend or brother, teaching the strong hero the importance of protecting those who are weaker than himself. Finally, in both Yonge and Kingsley, masculine suffering is seen as enabling self-expression, so that each novelist develops a connection between invalidism and authorship. In *The*

Heir of Redclyffe, for example, Charles Edmonstone, a lifelong invalid, follows an emotional trajectory that is close to the trajectory of the novel's plot. For Yonge reading is bound up with illness: she feels that novels are an indulgence for the sick. Her unobtrusive narrator gives the reader little guidance, and Charles, a voracious novel reader, fills this role, recognizing the conventions of romance and the Gothic at work and anticipating what will happen next. His restlessness and ennui, which stem from his life of confinement and illness, lead to his intriguing and are necessary to set the plot in motion. In this sense, his energy resembles that of the narrator as he mirrors the reader's emotional experiences. This connection between invalidism and authorship is viewed more positively in Yonge than it is in Kingsley, who sees volubility as being in tension with a self-assured masculinity. For example, his parody of the Spasmodic poets, the weak and opium-addicted Elsley Vavasour, is a negative example of the connection between authorship and masculine weakness. Yet Kingsley still relies on the spectacle of masculine suffering to motivate his plots. This chapter establishes the primacy of the pairing of the strong man and the weak man in the development of a theory of Christian chivalry that spanned high church and broad church thought.

In chapter 2, I shift the focus from issues of religion and Christian gentlemanliness to the issues of class raised in Dinah Mulock Craik's best-selling novel *John Halifax, Gentleman* (1856). There is a large social gap between the parlors of a genteel high church family in Yonge or the Crimea in Kingsley and the marginal world of dissenting trade and the tan yard found in the opening chapters of Craik's tale of rags to riches. Yet Craik also negotiates the question of what makes a true gentleman through a disabled male character who articulates emotions on the hero's behalf. *John Halifax, Gentleman* emphasizes the relationship between illness and narrative form as Phineas Fletcher, a confirmed invalid, narrates his eponymous friend's rise from rags to riches. I argue that Craik presents writing as a type of worthwhile labor by virtue of its painfulness. The invalid-narrator, who is accustomed to illness, is best able to turn his pain to account by giving it narrative form. Phineas claims that his memory has been "made preternaturally vivid by a long introverted life, which, colourless itself, had nothing to do but to reflect and retain clear images of the lives around it," and he thinks of John during his "seasons of excessive pain" when he is confined to the sickroom and "those four gray-painted walls; where morning, noon, and night slipped wearily away, marked by no changes, save from daylight to candlelight, from candlelight to dawn" (51). The form of the novel thus follows the form of

Phineas's illness and convalescence. John's story provides Phineas's otherwise monotonous life with a vicarious narrative shape, while Phineas breaks up the otherwise relentless story of John's work and success with a much-needed sense of rest and repose. Phineas elicits genuine tenderness from a character largely destined by his business career to be viewed with suspicion as a Bounderby-like social climber rather than a respectable self-made man. Yet for Craik the labor of writing is ultimately not as worthwhile as the labor of the industrialist, and John's robust life pushes Phineas to the margins of the tale.

Perhaps few genres are as concerned with normative behaviors and bodies as the schoolboy novel. In chapter 3, I argue that in striving to represent the typical English schoolboy in the midcentury novel, authors like Thomas Hughes and George Eliot pair their normative hero with an odd and often disabled companion who bears the emotional and narrative burden of the novel. In *Tom Brown's Schooldays,* Hughes uses the pairing to characterize his hero as an ordinary type of boy rather than an idiosyncratic individual. Tom Brown has "nothing whatever remarkable about him except excess of boyishness" (143). But his ordinariness is narratable only in contrast to the queerness of his companions, who include the "half-wit" Jacob Dodson, Diggs "the Mucker," Madman Martin, and of course the sickly and pious George Arthur. This pairing has a pedagogical side, teaching the strong hero chivalry and tenderness. To be a gentleman, the muscular Christian had to be capable of silently suffering moral pain, which he often felt as physical pain. His tender sympathy for his friend's sufferings proved that he, too, had the capacity to feel pain. Many muscular Christian novels end when the strong hero comes to know his weak friend's physical and moral pain firsthand. Kingsley's Amyas Leigh and G. A. Lawrence's parody of muscular Christianity, Guy Livingstone, are maimed or permanently disabled in shipwrecks and riding accidents to show that they, too, have the capacity for Christian suffering and to temper a strength that can easily bleed into brutality.

I argue that "The School-time" chapters of *The Mill on the Floss* are Eliot's rewriting of the schoolboy novel. Eliot pairs the robust Tom Tulliver with the hunchbacked Philip Wakem, but the result is not a lifelong emotionally educative friendship such as the one that Tom Brown and George Arthur enjoy. Indeed, the only moment when Tom and Philip can become friends at Mr. Stelling's boarding school is when Tom injures his foot. Instead of instilling a lifelong appreciation of the classics and sport in one another on the pattern of Tom Brown and George Arthur, the two develop an erotic rivalry that continues over Tom's sister Maggie. Eliot recognizes a tension between the schoolboy novel's promotion of health and athleticism, on the one hand, and its insistence on the affective power of disability on the other. She explores the somatic limitations of sympathy between two different men, extending to Tom Tulliver's adult career as a successful industrialist and his continued rivalry with Philip Wakem, which can be read as a critique of the John Halifax–Phineas Fletcher friendship. Tom rises in business at a rate that rivals that of John Halifax, but Eliot does not praise the career of the self-made man as Craik does. Rather, she questions the idea that masculine silence conceals a depth of character. Eliot suggests that the emotional differences between Philip and Tom are related to their physical differences: Philip's hunchback has rendered him overly sensitive and peevish, while Tom's more robust health has made him coarse and unfeeling. But, instead of having the two characters complement one another, Eliot questions the corporeal limits of sympathy. In Philip, she explores a potential limitation of her own theory of sympathy: when sympathy is grounded in a sense of exclusion, it may become debilitating, preventing one from making necessary connections to others. The Tom-Philip rivalry shows that the lifelong schoolboy friendship between men of physical differences is not as natural and inevitable as it once seemed.

Chapter 4 brings the story of the invalid-observer to the end of the century, suggesting that the position of the invalid as observer has become painful and ineffective as he is no longer called into friendship and action with the strong man. The mid-Victorian novel casts suspicion on the activities of observation and narration, demanding that the weak observer engage with the world through his friendship with the strong hero. By contrast, the fin de siècle dandy-invalid, typified by Huysmans' Des Esseintes in *A Rebours,* is content to recline on his sofa and observe. As Ralph Touchett complains to his cousin Isabel Archer, "What's the use of being ill and disabled and restricted to mere spectatorship at the game of life if I really can't see the show when I've paid so much for my ticket?" (169). The self-made man exists in James's novel, but no one cares to draw out his feelings. Only Henrietta Stackpole takes much trouble on behalf of Caspar Goodwood, the perpendicular Bostonian and head of a cotton mill. He has been hardened by his lack of interaction with a weak friend or a woman, but almost no one cares. James's novel takes it as a matter of course that invalidism and observation are interrelated, and Ralph Touchett's bequest and death frame the action of *The Portrait of a Lady* (1881). The painful and ineffective position of the invalid-observer heightens the pathos of the spectacle of male suffering, and his career as a narrator figure closes only in death. The aesthete figure can also combine the restraint of the strong man the susceptible constitution of the weak man. Some fin-de-siècle figures, like Dorian Gray or Jekyll and Hyde, seem to collapse the figure of the strong man and the weak man. Yet the pairing persisted beyond the nineteenth century.

In the conclusion, I gesture toward the routes that the pairing of the strong man and the weak man took in Edwardian and modernist literature, persisting as a feature of the schoolboy novel even as the pairing was increasingly pathologized and coded as queer in the wake of Sigmund Freud and Havelock Ellis. In the works of Edwardian authors such as E. M. Forster and Somerset Maugham, a protagonist with a clubfoot has often been taken as a code for the author's closeted homosexuality. This interpretation tends to gloss over disability. Reading the disabled protagonists through the pairing of the strong man and the weak man suggests instead that the authors are consciously rewriting a Victorian literary trope. Interestingly enough, some of the novels and films that follow the trope of the pairing of the able-bodied and the disabled boy have appeared in the last twenty-five years or so. Novels like John Irving's *A Prayer for Owen Meany* (1989), which often makes high school reading lists, suggest that these pairings, in which friendship transcends physical difference, are now seen as appropriate pedagogical tools.

In this study, I show how one particular and often eroticized relation between a feeling disabled character and his emotionally restrained friend structured the midcentury novel. Midcentury novelists drew on the idea that the weak body was naturally more verbally effusive, an idea that had its roots in the eighteenth-century man of feeling, in order to narrate the story of the taciturn strong man. The persistence of the pairing of the strong man and the weak man shows that, rather than being marginalized in a Victorian culture that valorized health and vitality, weakness and disability served a necessary function in shaping narrative form, and in forming ideals of Victorian manhood. Although the locus of my analysis is the mid-Victorian novel, the pairing of the strong man and the weak man did not disappear from literature at the end of the nineteenth century. It is part of my contention that our understanding of the weak male body as voluble and the strong male body as taciturn remains deeply Victorian.

Read through this lens, the activities of reading and authorship in the Victorian period are closely related to representations of the invalid male body as a feeling body. Disabled men became common narrator figures in a range of genres, suggesting an increasingly naturalized connection between the mental suffering resulting from bodily weakness or disability and literary proclivities. By 1915 Somerset Maugham could gesture toward the special authorial insight resulting from the painful psychological experience of physical difference almost as a matter of course. For his protagonist, Philip Carey, the perception of the influence of his congenital clubfoot at the end of *Of Human Bondage* solidifies the connection between the author's ability to observe and a marginalizing disability.

> He accepted the deformity which had made life so hard for him; he knew that it had warped his character, but now he saw also that by reason of it he had acquired that power of introspection which had given him so much delight. Without it he would never have had his keen appreciation of beauty, his passion for art and literature, and his interest in the varied spectacle of life. (607)

The task of the following chapters is to uncover the narrative patterns that made possible such a self-assured pronouncement of the powers of introspection and observation that stemmed from the experience of physical weakness and disability. The association of the pains and pleasures of observation with the physical pains and pleasures of disability, I suggest, has a history in the representations of masculine strength and weakness in the novel and still seems natural today.

CHAPTER 1

Charles Kingsley's and Charlotte Yonge's Christian Chivalry

Perhaps few authors have enjoyed such differing posthumous reputations as Charlotte Yonge and Charles Kingsley. Kingsley is known today as the author of swashbuckling stories for boys, Yonge as the author of pious family dramas for girls. Although Kingsley did in fact read and enjoy Yonge's work (Hayter 1), we can imagine the high church hero of *The Heir of Redclyffe* (1853), Guy Morville, as the type of highly strung, effeminate man that spurred Kingsley to denounce John Henry Newman's theology. Yet there are also few Victorian novels that give a higher place to self-denial, chivalry, and the importance of suffering for others than *The Heir of Redclyffe*. G. A. Lawrence's rather odd assertion in his novel *Guy Livingstone* (1857), whose hero is an Oxford blood, that "men . . . are most moved by the quiet and simple sorrows. . . . [W]e yawn over the wailings of Werter and Raphael, but we ponder gravely over the last chapters of *The Heir of Redclyffe*" (276) gives an idea of the power of Yonge's depiction of masculine suffering. In this chapter, I read Kingsley's novels of the Crimea, *Westward Ho!* (1855) and *Two Years Ago* (1857), alongside Charlotte Yonge's popular domestic drama *The Heir of Redclyffe*.[1] In doing so, I make a claim for the centrality of spectacles of masculine suffering in developing the hero's sense of Christian duty. This theory of Christian chivalry is refined through sickroom scenes and the care of an invalid friend or brother, which teaches the hero the importance of protecting those who are weaker than himself. Finally, in both Yonge and Kingsley, masculine suffering is seen as enabling self-expression, so that each novelist develops a connection between invalidism and authorship. Disability comes to be seen as an enabling condition for the writer, as the immobility caused by invalidism gives him a chance to refine his powers of observation and his wit.

This connection between invalidism and authorship is viewed more positively in Yonge than it is Kingsley, who sees volubility as in greater tension with a self-assured masculinity. Yonge uses the spectacle of male suffering and invalidism to train the reader emotionally. In the *Heir of Redclyffe*, Charles, the Edmonstone family's disabled brother, conjoins an effusive sentimentality with a demand for self-discipline in a sometimes unstable equilibrium. The boredom of the sickroom causes him to long for action; there is a restless energy in his ennui that resembles the narrative energy necessary to set the plot in motion. But as the novel draws to a close, Charles, like the other characters in the novel, must learn to restrain his feelings. The novel's emotional trajectory, from the opening's ennui to the climax's angry intensity and the ending's calm, thus follows Charles's affective development, developing a connection among narrative form, authorship, and disability.

By contrast, Kingsley critiques his intellectual author figures for their unmanly weakness, even when doing so may cast his own enterprise as a novelist under suspicion. At the same time, physical weakness was linked to authorship for Kingsley. This suspicion of intellectual activity was in fact a problem for Kingsley in defining muscular Christianity. Kingsley did not like the term *muscular Christianity*, which was coined as a dismissive term in the *Saturday Review* (Newsome 198). But when he was pushed to define the midcentury mania he had started, he called it "a healthful and manful Christianity; one which does not exalt feminine virtues to the exclusion of the masculine" (quoted in Newsome 210). The lack of a clear definition is part of the muscular Christian's ethos of acting rather than speaking. In *Tom Brown at Oxford*, Thomas Hughes claims that, although one might call his hero a muscular Christian, his own knowledge of the subject has been "gathered almost entirely from the witty expositions and comments of persons of a somewhat dyspeptic habit, who are not amongst the faithful themselves" (112). Indeed, he is not "aware that any authorized articles of belief have been sanctioned or published by the sect, Church, or whatever they may be" (112). The muscular Christian, it seems, is too busy boxing, hunting, rowing, and riding to write about his ethics, while those who do write tend to be of a less sound constitution. Since much of the muscular Christian's virtue lies in his ability to discern right from wrong without thinking about it, for the novelist to reflect on how this is so would only undermine his project.

This tension plays out in Kingsley's novel *Two Years Ago*. The Spasmodic poet Elsley Vavasour, an opium addict who must be rescued by the muscular Christian hero Tom Thurnall, has almost no insight into life; instead, his poems show a disconnect between what is happening in the world around him and his writing. Yet Kingsley is not as swift to dismiss the potential value of masculine weakness as he might initially seem. An improving friendship between an effeminate Tractarian curate who could have come from the pages of Charlotte Yonge and a muscular Christian hero who lacks in Christianity is at the heart of *Two Years Ago*. This friendship between a strong man and weak man, especially as it leads to Christian moral development, suggests a continued place for the self-searching associated with a weaker frame even in the work of an author often seen as glorifying unreflective masculine strength. Furthermore, in the novel, the poet character, Elsley Vavasour, suffers from disabilities that are connected to his emotional effusiveness, and his ability to write, even as his weakness undermines his masculinity for Kingsley.

Reading Kingsley's novels alongside Charlotte Yonge's family dramas helps us to see the neglected domestic aspects of his work. In locating the foil to the muscular Christian's strength close to home, in his weak brother, friend, or rival, I depart from criticism on muscular Christianity in particular and masochism in adventure fiction in general, which has tended to find the weak effeminized other in colonial settings. John Tosh has argued that nineteenth-century domesticity is difficult to square with homosociality and its emphasis on male adventuring and heroism (5). In her analysis of the adventure fiction of H. Rider Haggard, arguably the literary descendant of Kingsley's novels, Anne McClintock finds the masochistic strain most clearly expressed in the colonial context. More recently, John Kucich uses contemporary object-relations psychology as a challenge to the Freudian paradigm, arguing that figurations of masochism became a psychosocial language that addressed problems of social class and imperialism (2). Kucich argues that the adventure fiction of writers such as Robert Louis Stevenson and Rider Haggard "helped foster a fundamentally masochistic ethos of British masculinity, in which the ability to absorb pain stoically—or even ecstatically—was greatly prized" (9). By mastering himself, the British man became fit to master the colonial other. Analyzing Kingsley's works, James Eli Adams argues that the "figure of male suffering occupies a powerful boundary position within the structures of Victorian gender in which fierce attacks on the dominant culture may also articulate fantasies of self-empowerment, or in which, conversely, Victorian discipline may be registered at its greatest intensity by imagining the pleasures of self-abandon, or self-destruction" (147). In his analysis of *Westward Ho!*, Adams finds the tension between masculine desire and self-discipline expressed most clearly in the colonial situation. My reading of the value of pain and suffering in the mid-century novel places the context of male suffering much closer to home, in the homes and hunting grounds of England. The most important relationships that the muscular Christian develops in terms of offsetting his strength are not with effeminate natives, I argue, but with the weak friends or brothers that appear from the start of the novel. This shift in focus to the friend or brother who is closer to home brings to light just how integral masculine weakness and disability are to the articulation of theories of Christian masculine strength, and thus to the enterprise of novel writing and authorship itself.

Reading Yonge's novel alongside other best sellers of the 1850s highlights her initial popularity among men; her novels initially reached an audience far beyond that of the domestic dramas she is now known for. Although she became increasingly known as a girl's novelist at the fin de siècle, in the mid–nineteenth century Yonge's admirers included not only Kingsley and Lawrence but also William Morris, Tennyson, and William Gladstone (Hayter 1).[2] In *Two Years Ago* the heroine, Grace Harvey, is described as "reading Miss Young's [*sic*] novels, and becoming all the wiser thereby" (xix).[3] Yonge's initial popularity with male readers as well as women is due, partly at least, to her powerful portraits of masculine suffering.[4] She is especially interested in masculine disability and illness as a means of showcasing the potential for heroism within the home. Yonge's conviction that men could find ample room for deeds of daring within the home makes her iteration of the pairing of masculine strength and weakness less vexed than the examples found in Kingsley. This level of comfort with depicting men as suffering in both mind and body enables Yonge to depict a type of man whose responsiveness and sensitivity make his tenderness toward other men seem to be a natural extension of his Christianity.

Both Kingsley's and Yonge's novels are organized around contrasting pairings of men. In each case, the contrast is at once moral and physical. In *The Heir of Redclyffe*, the unbending, tall Philip and the spoiled, crippled Charles both learn from the sensitive, spry hero Guy Morville; the moral transformations are brought about by tender sickroom scenes in which men nurse each other. In *Westward Ho!* Kingsley pairs the sensitive court wit, Frank Leigh, with his strong sailor brother, Amyas. In *Two Years Ago*, the hero, the muscular Christian Tom Thurnall, is actually an atheist who benefits from the friendship of the effeminate high churchman Frank Headley, and who tries to save his childhood friend, poet Elsley Vavasour, from opium addiction and insanity. These novels all stage a spectacle of masculine suffering: the strong hero learns from his invalid friend the value of suffering and ultimately becomes ill or disabled himself. Physical suffering is tied to Christian moral growth for these strong heroes, who are shown to be not coarse men but feeling men through their friendship with a man weaker than themselves. The sickroom is the locus of their Christian chivalry, giving them an opportunity to show tenderness to a weak friend or brother. The oddity of the weak or disabled companion also delineates the contours of the hero's normalcy, especially in the muscular heroes, who are defined by their lack of physical and mental oddities. Reading the works of Charles Kingsley alongside those of Charlotte Yonge thus makes apparent a theory of Christianity and disability in which masculine suffering and chivalry are essential qualities of the Christian gentleman.[5] The ability to suffer is further linked to the ability to observe and articulate these observations, strengthening the connection between disability and authorship.

Spectacles of Masculine Suffering

In her work on masculinity and masochism, Kaja Silverman notes the long tradition of suffering male bodies on display, from Christ down through the Christian martyrs, in the Christian tradition (197). The novels of Yonge and Kingsley make the spectacle of masculine suffering a central element of their plots and use suffering to develop a theory of Christianity in which a man becomes a true Christian gentleman through his ability first to protect those weaker than himself and second to endure suffering in his own right. The weak or disabled male figure is thus central to both authors' formulations of Christianity. Yonge's high church Christianity, which was popularly caricatured as the property of high-strung, effeminate Oxford men, is more at ease with the figure of masculine suffering. Yet it is also essential to Kingsley's broad church, muscular Christianity, in which a normative healthy masculinity is defined against and dependent on a disabled masculinity.

Tennyson memorably satirizes this display of masculine Christian suffering in his dramatic monologue "St. Simeon Stylites." Simeon addresses God from atop the pillar where he has stood for thirty years, asking for the "meed of saints, the white robe and the palm" (20) in exchange for his suffering. He remained atop the pillar through "superhuman pangs" in "hungers and in thirsts, fevers and cold, / In coughs, aches, stitches, ulcerous throes and cramps" (11–13). In consequence of this suffering he has in fact become disabled. "[S]trong and hale of body" at first, he complains "half deaf I am" and "almost blind, / And scarce can recognize the fields I know; / And both my thighs are rotted with the dew" (28, 36, 38–40). There can be little doubt that Simeon has suffered physically, and put his Christian suffering on display, through his thirty years atop the pillar. The problem with Simeon's request for sainthood is that he makes it himself, which immediately undermines his claim in much the same way that a gentleman proclaiming himself as such is surely no gentleman.[6] In Kingsley's and Yonge's fiction, however, the use of masculine suffering becomes acceptable since it is suffering for others rather than for personal glory. Suffering on behalf of others, Kingsley and Yonge would argue, is true Christian suffering.

The popular writer Kenelm Henry Digby influenced both Kingsley and Yonge directly in their development of a theory of Christian chivalry as requiring quiet self-sacrifice. Digby was the author of the enormously popular conduct book and manifesto *The Broad Stone of Honour* (1823),[7] which drew on medieval romance and classic epic to inspire modern men to embrace the chivalry of heroes past. Kingsley has a chapter in *Two Years Ago* with the same title, detailing the southern gentleman Stangrave's struggle with the morality of slavery. Yonge names the town near Hollywell "Broadstone," and it is not difficult to hear echoes of Digby in the name Edmonstone. Digby writes, "Chivalry is only a name for that general spirit or state of mind which disposes men to heroic and generous actions, and keeps them conversant with all that is beautiful and sublime in the intellectual and moral world" (89). He prizes the same feeling that influences Yonge's heroes, elevating sentiment to a guiding principle for young men's conduct. There "is much to be apprehended from the ridicule which is cast upon sentiment" he cautions his readers. By contrast, he writes that there "is no danger in this enlightened age, as it is termed, of men becoming too heroic, too generous, too zealous in the defense of innocence, too violent in hatred of baseness and crime, too disinterested and too active in the cause of virtue and truth" (176–77). Both Kingsley and Yonge are interested in bringing the principles of Christian chivalry to modern times. Like the knighthood that Digby advises was formed for "the protection of the weak" (235) to the present day, central to their concerns are issues of how able-bodied young men should conduct themselves in fever epidemics and against issues like slavery. The protection of the weak, and especially weaker men, is the key to the development of a strong Christian gentleman in both instances.

Digby argues that the qualities necessary for the endurance of the true Christian knight are temperance, privation, labor, obedience, and suffering, all characteristics of the able-bodied man. The chivalrous Christian knight must be prepared to meet danger at all turns, and even a violent and sudden death will not find his spirit unprepared. Digby approvingly tells the story of an old Lord Gray, who, "to inure his sons for war, would usually in the depths of winter, in frost, snow, rain, and what weather so ever fell, cause them at midnight to be raised out of their beds and carried abroad hunting till the next morning, then perhaps come wet and cold home, having for breakfast a brown loaf and a mouldy cheese" (355). For Digby, to be able-bodied means to be able to endure an ascetic lifestyle. He scorns the "lectures upon constitutional weakness" that his contemporaries listen to, arguing that men of the past "knew, in defiance of all maxims, that among those who have attained to long lives, the greatest number have been men of abstemious and even austere habits; and the old heathen physicians were aware how much they conduced to the health of the body and the perfection of the mind" (350). True physical health for men involves immense restraint, continence, chastity, and a general ability to forgo indulgences of the flesh, instead focusing on braving danger and helping others.

Within this theory of Christian chivalry, the ability to tolerate pain without flinching is not only a sign of one's manliness but also a means of testing and developing Christian moral growth. The importance of pain in the moral development of the strong man helps to explain why the heroes of both Kingsley and Yonge become ill or disabled themselves or, if they remain in good health, why it is important for them to sympathize with the physical pain their friends experience. In this framework, physical illnesses and injuries are not emasculating but rather a proof of one's Christian gentlemanliness. Furthermore, the disabled characters, by virtue of their capacity for sympathy and their power of observation, are most often linked to writing and authorship.

The Heir of Redclyffe

Despite her seemingly tame domestic settings, Charlotte Yonge takes the idea that suffering, often physical, will mold the Christian character to an extreme. In 1865 a reviewer for *The Nation* described Yonge's masochistic authorial tendencies.

> [H]aving brought before us one or more fine creatures, she beats them; she binds them; she lets her other inferior creatures make butts of them; she sticks pins into them; she impales them; she makes them declare it is "so comfortable" to be impaled; she calls upon us to congratulate them; then in triumph she bears them out of our sight. (quoted in Juckett 117–18)

This pleasure in the spectacle of masculine bodies suffering is arguably grounded for Yonge in the passion of Christ, and the physical suffering of male saints. Yonge's Tractarian fiction participates in this display of the male body under duress.[8] Nor was Yonge alone in her assessment of the Christian value of pain. In an article on Christina Rossetti, Esther Hu argues that the Tractarians gave physical pain a positive valuation in terms that could apply equally to Charlotte Yonge's work. Hu writes, "The Tractarian view of suffering grounds itself in a startling conviction: God's character and purposes remain good even when his children endure pain. Thus Christ's incisions in the Christian soul show his compassion; suffering purges and purifies the soul as the Maker's hand fashions the soul's 'imperfect or decayed substance.'" Edward Bouverie Pusey, a leader of the Tractarian movement, exhorted that all suffering, "pain, sickness, weariness, distress, languor, agony of mind or body, whether in ourselves or others,"– should be treated with a spirit of reverence: in itself, "it were the earnest of Hell," but through Christ's mercy, "it is a purifying for Heaven. Earthly suffering prepares souls for eternity" (Hu 156). Yonge's depiction of physical suffering as leading to Christian moral growth is remarkably similar to Kingsley's vision of broad church Christian gentlemanliness. The novel's affective trajectory, from the opening's ennui through the upheavals of emotion to the ending's quiet restraint, is best represented by Charles, who, as the most accurate reader of the novel's plot is a stand-in for the narrator and the author.

For Yonge intense pathos arises from the disjunction between the expectation of a hardy and active masculinity and the actual weakness and suffering of the male characters in the novel. When Charles finds himself, like his mother and sister, unable to clear his cousin Guy's reputation, he exclaims, "I say there is no greater misery in this world than to have the spirit of a man and the limbs of a cripple" (239). Many of the novel's first readers felt the same way: the critic for the *North American Review* wrote that "the acute, satirical, but manly and kind-hearted cripple, Charles, is one of Miss Yonge's best creations. . . . The forced inaction to which he is subjected by his infirmity, in spite of all his natural vivacity and conscious ability, is one of the keenest trials of youth, and appeals strongly to the sympathy of a large class of readers. He goes on through the story in a course of improvement, moral and physical, which cannot be otherwise than gratifying to his friends and the public" (Anon., "Review of *The Heir of Redclyffe* and *Heartsease*" 447). Physical illness often leads to moral improvement in Yonge's work, and this is particularly the case with the men of *The Heir of Redclyffe*. Submission to God and filial piety are key high church values, and they are perhaps more of a trial to one who is physically and financially able to enjoy all the pleasures of youth.

Within the logic of Yonge's theory of Christian chivalry, the illnesses of the main male characters, Charles, Guy, and Philip, allow for the integration and reconciliation of wayward family members. As Miriam Bailin notes, the Victorian sickroom bears special significance as a place of respite from pettiness, where conflicts between and within characters can heal alongside the body (4–5). For Yonge chivalry is both the dutiful and the romantic response to physical suffering. Christian chivalry alleviates suffering as the sickroom takes on dramatic proportions. At the novel's climax, Guy braves a fever epidemic to nurse the cousin who has dogged his steps from the moment he entered Hollywell. Despite the "traces of repugnance" that Philip shows toward Guy during lucid intervals, Guy tends him through his fever, showing himself "an invaluable nurse, with his tender hand, modulated voice, quick eye, and quiet activity" (414). The antagonisms of everyday life are put aside in the sickroom, a space that offers a glimpse of the possible relationships between men in this historical and literary moment. So constant and tender are Guy's attentions to his cousin that the doctor proclaims that if "*le malade*" is saved, it will be "owing to the care and attention of *le chevalier*" (419), making the place of chivalry in the sickroom explicit. In declaring Guy, whose very name is one traditionally given to knights, a chevalier, Yonge brings the chivalry of the past into the present.

Yonge also highlights the homoeroticism of the sickroom as her ablebodied men nurse the sick.[9] In a queer moment on the morning of his marriage to Amy, Guy is found in her brother Charles's sickroom, looking back with sentiment over their relationship, rather than the scenes of his courtship: "I could not help coming once more," he says. "This room has always been the kernel of my home, my happiness here" (387). The wedding guests first see not the bride and groom but "Guy's light agile figure, assisting Charles up the step, his brilliant hazel eyes and glowing healthy complexion contrasting with Charles's pale, fair, delicate face, and features sharpened and refined by suffering" (376). The bride, meanwhile, stands behind them carrying Charles's crutch. Other characters notice the intense appeal of the men's bond: a neighbor says, "I was very much taken with that young Mr Edmonstone . . . he is about three-and-twenty, sadly crippled, but with such a pleasing, animated face, and so extremely agreeable and sensible, I do not wonder at Sir Guy's enthusiastic way of talking to him." She goes on to suggest that Guy may have been taken with Charles before Amy: "I could almost fancy it was admiration of the brother transferred to the sister" (570). Charles's invalidism necessitates close physical contact between the two men, which in turn underscores the eroticism and tenderness of the relationship.

Although the experience of restricted mobility and contentment within the domestic sphere is usually feminized, Yonge's theory of Christianity requires that men be similarly domesticated.[10] Duty, for John Keble, seems feminized in that it consists of finding moral fulfillment by seeking out prospects for self-denial in an already narrow sphere. In his popular book of poems, *The Christian Year* (1827), Keble writes:

> The trivial round, the common task,
> Would furnish all we ought to ask;
> Room to deny ourselves; a road
> To bring us, daily, nearer God. ("Morning" 53–56)

The formal restraint of Keble's tetrameter couplets here mimics the restrained and narrow lives that Yonge's characters nevertheless find spiritually rewarding.

This is especially the case for the men in *The Heir of Redclyffe*. While the novel's female characters are quite healthy, all of Yonge's major male characters fall ill and then struggle to find their duty as Christian men at home. Charles's knee joints flare up when family tensions run high, such that his illnesses serve as a barometer of tension in the narrative. The family's response to Charles also registers failures in Christian sympathy. The antagonism between Philip and Charles often centers on how Philip helps, or fails to help, his cousin. Charles tells a family friend about their altercations over what kind of help he needs. "Could you guess what a conflict it is every time I am helped up that mountain of a staircase, or the slope of my sofa is altered?" he asks. "Last time Philip stayed here, every step cost an argument, till at last, through sheer exhaustion, I left myself a dead weight on his hands, to be carried up by main strength. And after all, he is such a great, strong fellow, that I am afraid he did not mind it; so next time I *crutched* myself down alone, and I hope that did provoke him" (39 emphasis original). At the novel's crisis, Philip lets Charles slip down the stairs while the two are arguing over Guy's innocence. The accident results in a protracted illness that escalates family anxiety. The tensions that simmer in the narrative thus express themselves in Charles's illness.

Charles's illness is partly so suggestive because it is vague in nature. As Mary Wilson Carpenter has suggested, Charles most likely suffers from tubercular inflammations in the hip joint (*Health, Illness, and Society* 68). Yonge was writing at a time when surgeons such as Benjamin Brodie—whose work on diseases of the joints secured him the presidency of the Royal Society in 1858 (Acland 31)—were mapping the etiology of tuberculosis with increasing specificity, finding "the exact value of pain in the joints as evidence of organic disease" and altering the practice in such cases so as to "greatly reduce the number of amputations" (Acland 20).[11] But Yonge's novel does not overly medicalize Charles's disability. Instead, she remains fairly general as to exact symptoms, focusing instead on the duties invalidism creates for his loving family and the invalid himself. Yonge's lack of specificity on Charles's disability serves an important thematic function: it allows his invalidism to take on a moral and religious dimension. The spectacle of male suffering heightens the emotional interest of Yonge's novel, so that the affective undercurrents of the narrative are closely tied to the representation of disability.

Charles's passionate involvement on Guy's behalf acts as an affective outlet throughout moments of crisis. During an important conversation about Guy's future, Charles refuses "to go away with the womankind" and be shut out, demanding that Philip explain his accusations as soon as the door closes (237). At this moment, Charles acts as a stand-in for the reader, who also wishes to glean what is going on behind Hollywell's closed doors. When, in another conference by "the dressing room fire," Mrs. Edmonstone tries to break the news to Amy that she must give up Guy, Charles (who can hear all that transpires in the other room) bursts into the room "half dressed, scrambling on, with but one crutch, to the chair near which she stood, with drooping head and clasped hands," promising that it is only a rumor (236). Charles vents unexpressed feelings that Guy is being unjustly accused. He is allowed to make these remarks in part because, as an invalid, he has not learned the same self-control as the rest of the family, and his "early habits of disrespect to his father" resurface when his temper is roused (238). Charles's habit of disobedience in turn rouses the narrative. His intense affective engagement moves the narrative forward; Yonge establishes a link between reading and illness that allows Charles to function as a surrogate for both the narrator and the reader. Kingsley views the relationship between reading and disability with less optimism, making for a more strained relationship between masculine weakness and masculine strength.

Disability and Authorship

Illness and reading are complementary in Yonge's novelistic world. One enthusiastic German reader who eventually learned English by reading *The Heir of Redclyffe* countless times, wrote a fan letter to Yonge from her invalid couch: "It was in the summer 64 that I was in a water-place for the case of a lingering suffering of foot which forces me to lie on the couch now already three years, and there I read your book in a german translation and received it entirely into my heart" (Olga von Wilamowitz to Yonge, 24 January 1866).[12] Invalid men also enjoyed the story of Guy Morville, and Yonge's novel was the favorite reading of hospitalized soldiers during the Crimean war (Cruse 51). Yonge herself viewed contemporary novels, especially those in serial form, as "indulgences appropriate to the disabled, the convalescent, and the railway traveller" (Tillotson 60).

Charles is the novel's most voracious reader; his sister constantly strives "to keep down the piles of books and periodicals under which it seemed as if her brother might some day be stifled" (25). Charles is not subject to the same self-discipline as the other members of the Edmonstone home, and his access to novelistic conventions places him in a privileged narrative position. When the characters learn that their father's ward and cousin, Guy, will be coming to live with them, Charles promptly suggests that Philip should either ignore the family feud between Philip's and Guy's branches of the Morville family or "fight it out with his grandson, which would be more romantic and exciting" (12).

Being versed in novelistic conventions allows Charles to read the situations around him accurately. Although his disability thwarts his participation in family goings-on, his restricted mobility also gives him the perspective of an observer, from which he can critique what is happening around him. As the center of household management at Hollywell, Mrs. Edmonstone's dressing room doubles as Charles's sickroom and adjoins his bedroom, so that the invalid often knows things before he should:

"His room had a door into the dressing-room, so that it was an excellent place for discovering all from which they did not wish to exclude him" (193). Charles's point of view brings to mind that of Ermine Williams, the invalid in *The Clever Woman of the Family*, who sees "the world through a key-hole" but whose "circumscribed view" gains "in distinctness" (121).[13] In the same novel, Captain Alick Keith, who has been wounded in India, credits his long convalescence with developing his sensitivity and patience (421). Although Charles hardly attains the almost saintly wisdom of an Ermine Williams or a Margaret May, or even the patience and perspective of an Alick Keith, he is able to see the goings-on of the household more clearly than anyone else. As an invalid, he is also allowed to indulge his anger at certain situations more than able-bodied members of the family, and this affective response often proves to be the right one.

Unlike Ermine Williams or Margaret May, whose weak spines lead to a Christian outlook, Charles is an intriguer whose curiosity and sharp wit propel the plot forward. He must be trained through more suffering to learn his Christian duty. Charles's favorite pastime is "poking up the lion" (62) or bothering his sisters and cousins to pass the time. There is a restless energy in Charles's boredom that seems akin to the narrative energy necessary to set the plot in motion. Indeed, Charles's ennui eventually becomes an emotional attachment to the strong Guy that allows him to see that his friend has been wrongfully accused and to rouse himself out of his habitual peevishness and melancholy. When Charles is upset with Guy, "Having no other way of showing his displeasure," he remains downstairs "nursing his ill-humour" until he has forgotten "how slight the offence had been, and worked himself into a sort of insane desire— half mischievous, half revengeful—to be as provoking as he could in his turn" (62). Charles wants to see Guy's famed hereditary temper for himself, and the narrator comments that it becomes a "sport" with him "to try and rouse it," which has the greater relish because it keeps "the rest of the family on thorns" (62). Keeping his otherwise well-behaved family on thorns is another way of saying that Charles stirs up the conflict that sets the plot in motion.

While Charles's confinement to the couch allows him a privileged position as observer, his more serious illnesses prevent him from finding out all that goes on at Hollywell. Were Charles to retain his sharp powers of observation at all times, he would actually impede the plot by preventing the tryst between Laura and Philip. Instead, Charles falls seriously ill just after Laura and Philip become engaged and again when Guy is banished from the house on suspicion of gambling. Laura and Philip have reason to be glad when illness keeps him away from dinner, so that "not one suspicious eye could rest on them" (152). Having an invalid in the family also accounts for Laura's keeping a secret from her mother. "Mrs. Edmonstone had been so much occupied by Charles's illness," explains the narrator, "as to have been unable to attend to her daughters in their girlish days; and in the governess's time the habit had been disuse of flying at once to her with every joy or grief" (122). Nor can Charles, in such a state, defend Guy from Philip's accusations of gambling. When Charles is debilitated by illness just when Guy is banished, the narrator comments that "these gatherings in the diseased joint were always excessively painful, and were very long in coming to the worst, as well as afterwards in healing" and that he is constantly "either in a state of great suffering, or else heavy and confused with opiates" (266). Charles's illnesses literally change the course of the plot.

Yonge's theory of suffering as molding the Christian character demands that Charles give up the propensity for disobedience and melancholy that has generated so much narrative energy. He reflects to Amy that he owes his new character to Guy: "I know that his leading . . . brought out the stifled good in me. What a wretch I should have been; what a misery to myself and to you all by this time, and now, I verily believe, that since he let in the sunlight from heaven on me, I am better off than if I had as many legs as other people" (593). Charles most clearly expresses the kind of emotional trajectory that the novel's first readers experienced on reading Yonge's novel. In a letter to Dyson dated 23 February 1853, Yonge described John and Charlotte Keble's emotional engagement with her book in these terms: "It seems as if people were first angry, then sad, and then the peacefulness of the end grew on them; altogether the effect has been much more than I ever expected" (Coleridge 191). Yonge saw Charles as the beneficiary of Guy's noble influence. In letters written to Dyson during the composition of *The Heir of Redclyffe*, Yonge wrote, "I don't think Charles was in earnest enough before Guy came to take Philip as his *Bild*; it was Guy who made him in earnest, and by respecting Philip himself almost taught him to do so" (Coleridge 175). The novel's first readers sympathized with Charles's sentimental response. When the manuscript circulated among Yonge's close friends, the Coleridge family, Sir John (later Judge) Coleridge "said that when Philip came to inquire about Guy's debts, Guy should have kicked him downstairs" an opinion that Julian Yonge improved on "by saying that he would have horsewhipped him round the quad" (Coleridge 166). The reader's emotional progress seems remarkably similar to that of Charles. Indeed, it seems as if the novel arouses these emotions only to subdue them, as Charles must go through a course of improvement in which the ennui that has been the source of so much narrative energy throughout the novel is replaced with "the peacefulness of the end," as he reaches equanimity in recognizing and fulfilling his duty.

Charles chafes against his lot in life, but he, too, must learn the value of Christian self-resignation and self-sacrifice.[14] Despite his initial idle and mischievous nature, Charles is no more exempt from the demanding regime of self-renunciation and usefulness than are the rest of the Edmonstone family, men and women included. At the close of the novel, Charles decides that he will be Philip's "private secretary" when he is a member of Parliament and imagines himself "triumphing in his importance, when he should sit in state on his sofa at Hollywell, surrounded with blue-books, getting up the statistics for some magnificent speech of the honourable member for Moorworth" (574). As Elisabeth Jay points out, "By the end of the novel, Charlie, like his creator, has found through his writing public influence and a means of offering support to his family" (50). As readers turn the final pages of Yonge's novel, it seems appropriate that the most voracious novel reader in *The Heir of Redclyffe* should exchange the periodicals and light literature that once threatened to overwhelm his couch for blue books.

Westward Ho! *and* Two Years Ago

Kingsley is easily caricatured as an author who is only interested in presenting musclemen and who takes fright at the least tendency toward popishness, celibacy, or at any sign of masculine weakness. Readers of Kingsley's best-known muscular Christian novels, *Westward Ho!* and *Two Years Ago*, may come away mainly remembering his burly heroes, Amyas Leigh and Tom Thurnall.[15] But in each case the hero's hardy masculinity is buoyed by friendships with weaker men that reveal the hero's capacity for Christian selflessness in much the same way that the sickroom scene offers an opportunity for martyrdom in Charlotte Yonge. While Kingsley's field of action moves beyond the domestic sphere, the presence of a weak friend or brother still has the potential to soften the strong man. Kingsley sees the muscular Christian as in danger of becoming hardened and cynical if not for the possibility of friendship with weaker men. Most surprisingly, a Yongean high churchman is responsible for the moral conversion of Tom Thurnall in *Two Years Ago*. Tom's friendship with the effeminate curate Frank Headley both makes Frank more manly and softens the cynical Tom, whose worldliness puts him in danger of atheism. Similarly, Amyas Leigh, Kingsley's seafaring Elizabethan hero, is juxtaposed with his courtier brother, Frank Leigh, who teaches him the value of Christian chivalry, and also with his effeminate Jesuit cousin, Eustace Leigh. Kingsley pays lip service to women as objects of chivalry, but in fact men are often the object of other men's chivalry in his novels. Amyas Leigh spends much more time interacting with his weak courtier brother Frank than his Amazon bride-to-be Ayacanora, who has little need of his chivalry, and Tom Thurnall does not need to save Grace Harvey but the weak poet, Elsley Vavasour. Kingsley is more skeptical of the value of masculine weakness and disability than Yonge, but he continues to make the cultural connection between authorship and disability, even as he expresses his ambivalence about it.

Kingsley revises Yonge's pairing of the strong man and the weak man when he makes the high church curate, whose self-searching is strikingly similar to Guy's, the weak man to his muscular Christian strong man Tom Thurnall. Yet he does not censure the Yongean Tractarian curate as one might expect. Instead, Kingsley presents Frank Headley and Tom Thurnall as two opposite but equally commendable types of English manhood. Tom Thurnall, a strong, English everyman, lacks the sensitivity of Yonge's strong man Guy. But Kingsley does not valorize this lack; instead, he sees it as in need of softening through friendship with a weaker man before the strong hero is finally ready to marry. Thurnall is "sturdy, and yet not coarse; middle-sized, deep-chested, broad-shouldered; with small, well-knit hands and feet, large jaw, bright gray eyes, crisp brown hair, a heavy projecting brow" and a face that shows his "shrewdness and good-nature" (3). Kingsley writes that Frank, too, is handsome in his way, with "not an ungraceful line about him": "He was at one extreme pole of the different types of manhood, and that burly doctor who had saved his life at the other" (364–65). Both men are physically appealing while being cast as morally and physically opposite types of manhood.

Kingsley suggests that the association of the muscular Christian, or rather the muscular atheist hero, with the high church curate may be a morally improving one for both men as they learn the meaning of Christian chivalry through each other. Kingsley does not present the muscular Christian hero's temperament as entirely admirable or even Christian to begin with. He writes of Tom's time in Canada, Australia, the United States, and Mexico: "Fifteen years of adventure had hardened into wrought metal a character never very ductile" (20). Many near death escapes have not softened his heart toward God: "All the miraculous escapes of his past years, instead of making him believe in a living, guiding, protecting Father, have become to that proud hard heart the excuse for a deliberate, though unconscious, atheism" (520). "He had watched human nature under every disguise, from the pomp of the ambassador to the war-paint of the savage, and formed his own clear, hard shallow, practical estimate thereof" (20). Tom is in need of friendship with one more introspective than himself to soften his cynicism. The narrator soliloquizes to Tom,

> Will you make up your mind in the same foolishness of over-wisdom, that Frank Headley is a merely narrow-headed and hard-hearted pedant, quite unaware that he is living an inner life of doubts, struggles, prayers, self-reproaches, noble hunger after an ideal of moral excellence, such as you, friend Tom, never yet dreamed of, which would be to you as an unintelligible gibber of shadows out of dream-land, but which is to him the only reality, the life of life, for which everything is to be risked and suffered? (84)

The narrator advises his protagonist that he could learn something from the effeminate high churchman: "True, he has much to learn, and you may teach him something of it; but you will find some day, Thomas Thurnall, that, granting you to be at one pole of the English character, and Frank Headley at the other, he is as good an Englishman as you, and can teach you more than you can him" (85).

Although Frank is lacking in physical manliness, Kingsley suggests that there are admirable traits in his character that Tom cannot see. Displaying a Yongean capacity for self-sacrifice, Frank has given up a fashionable London curacy for the chance of doing more good in the remote seaside town of Aberalva. "For Frank was a gentleman, and a Christian, if ever one there was. Delicate in person, all but consumptive; graceful and refined in all his works and ways; a scholar, elegant rather than deep, yet a scholar still; full of all love for painting, architecture, and poetry, he had come down to bury himself in this remote curacy, in the honest desire of doing good" (35). Tom and Frank become fast friends in a successful if seemingly unlikely pairing of the strong man and the weak man.

> The two soon began to pass almost every evening together, pleasantly enough; for the reckless and rattling manner which Tom assumed

with the mob, he laid aside with the curate, and showed himself as agreeable a companion as man could need; while Tom in his turn found that Headley was a rational and sweet-tempered man, who, even where he had made up his mind to differ, could hear an adverse opinion, put sometimes in a startling shape, without falling into any of those male hysterics of sacred horror which are the usual refuge of ignorance and stupidity, terrified by what it cannot refute. (85)

Kingsley's protest against "male hysterics" is expected, but his faith in the improving friendship of a muscular atheist and a high church curate is less so, yet it underpins his portrait of strong masculinity.

Kingsley also follows Yonge in making the spectacle of masculine suffering in a epidemic an occasion for the hero to prove his Christian moral worth. Yet, unlike Yonge, whose hero martyrs himself in a fever epidemic, Kingsley's Frank Headley becomes physically hardier through his experience of corporeal suffering. In a dramatic scene, Headley bows over "almost double, crushing Thurnall's arm in the fierce gripe of pain," and asks him, "Can you conceive a sword put in on one side of the waist, just above the hip-bone, and drawn through, handle and all, till it passes out at the opposite point?" (337). Headley's description of his suffering here echoes the spear with which the soldier pierces Christ's side after he is crucified (John 19:34). Thurnall says that he has felt such a pain twice, suggesting his capacity for Christian suffering. Yet Kingsley feels somewhat uncomfortable with the intensity of this masculine suffering. His obtrusive narrator stops the conversation and ends the chapter with "There was no use in complaints. In half an hour Frank is screaming like a woman, though he has bitten his tongue half through to stop his screams" (338). The next chapter begins "Pah! Let us escape anywhere for a breath of fresh air, for even the scent of clean turf. We have been watching saints and martyrs—perhaps not long enough for the good of our souls, but surely too long for the comfort of our bodies" (339). Kingsley makes the connection between suffering and the development of Christian character explicit in this chapter in his allusion to the passion of Christ in his description of Frank Headley's own suffering, but, unlike Yonge, he does not dwell for long on the sickroom scene, preferring to concentrate on the two men's actions in the cholera epidemic instead, and how those actions develop their Christian sense of duty.

Kingsley thus shares Yonge's theory that the true Christian man is one who will endure physical pain on behalf of others. Summarizing Amyas Leigh's education in *Westward Ho!*, he writes that "his training had been that of the old Persians, 'to speak the truth and to draw the bow,' both of which savage virtues he had acquired to perfection, as well as the equally savage ones of enduring pain cheerfully" (8–9). Amyas uses his strength to protect the weak, and as a schoolboy he can hardly feel happy going home unless he has beat "a big lad for bullying a little one" (9). Men are gentleman for Kingsley by virtue of their capacity to spare others both physical and moral pain by bearing it cheerfully themselves. They do so through their actions rather than their words: when they speak the truth it is brief, and they are far more ready to protect the weak with their swords than with their tongues. Pain becomes expressive when words fail. The strong man's moral progress is expressed as an increasing ability to suffer on behalf of others.[16] The ability to feel moral as well as physical pain, then, is key to a man's becoming not only muscular but also Christian. Sensitivity is more typically the domain of the weak and nervous man, but his stronger friend must also be capable of feeling pain.

Whereas Yonge's Guy Morville has an innate sense of chivalry, Kingsley's strong heroes most often learn their chivalry through the teaching of a weaker man. The Frank and Amyas Leigh pairing in *Westward Ho!* is another instance of a pairing in which the weak man teaches the strong man chivalry.[17] Kingsley sees chivalry as the most admirable trait of an Elizabethan court wit such as Amyas Leigh's brother Frank. Despite the muscular Christian's distrust of the convoluted rhetoric of court wits, the narrator suggests that Amyas would do well to imitate their chivalry. Frank, a scholar and courtier who dresses in the latest fashions of Milan, is "as delicately beautiful as his brother" is "huge and strong" (25). The contrast between the brothers' physiques is borne out in the contrast between their characters. Amyas's stocky build goes hand in hand with his English commonsense. The English sailor trumps the Spaniard every time for "then, as now," he is a "quite amphibious and all-cunning animal, capable of turning his hand to everything, from needlework and carpentry to gunnery or hand-to-hand blows" (358). When Frank suggests to his brother that every realm should be ruled by a queen so that "weakness and not power" would "be to man the symbol of divinity," "love, and not cunning . . . the arbiter of every cause," and "chivalry, not fear, the spring of all obedience," Amyas grumbles, "Humph! There's some sense in that. . . . I'd run a mile for a woman when I would not walk a yard for a man" (308). The suggestion here seems to be that characters like Amyas would do well to import the chivalry being popularized on the Continent by figures such as Castiglione, with its emphasis on the protection of the weak and women. This chivalry can only be adopted on the condition that the effeminate tendencies of the foreign courtier are tempered with a dose of English commonsense and practicality. Kingsley thus allows his heroes to form the "Noble Brotherhood of the Rose" in worship of the local beauty of Bideford, Rose Salterne. He admonishes his readers that, despite what may seem like an "extravagant fondness for Continental manners and literature," this variety of "chivalry is only another garb of that beautiful tenderness and mercy which is now, as it was then, the twin sister of English valour" (160).[18] Chivalry is essential to the muscular Christian. As Thomas Hughes puts it, "[T]he least of the muscular Christians has hold of the old chivalrous and Christian belief, that a man's body is given him to be trained and brought into subjection, and then used for the protection of the weak" (*Tom Brown at Oxford* 113).

Seen as an element in a theory of physical suffering as molding the Christian character, Amyas Leigh's seemingly sudden blinding at the end of *Westward Ho!* is actually only one part of a larger theory of the place of physical suffering in developing the Christian gentleman. This Christian capacity to endure suffering exists in tenuous balance with the hero's capacity for brutality. Kingsley recognizes that there can be a dangerous lack of prudence and self-restraint in his strong men. With his love of sport and risk taking, the muscular hero runs the risk of becoming injured or disabled himself. Although there must be nothing odd about the body of the muscular Christian, a scar like the one that crosses Amyas's right temple, "the trophy of some Irish fight" (303), far from being an indication of weakness or effeminacy, is actually the visible sign of his courage and daring. This bravado, however, can be taken too far. The injuries the men sustain are commensurate with the risks they take, and often more damaging. In his overzealous pursuit of the Spaniards, Amyas tries to steer his ship between a wall of granite and a breaker and ends up blinding himself. Reflecting on his blindness, he compares himself to Samson in his strength and blindness: "I have been wilful, and proud, and a blasphemer, and swollen with cruelty and pride; and God has brought me low for it, and cut me off from my evil delight. No more Spaniard-hunting for me now, my masters. God will send no such fools as I upon His errands" (584). Amyas's blindness certainly ends his Spaniard-hunting days, and it is his impetus for setting up a domestic life with Ayacanora in a plot paralleling both Charlotte Brontë's *Jane Eyre* and Elizabeth Barrett Browning's *Aurora Leigh*.

This blinding, however, is not merely a symbolic castration of the hero, though it does have a chastening effect.[19] Instead, I would argue that it is also a battle scar, the visible indicator of his sometimes foolhardy acts of daring. Being chastened through this blinding is not necessarily a sign of Amyas's effeminacy but rather one of his ability to endure suffering like a gentleman as he sets up his own household back home in Bideford. In other words, the maiming and blinding of these heroes is not only a chastening but also proof of their manly ability to suffer morally and physically. Given that the strong man's self-mastery makes it almost impossible for readers to discern his physical or moral suffering, the presence of a weak or disabled man allows readers some insight into this pain that the sternness of the strong man's body would seem to deny. The importance of this pain in the moral development of the strong men helps to explain why so many muscular Christian heroes become ill or disabled themselves, or if they remain in good health why it is important for them to sympathize with the physical pain their friends experience. In Amyas Leigh's definition of a gentleman as one who would suffer anything to spare someone weaker than himself, for example, the concept of pain is integral to the midcentury notions of chivalry that bind the strong man to his weaker counterpart.

Charles Kingsley's Stuttering Muscular Christians

If Charlotte Yonge makes an implicit connection between invalidism and authorship in the character of Charles Edmonstone, Charles Kingsley's invalid-poets call into question the facility with which such masculine articulateness might be attained.[20] Language is not wielded effectively by either the weak poet figures or the strong heroes in muscular Christian novels. Kingsley's muscular Christians "stutter," to borrow Louise Lee's phrase. Kingsley repeatedly shows language to be an ineffective tool for bringing about the liberal social reformation that he hopes for. Lee argues that the Kingsley who wrote *Alton Locke* is a "Christian writer who attempts to use his spoken and written voice as a major social intervention but who repeatedly demonstrates, both implicitly and explicitly, that language itself is too unreliable to complete the task" (5). She draws a provocative parallel between Kingsley's experience as a lifelong stammerer and the inefficacy of language to bring about social change in his early industrial novels. This emphasis on silence is part of a new masculinity that appears in Kingsley's later historical fiction with its emphasis on muscular Christian heroes. Kingsley has "put aside the careful, prosing, educative side of his character," evident in novels like *Alton Locke*, "to fundamentally re-formulate his heroical template. In doing so, he also adopts a new fictional tactic in a bid to bring about linguistic and social coherence: the definition of the masculine social body is secured by silencing the voice and language of culture" (10). For these new heroes, "[N]ot talking is the new style of Kingsley's physically and mentally fortified manliness; emotional and verbal complexity is jettisoned to preserve the appearance of assured masculinity" (11).

Kingsley's heroes are able to appear manly and completely self-assured by virtue of their silence, a quality that is not a necessary precondition of manhood for Charlotte Yonge. But Kingsley has not jettisoned the voice of language and culture altogether in his novels of the mid-1850s. Instead, the task of representing this taciturn being linguistically has been shifted onto the weak characters, who continue to act as stand-ins for the narrator, despite Kingsley's ambivalence about them. The nervous, thoughtful, and effeminate poet figure of Alton Locke still exists in Kingsley's later fiction, and he continues to carry the verbal burden of the novel. It is just that he is no longer the main character. Instead, he is a friend of the muscular Christian, as the Spasmodic poet Elsley Vavasour is to Tom Thurnall, or a brother, as the court wit Frank Leigh is to Amyas Leigh.

The physically weak poet figure, who continues to be linked to the author, remains necessary as Kingsley's muscular Christian heroes become increasingly taciturn. The greatest difficulty in depicting the muscular Christian was how slow to speak he is. While Charlotte Yonge's men have little difficulty articulating themselves, in Kingsley taciturnity is a key part of strong manliness. James Fitzjames Stephen described this problem in his review of George Alfred Lawrence's 1857 novel *Guy Livingstone* (which is also narrated through the point of view of the muscular hero's disabled friend). "It is easy to say that a man has a 'huge frame' and 'iron muscles,' and to assign to him all the other conventional proofs of strength which novelists are so much in the habit of lavishing on their heroes," he wrote, "but it is a much more difficult and delicate matter to describe the influence which a constitution of that kind would produce upon habits of thought and feeling" (537). Stephen presumes that there is a connection between one's body and the way one thinks, but he finds it hard to imagine what "habits of thoughts and feeling" a "huge frame" and "iron muscles" would produce. It is much easier to describe the effect of the nervous or sickly body on the constitution, since novelists tend to associate nerves with quick feelings and loquacity. In fact Stephen speculated that the readers most drawn to muscular Christian works would be weak men themselves. He writes, "The hero with a simple massive understanding united with the almost unconscious instinct to do good, and adorned, generally speaking, with every sort of athletic accomplishment" (191) would appeal most strongly to "the febrile, irritable, over-excited part of the generation" and "such reading would be likely to calm or brace their nerves" (191–92). Stephen's speculation about the weak nerves of Kingsley's readership might well be true if one were to judge by the weak friends that are always drawn to the strong hero in the novels. Within the novel, the weak man is a kind of model for this nervous, excitable reader who must be calmed by the massive understanding and muscles of the hero.

In *Two Years Ago*, Elsley Vavasour provides Tom Thurnall with an opportunity to demonstrate his Christian chivalry and serves as a foil to the hero's strength. He also continues the cultural connection between disability and authorship. Vavasour is a parody of the Spasmodic poets of the 1850s.[21] First introduced as a surly youth called John Briggs (a dig at John Stanyan Bigg's unpoetic name), this onetime apothecary reinvents himself as Elsley Vavasour. Vavasour is a man who goes home to write tortured verses about a shipwreck instead of helping with the rescue, mistreats his wife and children, and eventually succumbs to opium addiction and ill-health after a Manfredic jaunt in the Welsh mountains. He sports a "highly-developed Byronic turn-down collar, and long, black, curling locks" and the sort of "bad complexion" that indicates a "sedentary life and a melancholic temper" (3). Yet this melancholic temper is more likely to generate narrative than the good-natured temperament of the muscular Christian. Vavasour's condition as an opium addict parallels that of his neighbor, the alcoholic and aptly named Trebooze of Treeboze, who Tom Thurnall is more successful in rescuing. After a bout of delirium tremens, he is "Terrified into sobriety" (530) and joins the militia. Kingsley's inclusion of these characters shows the extent to which his portrait of masculine strength depends on masculine weakness. Vavasour serves two important narrative functions: his odd masculinity serves to bring out the hero's normalcy, which would otherwise be difficult to narrate; and he takes on the linguistic burden of the novel.

The narrator of *Two Years Ago* takes immense pleasure in describing the language of the Spasmodic poets, but his pleasure is mixed with a deep suspicion that ornate language and metaphor are unmanly. The narrator has the pleasure of describing a chasm on the seashore through Elsley Vavasour's point of view: "Without, all simple, broad, and vast; within, all various, with infinite richness of form and colour.—An Hairoun Alraschid's bower, looking out upon the," but he directly interrupts the poet's train of thought: "Bother the fellow! Why will he go on analysing and figuring in this way? Why not let the blessed place tell him what it means, instead of telling it what he thinks?" (157). Earlier, when the narrator describes the wreck of the *Hesperus*, which Tom Thurnall miraculously survives, he imputes the extravagances of his prose to Vavasour, claiming that it is "through whose spectacles, rather than with my own eyes, I have been looking at the wreck, and to whose account, not to mine, the metaphors and similes of the last two pages must be laid" (50–51). Yet the preceding poetic description of the wreck is not consistently focalized through Vavasour's point of view, as the use of the proper names of the ship's crew, which he would have no way of knowing, makes clear. The muscular Christian is not unintellectual; rather, his intellect finds expression in practical projects rather than words. Yet this emphasis on taciturnity is in tension with the project of novel writing itself.

The poet figures in Kingsley's novels, despite his censure of them, share an uncomfortable proximity to the narrator, and perhaps even to Kingsley himself. As Lee points out, Kingsley the man was not much of a muscular Christian: "His stutter notwithstanding, he was in real-life a hyper-active, chain-smoking, manic depressive worrier whose penchant for over-work definitely contributed to his multiple nervous breakdowns and probably led to his early death at fifty-five" (13). Although Kingsley as a disabled author does not much resemble his muscular Christian heroes, he does resemble his minor characters: the neurotic, high-strung, opium-addicted spasmodic poet; and, in a more flattering light, the chivalrous, gentle, and loquacious court wit. Like the narrator, Kingsley's weak poets articulate what the hero cannot and define the contours of his normalcy and strength in contradistinction to their weakness. Kingsley's narrator expresses some ambivalence about this proximity to the effeminate poet. At one point in *Westward Ho!*, he chides Frank Leigh for his foppery, only to worry that he is becoming a fop himself. "Oh, Frank! Frank! have you come out on purpose to break the hearts of all Bideford burghers' daughters. And if so, did you expect to further that triumph by dyeing that pretty little pointed beard (with shame I report it) of a bright vermilion?" (39). After a rapturous description of Frank Leigh's dove-colored suit and broad, dove-colored Spanish hat with feather to match, the narrator exclaims, "There—I must stop describing you, or I shall catch the infection of your own Euphuism, and talk of you as you would have talked of Sidney or of Spenser" (40). Kingsley's narrator is uneasy with the effeminate dandiacal styles of Frank Leigh and Elsley Vavasour, yet they enable him to fill out the contours of his heroes, who are ordinary to the point of being unnarratable.

Tom Thurnall is a mouthpiece for Kingsley when he argues that the poetry of healthy manhood would focus on natural history or perhaps war. He seems to be a mouthpiece for Kingsley's views of authorship when he advises Vavasour that "it may be a very materialist view of things, but fact is fact, the *corpus sanum* is father to the *mens sana*—tonics and exercise make the ills of life look marvelously smaller" (195) and recommends a course of boxing, shooting, sailing angling, gardening, walking, dumbbells, beef, and ale (196–97). He proposes a new, more pragmatic, subject for the verses of the author of *The Soul's Agonies*, science and the natural world (163), further suggesting that the poet should get a high desk made and compose his verses standing up (196–97).[22] When the Crimean War begins, he suggests that war poetry would be a properly manly and active topic for his friend: "And if it comes to that, why not come to the war, and see it for yourself? A new country—one of the finest in the world. New scenery, new actors,—Why, Constantinople itself is a poem! Yes, there is another 'Revolt of Islam' to be written yet. Why don't you become our war poet?" (457).

This active topic for poetry suggests that Kingsley's theory of Christian chivalry depends on brave actions, not brave words. The narrator of *Westward Ho!* is suspicious of the eloquence and intellect of the silver-tongued Sir Walter Raleigh, poet Edmund Spenser, and Philip Sydney and other members of Frank's circle (195). By contrast, Amyas only makes a single speech to his crew, and when he does so he speaks "simply and manfully" (387). The novelist does not record his words. Instead, he commends his hero's more practical knowledge: "Luckily for him," Amyas is "no 'genius,'" but he is "as cunning as a fox in all matters of tactic and practice, and would have in these days," claims the narrator, "proved his right to be considered an intellectual person by being a thorough man of business" (106). Kingsley's praise establishes the businessman as the kind of strong, silent hero that Dinah Mulock Craik describes a year later in *John Halifax, Gentleman*. Yet, for Kingsley, the silence that the narrator recommends as an indicator of a healthy manhood is not reproducible for the narrator, who constantly finds himself enamored of the language of his suspicious poet characters, Elsley Vavasour and Frank Leigh.

While Kingsley does advise brisk exercise as an antidote to male hysterics, this in itself is not a sufficient condition for Christian moral growth. Reading Kingsley in the context of Charlotte Yonge renders his emphasis on the morally improving potential of physical suffering, and of chivalrous friendship with men weaker than oneself, newly apparent. For Kingsley and Yonge, moral growth does not stem from physical strength alone. Rather, physical suffering, or close friendship with one who is physically suffering, is the catalyst for moral growth. For these midcentury novelists, weakness and disability are necessary conditions for Christian manliness; the strong protagonists of Kingsley and Yonge do not stop at friendship with a weak man, for they often suffer physically themselves. The spectacles of masculine suffering that they stage in their novels suggest that the experience of physical pain is a precondition for moral growth. The pairing of the strong man and the weak man is thus essential to their theories of Christian moral development. Indeed, on a broader scale, masculine suffering seems to be a precondition for writing, as Kingsley and Yonge persistently connect disability to emotional effusiveness and the potential for authorship. This emotional effusiveness is sometimes threatening enough that it needs to be tamped down, as it does for Charles Edmonstone in *The Heir of Redclyffe* and as Elsley Vavasour's tragic end amply demonstrates in *Two Years Ago*. Yet Kingsley and Yonge identify a cultural connection between masculine disability and authorship that their contemporaries were to elaborate even further in some of the best-selling works of the century.

CHAPTER 2

Invalidism and Industry in Dinah Mulock Craik's *John Halifax, Gentleman*

It may seem like quite a leap to move from the parlors of a genteel high church family found in Charlotte Yonge, or the adventures of the Crimea and the Spanish Armada in Charles Kingsley's novels, to the world of dissenting trade, the tanyard, and Quakerism found in the opening chapters of *John Halifax, Gentleman* (1856). Different as Amyas Leigh and Guy Morville may seem, one quality they are assured of is their gentlemanliness. The question of what makes a gentleman is at the forefront of Dinah Mulock Craik's novel, which negotiates the gentlemanly ideal through the same narrative pairing of disability and strength found in Yonge and Kingsley.

In its depiction of an intense homoerotic friendship between a strong man and his disabled friend, which in turn facilitates the strong man's rise to power, *John Halifax, Gentleman* is perhaps the paradigmatic example of the friendship of the strong man and the weak man. In Craik's novel, the invalid friend, Phineas Fletcher, actually narrates the rags-to-riches story of the novel's eponymous hero, John Halifax. The novel's central claim, that one need not be well born to be a true gentleman, leads Phineas to catalog the social movements that enable John's class mobility, from the French Revolution a decade after John's birth in 1780 to the passing of the First Reform Bill in 1832, shortly before his death.

This story also leads him to an emotional outpouring of admiration and affection for his successful friend. While Yonge and Kingsley focus on the moral and religious burdens of their heroes as Christians with little need to prove their gentlemanliness, Craik's self-made man straddles social classes through the values of earnestness, hard work, and perseverance, which the novel argues are values that transcend class affiliations. Because John, with no birth or wealth to recommend him, must prove himself a gentleman through his hard work and self-restraint, Phineas carries more of the narrative burden in Craik's novel than Charles Edmonstone does in Yonge's. Although John Halifax is the hero of the novel, Phineas Fletcher is its affective center.

Craik links the physical differences in the two men to their affective differences. Robert McRuer argues that in contemporary American culture disability and queerness are both popularly supposed to be legible on the body, while heterosexuality and able-bodiedness are invisible (2). Following this logic, Phineas's weakened frame is certainly the legible sign of his queer affective difference. Phineas remains in the Halifax household even after John marries as a kind of bachelor uncle and continues to narrate John's life. As a self-described invalid bachelor with his own "crotchets," Phineas continues to recognize and articulate forms of desire that the rest of John's household does not, occupying what Sedgwick would call an "avuncular" narrative position, which challenges the patriarchal reproductive norm.[1] "Because aunts and uncles" writes Sedgwick, "are adults whose intimate access to children needn't depend on their own pairing or procreation, it's very common, of course, for some of them to have the office of representing nonconforming or nonreproductive sexualities to children" (*Tendencies* 63). Aunts and uncles, rather than being part of a direct line of biological reproduction, are "elements in a varied, contingent, recalcitrant but reforming seriality" (63). Furthermore, a disabled avuncular narrator like Phineas occupies a marginal position in the household through which he can critique bourgeois domesticity without wholly disrupting it.[2] While Phineas does delineate the boundaries of normative domestic manhood, he does not quite disrupt these bounds. Instead, he remains a member of the patriarchal household while occasionally offering a critique of it. Phineas's role in the latter half of the novel is to provide an alternative emotional perspective on events in the household.

Phineas's narration establishes a relationship between weak bodies and storytelling. It was coming to seem natural to the mid-Victorians that a disabled invalid would be a good observer, having so little else to do, and that effusiveness and emotional outpourings were the symptoms of a weak body. A stronger body, like John's, could restrain the outpourings that were excusable in an invalid. Yet Craik turns even Phineas's volubility to account, showing that his labor in narrating John's life is worthwhile precisely because it is associated with the physical pain he experiences as an invalid. Phineas's narration thus lends support to recent theories of authorship in the mid–nineteenth century; as Catherine Gallagher shows, authors like Dickens and Trollope were interested in showing their writing to be worthwhile labor by virtue of its painfulness (*Body Economic* 83–84).[3] Phineas, too, claims authority for himself through his experience of physical suffering.

The Businessman as Hero

By contrast to the painful labor of the voluble invalid, the taciturn labor of the strong man is modeled on the Carlylean captain of industry. The influence of Thomas Carlyle on muscular Christian writers like Charles Kingsley and Thomas Hughes has been well documented, yet Dinah Craik, too, seems to have been influenced by the Carlylean hero in her portrait of John Halifax, a true captain of industry if there ever was one. Norman Vance writes that Carlyle was the progenitor of a new type of hero: the muscular hero who manfully takes up the challenges of daily life without grumbling. Carlyle's doctrine was "stern but liberating," "effectively jettisoning the vexed questions of theology in return for sturdy practicality and a romantic-intuitive assurance that all was well which could be dignified by religious language," including a respect for nature and the body (Vance 62). The influence of Carlyle's conception of the businessman as hero in *Past and Present* (1843) can also be seen not only in muscular Christian adventures but also in Craik's sentimental novel. Within the theory of businessman as hero, to be able-bodied is linked to the ability to make good business decisions; like John Halifax, the businessman is clearheaded and vigorous, unaffected by an anxious intellectualism that could affect his nerves and cloud his ability to act in the moment. Carlyle, like Craik, envisions an ethics of business driven not by mammonism, "cash-payment," or "mere Supply-and-demand" (233, 234) but by beloved captains of industry who will lead the working class through chivalry. Carlyle writes of these captains of industry, "The Leaders of Industry, if Industry is ever to be led, are virtually the Captains of the World; if there be no nobleness in them, there will never be an Aristocracy anymore" (232–33). Carlyle continues by asserting the continuing relevance of chivalry in an industrial society: "No Working World, any more than a Fighting World, can be led on without a noble Chivalry of Work, and laws and fixed rules which follow out of that—far nobler than any Chivalry of Fighting was" (234). Carlyle's formulation of the captain of industry as a leader, and his praise of the noble chivalry of work, could just as easily be Phineas Fletcher's descriptions of his hero, John Halifax.

If Carlyle's hero was a captain of industry who led through chivalry, he led by his actions, which are often described in physical terms of strength, rather than his words. Carlyle separates the ideal man from his own narrative voice, which must fall prey to the very dangers of overtalking and overthinking that he warns readers against. Indeed, Carlyle's clearest articulation of his ideal strong man comes only when he defines him against the weak man. In his lectures, published as *On Heroes, Hero-Worship, and the Heroic in History* (1840), he sees Rousseau as the anti-strong man.

> He is not what I call a strong man. A morbid, excitable, spasmodic man; at best, intense rather than strong. He had not "the talent of Silence," an invaluable talent; which few Frenchmen, or indeed men of any sort in these times, excel in! The suffering man ought really "to consume his own smoke"; there is no good in emitting *smoke* till you have made it into *fire*,—which, in the metaphorical sense too, all smoke is capable of becoming! Rousseau has not depth or width, not calm force for difficulty; the first characteristic of true greatness. A fundamental mistake to call vehemence and rigidity strength! A man is not strong who takes convulsion-fits; though six men cannot hold him. He that can walk under the heaviest weight without staggering, he is the strong man. We need forever, especially in these loud-shrieking days, to remind ourselves of that. A man who cannot *hold his peace*, till the time come for speaking and acting, is no right man. (170–71 emphasis original)

Carlyle uses the vocabulary that was used to define the Spasmodic poets—nerves, uncontrollable convulsions, and a related need to speak—to characterize the weak man. An industrial metaphor of fire and smoke, used repeatedly in later Victorian novels to describe the captain of industry, captures the psychological state of the weak man who is unable to tamp down his excitement or keep quiet. This tension is reflected in Craik's novel, in the pairing of the excitable, disabled narrator, Phineas Fletcher, and the stalwart, silent hero, John Halifax.

Both Craik and Carlyle rely on metaphors of water and liquidity to describe the strong hero, who says little but who possesses unfathomable depths. In *On Heroes and Hero-Worship*, even the poets and prophets end up sounding like inarticulate men who have kept the best part of their thoughts to themselves through incredible self-restraint. Shakespeare possesses "such a calmness of depth; *placid* joyous strength; all things imagined in that *great* soul of his so true and clear, as in a tranquil, unfathomable sea!" (96 emphasis original). Mohamet is "A man rather taciturn in speech; silent when there was nothing to be said; but pertinent, wise, sincere, when he did speak" (49). Robert Burns is so articulate that waiters and ostlers will stop what they are doing to catch a word, but actually the Scottish poet speaks very little despite his remarkable gift (176). In a rather unlikely description of Norse epic, Carlyle claims that Snorri Sturluson writes the story of Odin "in the quietest manner, almost in a brief business style" (21). These men are silent because they have so much to say stored up inside them that words could hardly capture their depths. Oliver Cromwell is "The inarticulate Prophet; Prophet who could not speak. Rude, confused, struggling to utter himself, with his savage depth, his wild sincerity" (200). Poetry for Carlyle is really music, "a kind of inarticulate, unfathomable speech, which leads us to the edge of the infinite, and lets us for a moment gaze into that!" (78). These imagined depths, captured in a watery metaphor of Shakespeare's "tranquil, unfathomable sea," are much greater for being unspeakable. In other words, if Carlyle were able to describe the greatness of these men in plain English, their greatness would seem rather diminished. Carlyle's own articulateness—not only did he write sophisticated analyses of these men, but he also originally delivered *On Heroes and Hero-Worship* as a series of six lectures in Edinburgh—belies his praise of silence. Yet the author's verbosity seems acceptable to his readers despite this contradiction because they accept that someone must take on the task of praising the strong man, who would be undermined in singing his own praises. It is this very tension between the need for silence and the need to praise that very silence that Craik captures and resolves in her pairing of a disabled narrator and a strong man as hero.

A Love Surpassing Woman

Craik's novel thus solves a contradiction inherent in Carlyle's praise of the strong, silent type by setting the strong man's weak friend the task of singing his praises. John and Phineas act as foils to one another: John is a strong, silent, self-made man, whereas Phineas is a weak, voluble invalid. A descendant of the Carlylean captain of industry, John is a gentleman because of his tremendous self-restraint and silence. Carlyle's captain of industry is a businessman who takes up the challenges of contemporary industry manfully and, most important, silently. Craik's solution to the problem of how to narrate the story of a man who is so sparing of his words is to have Phineas, the hero's friend and companion, articulate those desires that he cannot or will not, including praising his friend's achievements. Arlene Young wryly remarks that "John Halifax's gentlemanliness is in part represented by his restraint and understatement—characteristics not always shared by his creator or the narrator in their celebrations of his glory" (39). Phineas is able to be so extravagant in his praise of his friend in part because he is recognizable as a descendant of the man of feeling. Craik sets her story at the turn of the century, and her story dramatizes the cultural shift from the man of feeling to the self-made man. Her thematic pairing of the businessman and the invalid thus speaks to a specific juncture in the history of masculinity, as well as enabling her to tell the story of the ascendance of the self-made man. Phineas's narration also functions on a literary register, providing an implicit defense of the literary world as it humanizes the ideal of the self-made man.

The different kinds of energy that Phineas and John bring to the novel as narrator and protagonist act as pulses to one another. Phineas's intense longing for John during the weeks and months he spends in his sickbed can be read, like Charles Edmonstone's ennui, as a longing for action and plot. John's highly plotted life offers Phineas's life a kind of vicarious narrative shape. By contrast, John's relentless course of self-improvement is tempered by Phineas's aimless indolence, which offers John, and the readers, a sense of much needed repose. In the mid–nineteenth century, the cult of the invalid seemed a natural response to the cult of the businessman-hero who never took a rest. Maria Frawley argues that hypochondria was particularly associated with businessmen in the 1840s: "Made ill by overwork, or otherwise inclined to nervous disorder, the male could all too easily become a hypochondriac and in doing so sacrifice rational understanding to an unchecked imagination and self-control to unrestrained desire" (97). The pairing of the strong man and the weak man, then, is the novelistic version of a wider cultural phenomenon: the cult of the invalid that was the response to the constant demands of industry.

To be an able-bodied man demands physical strength solidified through tremendous self-restraint, temperance, sexual continence, and the ability to labor and endure physical hardship. Craik's depiction of John concentrates on the muscular upper body that characterizes the strong man. Especially in their boyhood days, the physical differences between John and Phineas are conducive to an intense physical and emotional friendship as John supplies the physical strength and mobility that Phineas lacks and Phineas articulates the recesses of John's emotions. The first thing Phineas notices on seeing John is his physical prowess: "[I]n person" says he, "the lad was tall and strongly built; and I, poor puny wretch! So reverenced physical strength. Everything in him seemed to indicate that which I had not: his muscular limbs, his square, broad shoulders, his healthy cheek" and "his crisp curls of bright thick hair" (31–32). Phineas admires John's facial features, down to his "square, sharply-outlined, resolute chin," which "gives character and determination to the whole physiognomy" if not the whole man (31). Similarly, John's "muscular limbs" and his "square, broad shoulders" impress upon Phineas the stolidity of his character (32).[4] John, standing at a full five foot eleven and a half inches compared to Phineas's five foot four, is a man. Phineas links John's manhood to his strong physique and his verbal reticence; for John to proclaim his manhood would be to undermine it, and there is no need for him to do so when his body bespeaks his manhood so clearly. On his eighteenth birthday, Phineas remarks, "Manhood had come to him, both in character and demeanour, not as it comes to most young lads, an eagerly-desired and presumptuously-asserted claim, but as a rightful inheritance, to be received humbly, and worn simply and naturally" (78).

In her depiction of John Halifax, Craik shares the muscular Christian's emphasis on able-bodiedness as an indicator of a healthy morality.[5] If Craik was impressed with Kingsley's work, she was even more taken with that of Thomas Hughes. While she found George Eliot's *The Mill on the Floss* to be decidedly unwholesome, and troubling, she thought *Tom Brown's Schooldays* was the perfect antidote to any such intellectual morbidity.[6] After much reflection, she decided that Hughes's novel would be the perfect birthday present to send to her brother Ben, who was then working as a civil engineer in Brazil: "I was puzzling a long time what on earth to send you:—till I thought of Tom Brown. And it is such a beautiful book—'one that no gentleman's library should be without.'—I read it over again last Sunday with infinite delight" (Letter to Benjamin Mulock, 28 April 1860, in Craik, *Letters to Benjamin Mulock*). Craik and her circle were greatly impressed by Hughes's novel, especially the sporting scenes. Craik wrote to Ben, "Clarence [Dobell] got on board an Oxford boat & saw all close: his description was really like a bit of Tom Brown. Annie [Miers] read the "boat-race" in Tom Brown in the omnibus & was so excited by it, she said, that she was near crying—greatly to her confusion" (Letter to Benjamin Mulock, 1 April 1860). John Halifax is not a muscular Christian, but the extent to which he shares the muscular Christian's virtues demonstrates the overlap between what traits the Victorians thought made a good businessman and what made a good Christian gentleman.

Craik also uses a biblical precedent—the friendship of Jonathan and David—to give her readers a familiar framework for thinking about the central relationship in her novel. Phineas calls his beloved David and thinks of himself as Jonathan after the Old Testament story of the friendship between the King of Israel and the warrior, and he spends much of the first third of the novel being carried about by John. At the end of the first chapter Phineas recalls the passage from Samuel on this friendship—"the soul of Jonathan was knit unto the soul of David, and Jonathan loved him as his own soul"—and claims that "this day, I, a poorer and more helpless Jonathan, had found my David" (39).[7] Indeed, the biblical language gives Phineas a way to describe some of the most intensely erotic moments in the novel. When Phineas's father, the Quaker tanner Abel Fletcher, offers John his first job, Phineas exclaims, "I did not 'fall upon his neck,' like the princely Hebrew, to whom I have likened myself, but whom, alas! I resembled in nothing save my loving. But I grasped his hand, for the first time, and looking up at him, as he stood thoughtfully by me, whispered, 'that I was very glad'" (50). For Craik the affective intensity of this bond is a way to demonstrate true manliness. Friendship with a weaker man in particular allows the stronger man to demonstrate his gentleness and thus his gentlemanliness.

Craik's portrait of the tender relations between John and Phineas is at times extravagant in its homoeroticism, yet these homoerotic elements allow for the softening and humanizing of the man of industry.[8] Phineas draws out the scene of their first parting by calling John back to his door.

> "Not goodbye just yet!" said I, trying painfully to disengage myself from my little carriage, and mount the steps. John Halifax came to my aid.
> "Suppose you let me carry you. I could—and—and—it would be great fun, you know." He tried to turn it into a jest, so as not to

hurt me but the tremble in his voice was as tender as any woman's—tenderer than any woman's I ever was used to hear. I put my arms round his neck; he lifted me safely and carefully, and set me down at my own door. (37–38)

The intense homoeroticism of this scene is repeated throughout the first third of the novel and lays the foundation for Craik's humanization of the man of industry.

Craik argues that true tenderness is a masculine quality. John treats Phineas as tenderly as if he were his lover, and Craik does not shy away from the comparison. "If I had been a woman," confesses Phineas, "and the woman that he loved, he could not have been more tender over my weakness" (92). Phineas claims that tenderness is "a quality different from kindness, affectionateness, or benevolence; a quality which can exist only in strong, deep, and undemonstrative natures, and therefore in its perfection is seldomer found in women than in men" (53). The notion that women of the same age are less tender friends than men is borne out in Craik's earlier novel of disability, *Olive* (1850). Throughout the novel, Craik pairs her heroine with potential friends who turn out to be less than sympathetic, and whose beauty contrasts with Olive's spinal deformity. Where John and Phineas share a tender adolescent friendship, Olive's peers are sometimes cruel to her as a young woman. An offhand comment from her close friend crushes her: "Jealous of Olive—how very comical!" The friend continues "To think of Olive's stealing any girl's lover! She, who will probably never have one in all her life—poor thing!" (66). While some older women show Olive sympathy, including Harold's mother, Mrs. Gwynne, and she develops a close relationship with her mother when Mrs. Rothesay goes blind, her peers evince little sympathy based on her disability.[9]

John's devotion to his friend proves his character, acting as a safeguard against the hero sowing too many wild oats. At the same time that he acts as a vehicle for the expression of John's emotional life, Phineas also reins in any unseemly impulses or desires that might simmer in his friend's muscular frame. John confesses that he is not sure whether he is ready to meet the challenges of the world.

"I don't know. I'm not clear how far I could resist doing anything wrong, if it were pleasant. So many wrong things are pleasant—just now, instead of rising tomorrow, and going into the little dark counting house, and scratching paper from eight till six, shouldn't I like to break away! Dash out into the world, take to all sorts of wild freaks, do all sorts of grand things, and perhaps never come back to the tanning any more." (82)

John's punishment for his single lapse of judgment as a youth in spending an evening watching Sarah Siddons perform as Lady Macbeth is to carry his friend ten miles to the theater and another ten miles back home to Norton Bury after his money is stolen (91–97). This incident is the clearest indication in the novel of the private inner struggles that John undergoes to restrain his desires and is indeed the only wild oat that John sows in the whole novel.

Extraordinary Laconism

Craik ties John's self-control up in his taciturnity: his "extraordinary" laconism manifests itself at key moments throughout the text (138). He first proves his worth to Phineas's father through his determined silence. When Abel Fletcher asks if he is a lad to be trusted, John seems to feel that this is a "critical moment," and he gathers "all his mental forces into a serried square, to meet the attack" (34). He meets it, and conquers it, "in silence," neither answering nor declining his eyes (34). John's lack of response answers well with the tanner, who leaves him to escort his crippled son home. John's moral strength in remaining silent is only equaled by his physical strength, which he uses to carry his charge. As the two young men wait for the rain to pass before starting home, John again makes no "attempt to talk" (34). Later in their friendship, when Dr. Jessop diagnoses Phineas's unspecified illness as incurable, John only listens with his hand on his friend's shoulder, and a "grave, sweet look," which provides "dearer sympathy" to his friend "than any words" (81). John teaches Phineas how to restrain his melancholic temperament, as the two "draw a curtain over inevitable grief" and lay "it in the peaceful chamber of silence" (81). Despite this protest, at times it can seem that Phineas keeps very little to himself.

Phineas's effusive praise stands in stark contrast to John's forthright speeches, which are rarely quoted in full. Instead, Phineas narrates these incidents through the sentimental lens that John's own speech presumably lacks. He tells us John speaks well enough to quell riots, stop a run on a bank, and dissuade highwaymen from robbing him. He also wins a wife partly through his eloquence. Phineas never records the words with which John courts Ursula, but he explains that when "his tongue was once unloosed, few people could talk better than John Halifax." This is not to say that he is "one of your showy conversationalists." As Phineas puts it.

> [L]anguage was with him neither a science, an art, nor an accomplishment, but a mere vehicle for thought; the garb, always chosen as simplest and fittest, in which his ideas were clothed. His conversation was never wearisome, since he only spoke when he had something to say; and having said it, in the most concise and appropriate manner that suggested itself at the time—he was silent; and silence is a great and rare virtue at twenty years of age. (160)

John's language is the transparent expression of his soul, unobscured by any showy "garb." In fact he shows great suspicion of using any "vehicle" at all to express himself.

Craik's consistent emphasis on the taciturnity of the gentleman casts suspicion on literary enterprises, including her own novel. On a pragmatic level, John needs to be literate in order to rise in business; on an imaginative level, he and Phineas, who read *Romeo and Juliet* to one another, as well as the poems of Wordsworth and the Elizabethan Phineas Fletcher, for whom Phineas is named, take an intrinsic pleasure in storytelling. Phineas is aligned with literature in both its humanizing and its suspicious forms. His early attempts to pull John into his life and thus the narrative take on a literary register. Irresistibly drawn to John, Phineas uses his talents as a conversationalist to draw him into the narrative, talking to John of books, which make his only world, and of which John knows little (40). When John tries to leave again after the cantankerous family servant, Jael, objects to this ragged boy as company for her master's son, Phineas soliloquizes, "Gone! It was not to be thought of" and smooths the matter over with John by offering to tell him the folktale of Dick Whittington, the boy who rises from rags to become mayor of London (43). On one afternoon outing, Phineas teaches John to write cursive with a rose stem in the gravel (72). At every opportunity, he sends John "a little note, written carefully in printed letters," which he knows John can read, and also "a book or two, out of which he might teach himself a little more" (65). John's education is complete when, with new clothes and a figure "increased both in height, compactness and grace" (66), he demonstrates to his friend that he has taught himself to "read and add up" out of Phineas's books and consequently now goes around collecting money instead of skins for Abel Fletcher (67).

Mary Poovey's influential argument that the labor of the man of letters parallels the domestic labor of the woman—both are invisible, humanizing, and comforting, potentially disguising "the inequities and hypocrisies of class society" because they carry "the symbolic authority of moral superiority"—is pertinent here (122–23). As a feminized invalid, Phineas supports John's rise to power, potentially papering over anxieties about the self-made man's rise. Phineas does not set himself up as a man of letters, he only once refers to the physical writing of the novel only to dismiss it as "foolish," though perhaps "less foolish and harmful" to him as an invalid than to most (50)—his literary labor, like the housewife's domestic labor, is successful because it remains hidden. Both are labors of love.

The Grand Old Name of Gentleman

By establishing a tender friendship between Phineas and John, and then narrating John's rise to power through Phineas's point of view, Craik allays Victorian anxieties that the self-made man is an uncaring social climber who is only interested in getting on in a narrowly material sense. Phineas praises and humanizes the businessman, yet through his marginal position he also subtly undermines the patriarch's values. As Silvana Colella argues in an essay on *John Halifax* and gift theory, Phineas is a "pure conscience, a self untainted by the market and therefore able to validate the beauty and purity of business properly understood, from his privileged position outside the arena of commercial strife" (402). Yet Phineas is important not only as an antidote to Victorian suspicions of self-interest but also as someone who will speak on behalf of the self-made man who cannot praise himself. Craik's epigraph to *John Halifax*, from Tennyson's *In Memoriam*, sets up the idea that a gentleman is silent.

> And thus he bore without abuse
> The grand old name of gentleman
> Defamed by every charlatan,
> And soil'd with all ignoble use (CXI 21–24)

Craik quotes only the first two lines of the quatrain in her epigraph, but her work shares Tennyson's anxiety about the status of the gentleman, whose very name can be "soil'd" by being used too freely. Given the concern about men (and authors) who speak too much or too freely that Craik and Tennyson share, we can see that both Phineas and the speaker of the poem are in a difficult position when they proclaim their friends gentlemen.

Like Craik, Tennyson uses an intense, homoerotic friendship between two men—a weak speaker who cannot help but praise his strong friend—to shore up the strong friend's status as a gentleman. Tennyson's speaker is deeply suspicious of the power of language to capture his friend's true greatness of character.

> I leave thy praises unexpressed
> In verse that brings myself relief,
> And by the measure of my grief
> I leave they greatness to be guess'd; (LXXV 1–4)

Lyric for the speaker can only gesture toward the full manliness of his friend's character. While his love is a reflection of his beloved friend, his "words are only words, and moved / Upon the topmost froth of thought" (LII 3–4). Not only is language inadequate to capture Hallam's greatness, but it also redounds on the character of the speaker, who cannot exert the manly self-control necessary to keep his pain private. To those who suggest that his grief is too public, as he makes a "parade out of pain," the speaker protests, "I do but sing because I must" (XXI 10, 23). Tennyson's effeminate speaker presents his own weakness by continuing to express his grief in lyric form in contrast to the silent strength of his friend.

This tendency to equate manly self-control with silence takes a comic turn in Dickens. The way to tell that a man is a gentleman in the Victorian novel is not by what he says but by what he does. You can rarely trust what the long-winded industrialist has to say in Victorian fiction. Things go terribly awry when the self-made tries to narrate his own story. In *Great Expectations* (1861), Pip tells the melancholy story of his attempt to be a gentleman from the time when he has already realized the pitfalls of that enterprise. In *Hard Times* (1854), Bounderby's verbosity makes him an object of suspicion from the moment the scene first opens on him as he tells Mrs. Gradgrind of the trials of his childhood, which, he says, was pretty fairly divided between the cot of his infancy, an egg box, and the bed of his youth, the muddiest of ditches. As the narrator comments, he was a "man who could never sufficiently vaunt himself a self-made man. A man who was always proclaiming, through that brassy speaking-trumpet of a voice of his, his old ignorance and his old poverty. A man who was the Bully of humility" (53). The trials that Bounderby claims to have suffered are not so different from those that Phineas catalogs of John, who sleeps in ditches and lives in a garret long after he is well on his way to becoming a respectable businessman. Dickens's satire of Bounderby's oft-repeated claim, "I never wear gloves. . . . I didn't climb up the ladder in *them*. Shouldn't be so high up, if I had" (58), or, as he tells his friend's wife, "I was to pull through it, I suppose, Mrs. Gradgrind. Whether I was to do it or not, ma'am, I did it. I pulled through it, though nobody threw me out a rope" (55), resonates with Phineas's earnest claims that his friend John started with no capital but his head and his own two hands, and was indebted to no forefathers for his history (17). Craik's portrait of John in these moments would teeter dangerously close to Dickens's satire of the self-made man were it not for the key point that John never praises himself. The sentiment that Phineas infuses these comments with as John's friend and admirer allows Craik to admire John unabashedly in a way that no omniscient narrator, and certainly not John himself, could. In Dickens, when Mrs. Pegler enters the scene late in the novel and claims Josiah as her own son, and it becomes apparent that the Coketown manufacturer has antecedents after all, the blow literally takes the wind out of Bounderby.

John Halifax anticipates Samuel Smiles's 1859 formulation of the self-made man, whose value lies not in his wealth but in his character, which allows him to rise to the top of his chosen industry regardless of how low on the ladder he begins.[10] Thus, although a man can be a gentleman in rags if he has the right character, if he does indeed have the right character riches are likely to follow. In Smiles's estimation, "The crown and glory of life is character. It is the noblest possession of a man, constituting a rank in itself, and an estate in the general good-will; dignifying every station, and exalting every position in society" (314). Through self-culture, any man could obtain the character of a gentleman regardless of his station in life. In his advice to young businessmen in the early part of the century, Thomas Tegg emphasized self-regulation: "The first rules are these: Tell truth; be sober; be punctual; rise early; persevere; avoid extravagance; keep your word; and watch your health" (141). The self-made man's success was bound up in his vital power, and the regime required to keep him in tip-top shape—from the time he woke up to bathe in cold water to the wee hours of the morning when he taught himself Latin or double-entry bookkeeping—could at times seem exhausting.

Much like Craik, Samuel Smiles admonishes his readers that a man's success as a gentleman is known not only by his upright dealings in industry but also by the way in which he treats those weaker than himself. As Smiles argues, "Gentleness is indeed the best test of gentlemanliness. A consideration for the feelings of others, for his inferiors and dependents as well as his equals, and respect for their self-respect, will pervade the true gentleman's whole conduct" (333). Smiles goes on to tell an anecdote about the remorse of a man who strikes a passerby who treads on his foot without realizing that he is blind, and he notes that the gentleman will always give others the benefit of the doubt, for he "will rather himself suffer a small injury, than by an uncharitable construction of another's behaviour, incur the risk of committing a great wrong" (333). Although the only advantages that the self-made man possesses may be, like John's, his head and his own two hands (40), he will keep this capital in mind when considering "those whose advantages in life have not been equal to his own" and be "forebearant" of their "weaknesses," "failings," and "errors" (333). The idea of the gentleman is thus dependent on the existence of a physically or morally weaker person on whom he can lavish his gentleness.

Craik's pairing of John and Phineas allows her to subdue the relentless self-discipline of the self-made man through the more restful tempo of the invalid's life. One of the reasons that Phineas is so necessary as a narrator is that John develops a tremendous amount of self-restraint, and in order to make this restraint heroic Phineas must show the reader the extent of the feelings he is reining in. Like Carlyle's, Craik's affective metaphors are hydraulic: John's emotions are liquid substances (tears, boiling blood) that must be kept under pressure lest they explode. Accused of being tempted to spend his first earnings from the tanyard at the local pub, though his face is "crimson and quivering," John smothers "down a burst of tears" with difficulty (49). Phineas speculates that perhaps "this self-control was more moving than if he had wept—at least it answered better with my father" (49). This metaphor of self-restraint as a controlled but potentially dangerous liquid continues throughout the novel. When Ursula's gentleman cousin refuses to have the man of the people dine with them, although he speaks "savagely and loud," John remains silent. "He had locked his hands together convulsively," says Phineas, "but it was easy to see that his blood was at a boiling heat, and that, did he once slip the leash of his passions, it would go hard with Richard Brithwood" (209). When John is having difficulty supporting his young family financially, Phineas observes, "Sometimes even a hasty word, and uneasiness about trifles, showed how strong was the effort he made at self-control" (271). The control that John exercises over his liquid emotions is similar to his dexterously managed conversion of the mill to steam power, which is effected without worker agitation, explosions, or steam-related industrial accidents.

Key to this conversion are the Victorian ideals of chivalry that characterize the relations between strong and weak men, or, in this case, men and masters. Phineas calls on Victorian ideals of chivalry similar to those of Kingsley and Yonge, which humanize the relationship between the strong and the weak, and the rich and the poor, to think about his relationship with John: "And though he never failed to maintain externally a certain gentle respectfulness of demeanor towards me, yet it was more the natural deference of the younger to the elder, of the strong to the weak, than the duty paid by a serving-lad to his master's son" (58). In this passage, class hierarchy enables the intense homoeroticism that exists between the two boys. The labor relations between the boys, as John is hired to help Phineas home, thus become personal relations. This is a common pattern in mid-Victorian thinking about how the gentleman comports himself in business. Mary Klages argues that Phineas and then Muriel, John's blind daughter who dies in youth, both allow the captain of industry to demonstrate his gentle and thus gentlemanly nature. According to Klages, gentility, for Craik, "is related to gentleness and is marked by the deployment of a proper Christian moral sensibility and concern for the welfare of others in all areas of endeavor, including the economic realm. What makes John Halifax, the book's hero, into a 'gentleman' is not the wealth he gains through his honest work, but the love he generates and earns through his treatment of his family and, by extension, his workers and dependents" (64). Similarly, Patrick Brantlinger argues that for writers like Carlyle, Dickens, and Arthur Helps, Craik's contemporaries, the best industrial relations are personal relations (111).

The idea of treating those who are weaker, be they women, workers, or invalid men, with chivalry also brings the private sphere into the public sphere. In *The Industrial Reformation of English Fiction*, Catherine Gallagher argues that realistic novels of the mid-Victorian period simultaneously associate and disassociate the public and private sphere. "Industrial novels, especially those of the 1850s," she writes, "display this normal tension in an exaggerated form. They make the connection between the family and society one of their main themes and primary organizing devices, but they simultaneously emphasize that the family must be isolated and protected from the larger social world" (114–15). By contrast, Craik's novel actually reveals the two separate spheres to be compatible. Throughout the novel, Craik shows that treating people with kindness is the best way to get ahead in the business world. For example, John gains his first job in the tanyard through his kindness to Phineas. Similarly, John's workers eventually accept steam power not because John has explained that it is a good business decision but because they have seen how tenderly John treats his blind daughter, Muriel, who spends every afternoon in the mill with her father. Phineas reflects that "the quiet way in which the Enderley mill people took the introduction of machinery, and the peaceableness with which they watched for weeks the setting up of the steam engine, was partly owing to their strong impression of Mr. Halifax's goodness as a father, and the vague, almost superstitious interest which attached to the pale, sweet face of Muriel" (334). John explains to his young boys that the most productive laborers are those who work from love. He says, "Our people will work the better, because they will work from love. Not merely doing their duty, and obeying their master in a blind way, but feeling an interest in him and all that belongs to him; knowing that he feels the same in them" (308). Here economic power has an affective base that is similar to the emotional register through which Phineas has been describing John's work all along. John's business strategy thus validates Phineas's narrative strategy.

Pain and Productivity

Phineas gives his disability a kind of economic value by turning it into a story. His pain becomes productive as he uses it to write John's story. In nineteenth-century economic thought, as Catherine Gallagher argues, labour was only valuable insofar as it was physically demanding or painful and yet provided the means to sustain the body.[11] Unlike some forms of manual labor, authorial pain may be psychological. Gallagher argues that nineteenth-century thought connected labor to physical pain and nourishment insofar as a man was supposed to earn as much as would keep him nourished to continue working. But for Craik good writing, as well as good labor, was physically painful. Phineas not only claims writing as painful labor but he claims that it is physically painful. Yet this physical pain is perhaps even more conducive to narrative than mental anguish.

Phineas links his illness to the wide sympathies that make him a good storyteller. He describes himself as susceptible to impressions, feeling "more quickly and more keenly" than his "strong and self-contained friend" (59). As he explains, illness and a "long introverted life" have made his memory "preternaturally vivid": "colourless itself," his memory has "had nothing to do but to reflect and retain clear images of the lives around it" (50). Phineas's invalidism, which allows him to write his friend's story, is a good example of the kind of pain that Gallagher argues gives all labor, including literary labor, its value in nineteenth-century economic thought. John's "active busy life" gives a vicarious narrative structure to Phineas's idleness. In the opening chapters of the novel, Phineas struggles to keep John within the purview of the narrative. When John says "goodbye" after escorting Phineas home on that first rainy day, Phineas says, "I started. The word pained me. On my sad, lonely life indeed, though ill-health seemed to have doubled and trebled my sixteen years into a mournful maturity—this lad's face had come like a flash of sunshine" (37). Phineas claims, "I had been revolving many plans, which had one sole aim and object, to keep near me this lad, whose companionship and help seemed to me, brotherless, sisterless, and friendless as I was, the very thing that would give me an interest in life, or, at least, make it drag on less wearily" (40). Here the "interest in life" that Phineas hopes John will bring him seems akin to the narrative interest of the novel itself.

The pleasure of John's presence gives Phineas's life a vicarious narrative shape and tempers his physical suffering. Phineas describes his pain as rendering time indistinguishable. He experiences intense isolation and ennui during his illnesses: "Summers and winters slipped by, lazily enough, as the years seemed always to crawl round at Norton Bury. How things went in the outside world, I little knew or cared. My father lived his life, mechanical and steady as clockwork, and we two, John Halifax and Phineas Fletcher, lived our lives—the one so active and busy, the other so useless and dull. Neither of us counted the days, nor looked backwards or forwards" (78). Phineas claims that his life is "useless and dull," but the days and seasons that slip "wearily away" for him allow Craik to mark the passing of time that transforms John from vagabond to successful businessman (51). Phineas's wearisome life also allows the reader a sense of repose from what would otherwise be a relentless catalog of John's actions and achievements.

Phineas describes the pleasurable monotony of living in John's household using another watery metaphor, comparing the passage of time in retrospect to a calm stretch of sea. Whereas Yonge's Charles Edmonstone finds the ennui of being ill tiresome, and works to stir up the action of the narrative, once he is an established member of John's household and secure of his friend's presence forevermore, Phineas is happy to enjoy the "delicious monotony" (275) of life in the country. Once in John's household, Phineas claims that "sickness did not now take that heavy, overpowering grip of me, mind and body, that it once used to do. It never did when John was by. He gave me strength, mentally and physically. He was life and health to me, with his brave cheerfulness—his way of turning all minor troubles into pleasantries, till they seemed to break and vanish away, sparkling, like the foam on top of the wave" (124). They lived those years, he reminisces, in "such unbroken, uneventful peace, that looking back seems like looking back over a level sea, whose leagues of tiny ripples make one smooth glassy plain" (356). The pattern of the narrative for the last two-thirds of the novel, then, seems to follow that of Phineas's convalescence. Here, the hydraulic metaphors that Craik uses to describe John's pent-up emotions give way to the more peaceful flow of Phineas's emotions, which sail smoothly over troubled waters.

Narrative Crotchets

Phineas's marginal position in John's household as a disabled bachelor uncle lends him a different perspective on the family's workings for the rest of the novel. The critic R. H. Hutton remained unconvinced of Phineas's masculinity and thought that he was more of an aunt than an uncle. "During the early part of the tale," writes he, "it is difficult to suppress a fear that Phineas Fletcher will fall hopelessly in love with John Halifax, so hard is it to remember that Phineas is of the male sex. Afterwards, when he professes to be an uncle, the reader is constantly aware that he is really an aunt, and a curious perplexity is apt to arise in the mind on the subject" ("Novels by the Authoress of 'John Halifax'" 475). This claim was later echoed by second-wave feminists, who argued that Phineas was a stand-in for the woman writer's crippling situation in a patriarchal society.[12] Hutton's claim that Phineas is really a maiden aunt suggests that Phineas is radically feminized. However, this extreme view of Phineas as a maiden aunt rather than an uncle was not shared by other reviewers.

As Eileen Cleere points out in her work on avuncularism in the nineteenth-century novel, a careful reading of the importance of aunts and uncles reveals an alternative perspective to the nuclear family as the organizing principle of the industrial novel (3). Cleere argues that uncles, who often die conveniently so that a niece or nephew can inherit and who generally earn their wealth through industry and in the colonies rather than through patriarchal inheritance, come to stand for an alternative set of economic possibilities in the Victorian novel (8). Disability, which is often paired with an avuncular position, similarly stands for an alternative set of economic and affective possibilities in the novel. Phineas is the perfect example of a character whose different investment in the economic systems that undergird the novel—he provides the repose and affective engagement necessary to balance the relentless work and self-restraint of the self-made man—further structures the novel's narrative form. This phenomenon is not limited to Craik's work. In *Doctor Thorne* (1858), Trollope gives us another uncle whose disinterestedness counterbalances the taint of the money that his niece, Mary Thorne, stands to inherit from her other uncle, the self-made man Roger Scatcherd. John Halifax is the paradigmatic good self-made man while Roger Scatcherd, an alcoholic and workaholic, is the paradigmatic bad self-made man. Nevertheless, the avuncular perspective seems necessary in both novels to allow for a strengthening of the disinterested affective ties that an investment in business threatens to destroy.

Phineas's voice as a narrator is largely collaborative rather than completely undermining of John.[13] Although he criticizes John's parenting as too harsh on occasion, his critique is not meant to topple John's position as *pater familias* or mill owner. Rather, Phineas's voice supplements John's self-control. If John's position were completely self-contained and unassailable, Phineas would not be necessary. Phineas's voice is indeed collaborative, as he provides the necessary function of praising and narrating John's life, but rather than radically revising patriarchy Phineas subtly critiques John's position as domestic patriarch while allowing his family and his mill to remain intact. As the narrator, Phineas critiques John's unbending will only to the reader, and many years after the events he is narrating have passed. He thus gives vent to emotional outbursts that suggest the difficulty of maintaining the tremendous self-restraint of the self-made man, while ensuring that John's path remains along the straight and narrow since his commentary can have no possible effect on the events of his life after so many years have passed. His romantic friendship with John and later his domestic position in the Halifax household move the industrial novel in the direction of the domestic novel, softening the contours of the public sphere with the feeling of the private sphere. As a disabled uncle figure rather than a strong father, Phineas offers an alternative and much more intense affective engagement from that of the patriarch of home and industry, whose very self-restraint assures his position as father. Phineas's disability—at once privileged as the main point of view in the novel and marginalized as the voice of a character narrator who is not the main character—is thus a source of tension and narrative energy.

John's tremendous self-restraint threatens to bar him from marriage precisely because he cannot step outside his manly taciturnity to woo his wife. Phineas, as the more loquacious weak man, accomplishes this wooing on his behalf. In a role reversal, John lies dying of a broken heart because of his unrequited love for the mayor's daughter. Phineas uses his pain as a reason to lash out at Ursula. When she protests that she is sorry that no one told her John was ill, Phineas exclaims: "'You? How could it affect you? To me, now'—and my savage words, for they were savage, broke down in a burst of misery—'Nothing in this world is to me worth a straw, in comparison with John. If he dies—'" (216). Phineas effectively teaches Ursula to love John through the depth of his feeling for his strong companion. Repeating the liquid metaphor for affect, he writes, "I let loose the flood of my misery, I dashed it over her, that she might see it—feel it; that it might enter all the fair and sightly chambers of her happy life, and make them desolate as mine. For was she not the cause?" (216). Phineas blames Ursula for the potential loss of his friendship, but the result is that his intense homosocial bond with John underwrites John's marriage.

Phineas is able to remain a collaborative voice in the Halifax household partially because he critiques John's methods of raising his family mainly in retrospect. As a disabled bachelor uncle in a model household, "Uncle Phineas" gives vent to the emotional tension that John and his wife fail to articulate. Phineas's narrative "crotchets" often manifest themselves in his reactions to the love affairs of John's children. He characterizes himself as an "old bachelor" who is "prone to moralize over such things" as the duty of women not to engage in coquetry since it can turn men off the entire sex (410). When John's eldest son, Guy, tells his parents that he is in love with a woman of whom they do not quite approve, a French governess (and who, as it turns out, is in love with his younger brother Edwin), Phineas claims that he can sympathize with all the parties. "Those who in the dazzled vision of youth see only the beauty and splendor of love—first love, who deem it comprises the whole of life, beginning, aim, and end—may marvel that I, who have been young, and now am old, see as I saw that night, not only the lover's, but the parents' side of the question," he writes. "I felt overwhelmed with sadness, as, viewing the three, I counted up in all its bearings and consequences, near and remote, this attachment of poor Guy's" (403). Phineas imagines that he must convince an audience of young, love-struck readers of the validity of his narrative perspective, which allows him a wider range of sympathies than his friend John.

Phineas claims that he can sympathize with all kinds of love as one who has been deprived of romantic love. He is especially emphatic on the point of love in the face of a great disparity in age when Lord Ravenel falls in love with John's much younger daughter Maud. Phineas muses in retrospect:

> Of all kinds of love, there is one which common sense and romance have often combined to hold obnoxious, improbable, or ridiculous, but which has always seemed to me the most real and pathetic form that the passion ever takes; I mean, love in spite of great disparity of age. Even when this is on the woman's side, I can imagine circumstances that would make it far less ludicrous and pitiful; and there are few things to me more touching, more full of sad earnest, than to see an old man in love with a young girl. (446)[14]

Phineas does not directly state his opinion of May-December marriages to John, but he slips up and calls John's daughter "poor Maud" because it seems that she will never know of Lord Ravenel's love for her. He explains this slip as one of his crotchets: "I really could not tell; it was a mere accident, the unwitting indication of some crotchets of mine, which had often come into my mind lately. Crotchets, perhaps peculiar to one, who, never having known a certain possession, found himself rather prone to overrate its value" (455). Narrating in retrospect, Phineas undermines his earlier feelings as the reaction of one who has never experienced love, but he nevertheless allows them to stand as a counterpoint to John's interference in his children's love affairs, which he disapproves of when they involve titled lovers. Although Phineas claims that he may be prone to overrate that certain possession that he has never experienced, heterosexual love, he has of course experienced romantic friendship.[15] His position as "brother" and "uncle" in John's household is the legacy of that early romantic friendship, and it is this avuncular position, won in part by his disability, that allows him to sympathize with John's children.

If Craik's portrait of the potential for friendship across physical and temperamental differences is idyllic in the John-Phineas bond, her portrait of John's sons hints that such a bond may not always result from differing sympathies. John's sons, Guy and Edwin, are typed as psychologically if not physically opposite. Even in their boyhood, Edwin is intellectual and Guy is sociable. At the mention of learning how steam power works, "Edwin lifted up from his slate bright, penetrating eyes. He was quite an old man in his way—wise even from babyhood." Guy, by contrast, is "much the naughtiest" but with the "frankest, warmest, tenderest boy-heart, always struggling to be good, and never able to accomplish it" (335). These personalities remain fixed in adulthood: "With his easy, happy temper, generous but uncertain, and his showy, brilliant parts, he was not nearly so much to be depended on as the grave Edwin, who was already a thorough man of business, and plodded between Enderly mills and a smaller one which had taken the place of the flour mill at Norton Bury, with indomitable perseverance" (361). Craik has sometimes been read as presenting too idyllic a picture of the possibilities of friendship between the able-bodied and the disabled, a pairing that Eliot revised in *The Mill on the Floss* and Charlotte Yonge responded to in her late 1886 novel *Chantry House*, which suggests that the more scholastic, steady temperament might be better suited for success in business.[16] Craik's positioning of the weaker, more intellectual brother as the one who will take over the family business thus complicates her initial claim that taciturn strong types are the best businessmen. In contrast to Edwin, Guy and their neighbor and eventual brother-in-law, Lord Ravenel, are only prepared to enter into the business after a stint in the United States hones their business sense.

John Halifax, Gentleman is a novel that praises self-restraint, silence, and an upright physical body as an indicator of an upright character through the eyes of a physically weak man who is prone to effusions. How do these values redound on Phineas? John does once chastise Phineas for his propensity to gossip. When Phineas wants to question their landlady Mrs. Tod about the handsome woman he and John have caught a glimpse of, Ursula, John gives "his veto so decidedly against seeking out people's private affairs in such an illicit manner" that Phineas confesses, "I felt quite guilty, and began to doubt whether my sickly, useless, dreaming life, was not inclining me to curiosity, gossip, and other small vices which we are accustomed—I know not why—to insult the other sex, by describing as 'womanish'" (148). It seems that, as an effeminate invalid, the narrator is not expected to have strength enough to bear the same moral burden as the novel's eponymous hero. Phineas's weakness in narrating John's story is in some ways an extension of his physical weakness: his record of John's history is both a testament to his friend and a betrayal of his confidences. Writing, as well as speaking, is suspect in Craik's work. Yet the strictures against writing and gossip are not so absolute that Phineas becomes completely pathologized in the world of the novel. Craik sets up her narrative structure so that Phineas provides the necessary emotional and verbal counterpoint to John's taciturnity and self-restraint.

Craik's novel has been dismissed over the years as a pious representation of the perfect Victorian gentleman. Her rags-to-riches story is at best a facile Victorian fantasy of the potential of self-help; her representation of the John-Phineas relationship is embarrassing or excessive in its intimacy, or at best a noteworthy celebration of homoeroticism that must fade into the background once the main characters reach adulthood. Yet Craik's portrait of the friendship of the strong man and the weak man is nonetheless a powerful one. The John-Phineas relationship crystallizes the dynamic of the voluble weak man and the strong businessman-hero, shedding light on later iterations of the pairing in canonical novels. George Eliot and Henry James were both critical of Craik's work. Eliot claimed that she was a "writer who is read only by novel readers, pure and simple, never by people of high culture" (*George Eliot Letters* 3.302), while James, in his review of her later novel, *A Noble Life*, wryly remarked on that "lively predilection for cripples and invalids by which she has always been distinguished" (169).[17] Yet so powerful were representations like Craik's, that each novelist felt compelled to rework the pairing of the strong man and the weak man, with Eliot turning the friendship into a rivalry and James relying heavily on the figure of the invalid yet portraying him as indifferent to the strong man. In a critical climate that has largely underestimated the value of Craik's work, it would be hard to overestimate the influence of her pairing of the strong man and the weak man on later Victorian fiction.

CHAPTER 3

Tom Tulliver's Schooldays

In George Eliot's *The Mill on the Floss* (1860), Tom Tulliver, who stands half an inch taller than John Halifax at a full six feet (352), is not all that different from Craik's paradigmatic self-made man. Like John Halifax, Tom is not afraid to get his hands dirty or deal with cheese, keeps a humble room in his friend's house, and studies bookkeeping at night. Nor are his financial and moral rewards considerably less than those of Craik's hero: he manages to pay off 320 pounds of his father's debt, equivalent to a year's income for a middle-class family,[1] by the tender age of nineteen (364)— an age when John Halifax has only just been promoted from driving a cart full of skins to and from the tanyard to collecting money for Abel Fletcher. Perhaps the prime difference between Tom Tulliver and John Halifax is in how they treat their disabled companions. While John lavishes his tenderness on Phineas, Tom treats the hunchbacked Philip Wakem with suspicion and scorn.[2] In its complex exploration of male friendship, education, and self-help in the business world, *The Mill on the Floss* rewrites some of the most important issues facing men at midcentury.

Yet critics, from the novel's first reviewers onward, have focused on the trials and tribulations of the heroine, Maggie, reading *The Mill on the Floss* almost exclusively as a female bildungsroman. *The Mill on the Floss* enjoyed its greatest critical popularity during the second wave of feminism. Elaine Showalter found that Maggie, overwhelmed by the patriarchal rigidity best represented by Tom, is ultimately unable to recognize and act on her feelings (*A Literature of Their Own* 128). Nina Auerbach argued that the intimations of the Gothic that tinge Eliot's realism converge in Maggie, whose sexuality and desires are consistently associated with witchery, vampirism, and demonism (150). Mary Jacobus focused on Maggie's intellectual engagement with Tom's education, arguing that Maggie finds room for linguistic play in an otherwise exclusionary masculine education in the classics.

But Maggie's struggles are complexly interwoven with a sustained critique of midcentury masculinity. In fact the first chapters of the novel do not detail Maggie's time at Miss Firniss's boarding school, or her time as a governess in the style of *Jane Eyre*, but rather a story that we might call "Tom Tulliver's Schooldays." Tom's story is in part a recasting of the schoolboy genre exemplified by *Tom Brown's Schooldays*, taking us from the family mill to the boarding school to the warehouse. *The Mill on the Floss* pairs the robust Tom Tulliver with the hunchbacked Philip Wakem, but the result is not an emotionally educative friendship such as the one that Tom Brown and George Arthur enjoy. Eliot recognizes a tension between the schoolboy novel's promotion of health and athleticism, on the one hand, and its insistence on the affective power of disability on the other. Her innovation in the genre is to turn what should be a tender lifelong friendship between two physically different boys into a bitter enmity. A Sedgwickian rivalry for Maggie's affections has important consequences for Eliot's vision of sympathy. While many of her contemporaries celebrate the friendship of the strong man and the weak man as productive of sympathy and understanding, for Eliot this is not the case. She suggests that the physiological differences between the two boys engender their affective differences: as a hunchback, Philip is morbid, peevish, sensitive, and sympathetic, while Tom's straight back matches his unbending morals. But instead of having the two sensibilities complement one another, Eliot explores the somatic limits of sympathy. In Philip, Eliot anatomizes a potential failing of her own theory of sympathy: when sympathy is grounded in a sense of exclusion, it is liable to turn peevish and egotistical. The Tom-Philip rivalry serves to demonstrate that male friendship across physical differences is not inevitable, and that an increased capacity for sympathy is not necessarily the natural consequence of an enervated frame.

Schoolboy Friendship

Eliot's publisher, John Blackwood, recognized the contrast between Tom Brown and Tom Tulliver, early on, writing that "the hero is a wonderful picture of a boy and lifelike contrast to the sort of Tom Brown ideals of what boys are" (Letter to William Blackwood, quoted in Eliot, *George Eliot Letters*, 3.234). George Lewes was actually reading *Tom Brown at Oxford*, which began serialization in *Macmillan's Magazine* in November 1859, aloud to Eliot as she began *The Mill on the Floss* (3.193). Eliot's novel is deeply responsive to Hughes's portrait of a hardy, unreflective boy whose education is meant to make him an Englishman first and foremost. She engages several motifs from the schoolboy genre, including the characterization of the hero as an ordinary boy whose indifferent performance at school belies his cleverness in practical matters, the pairing of the normative schoolboy with an odd or weak friend who reveals his true character, and the involvement of the schoolfriend's sister as a means of mediating the relationship between the two boys.

The story of how reforms in public schools at midcentury contributed to the ideal of a vigorous, healthful manhood is a familiar one. Practically speaking, athleticism developed in public schools, and in schools aspiring to public school status, as a response to a shared set of disciplinary problems across several different educational institutions. G. E. L. Cotton, fictionalized as the young headmaster in *Tom Brown's Schooldays*, became headmaster of Marlborough in 1852 and was faced with a number of disciplinary problems, including "poaching, trespassing, and general lawlessness" (Mangan 22). Historian J. A. Mangan suggests that while he may have extolled the moral virtues of athleticism in Hughes's novel, in life an emphasis on organized sport was considered a solution to a practical disciplinary problem, a direction for sexual energy, and a way to form a virtuous and manly character in young boys.

While the role that organized sport in the public school played in developing a culture of masculine industry and vitality is well known, the concurrent presence of masculine weakness and disability has received little scholarly attention. The presence of masculine weakness and disability could serve as a foil to a normative, strong masculinity or it could be seen as a call to action to strengthen weak or underprivileged boys. One headmaster, Hely Hutchinson Almond of the Scottish Loretto School (from 1862 to 1903), emphasized health to the extent that he actually ended up attracting feeble boys as pupils. This was hardly his intent in bringing the sporting principles of Oxford to the unhealthy, bookish Scottish educational system in the 1860s. For all his emphasis on physical exercise, hygiene, and rational dress (short trousers, sensible boots, an open-necked shirt, and no coat or tie), according to Mangan "to a degree Loretto resembled a remedial health centre with its wholesome and plentiful food, daily cold baths, open windows in dormitory and classroom, regular physical activity throughout the day (morning and afternoon) and clothes and footwear designed for sensible living." It became a "place for he special care of poor physique and weak constitution," somewhat to Almond's dismay (55). Yet he also took pride in the school's positive impact on the constitution of weak boys.

> A narrow-chested poorly-nourished boy came here in 18[8]4. He improved greatly in the next two years, chest from 29 ½ inches to 35, weight from 6 stone 11 to 8 stone 4, and I was quite happy about him. He was also tall for his age growing from 5 f 1 ½ to 5 ft 7 in the time. He never appeared in our medical books except for a weak knee till November 3rd 1887. (quoted in Mangan 55)

Almond had expected to run a school, not a sanatorium. Yet, this unexpected proliferation of weakness in a school run on muscular Christian principles dovetails with the presence of the weak man or boy in muscular Christian fiction, where it seemed almost impossible to do away with the presence of masculine weakness despite all the trumpeting of the virtues of masculine strength.[3]

Tom Brown's Schooldays

In *The Mill on the Floss*, Tom Tulliver is a critique of and commentary on the Tom Brown and Tom Thurnall types of the muscular Christian and schoolboy novels of the 1850s.[4] He shares the name and character traits of these other Toms, including his fair Saxon looks, his stubbornness, his practical good sense, and his athleticism. Both of these protagonists excel at sport. "At Mr Jacobs' Academy," the narrator tells us, "life had not presented itself to him as a difficult problem: there were plenty of fellows to play with, and Tom being good at all active games, fighting especially, had that precedence among them which appeared to him inseparable from the personality of Tom Tulliver" (140). Maggie sums up Tom's practical intelligence simply: "[F]or all he doesn't like books," she says, "he makes beautiful whip-cord and rabbit-pens" (34). Tom Brown's summary of his ambitions at Rugby could just as well be Tom Tulliver's. He claims, "I want to be A 1 at cricket and football, and all the other games, and to make my hands keep my head against any fellow, lout or gentleman" (313). This portrait of the development of physical and moral character as in tension with an anxious intellectualism is taken to an extreme in Arthur Clough's poem *The Bothie of Tober-na-vuolich*, when the hero, Philip, abandons his first at Oxford and future career in England to emigrate to New Zealand with "Tool-box, plough, and the rest" to hew, dig, and subdue "the earth and his spirit" (IX.195–96). To be a respectable English schoolboy is to have nothing but an athletic record to distinguish oneself from millions of other boys. This fair-haired Saxon athlete with more practical good sense than intellectual ability is at once peculiarly English and a universal type.

Perhaps no boy is presented as more normal than the eponymous Tom Brown, who has "nothing whatever remarkable about him except excess of boyishness" (143). Hughes makes Tom Brown seem extraordinary in his ordinariness. Although readers have the sense that Tom has many unnamed ordinary boys as friends, the narrator spends the most time describing Tom's odd friends, who give the novel color while making Tom seem average by contrast. As Jenny Holt argues, one major preoccupation of public school literature is to "demarcate 'normal' and 'deviant' adolescent behaviour" (10). There is a physical as well as a moral dimension to this demarcation of deviant and normal adolescence. Most of the critical attention on male friendship in the novel has dwelled on the relationship between the healthy Tom and the sickly and pious George Arthur. Claudia Nelson emphasizes the spiritual and moral aspect of the relationship, arguing that the Tom-Arthur relationship was idealized at midcentury, as Arthur guarded Tom's purity, and pathologized and coded as queer toward the end of the century (52–53). Yet the Arthur-Tom relationship is only one of several queer friendships in the novel that throw Tom Brown's normalcy into relief. For the most part, the reader does not enter very far into their consciousness; instead, they are defined by their peculiarities, which are narratable in a few short sentences. Almost all the minor characters are marked by some physical or cognitive disability: Old Benjy has the rheumatiz, Jacob Dodson is cognitively disabled, and George Arthur is an invalid. Dennis W. Allen argues that Hughes's novel contains "surprisingly little physical description of the characters" for a book so concerned with the education of the body (115).[5] While there is little description of muscular Christian bodies, there is surprisingly much more description of weak or abnormal masculine bodies. This narrative focus on weak bodies allows Hughes to define the normal body, like the normal character, by means of what it is not.

In his country life, Tom Brown establishes the pattern of making friends with the odd man out that will characterize his school life.[6] This is the pattern with Tom's first friend, Old Benjy, an old servant of the Brown family who becomes his dry nurse. Old Benjy is a "cheery, humorous kind-hearted old man, full of sixty years of Vale gossip, and of all sorts of helpful ways for young and old, but above all for children" (26). Later in the narrative, instead of describing the typical boyish games and camaraderie that Tom enjoys with boys like the "stolid" Job Rudkin or the exemplary Harry Winburn, "the quickest and best boy in the parish" (51), Hughes devotes the most narrative space to Tom Brown's friendship with a cognitively disabled boy. Jacob Dodson is popularly (and problematically) called Jacob "Doodle-calf." Jacob is a "half-witted boy" who ambles about "cheerfully, undertaking helpful odds and ends for everyone," which he manages "always hopelessly to embrangle" (51). "Everything came to pieces in his hands, and nothing would stop in his head" (51). Despite his oddness, Jacob is actually the character who unwittingly enables Tom to make friends with the ordinary village boys, when they get into a scrape loitering around the village school. Jacob also registers emotions that the other boys cannot. When Tom leaves for Rugby, every village boy gives him "some small little present of the best that he had" until his box is full of "peg-tops, white marbles . . . screws, birds'-eggs, whipcord, jew's harps, and other miscellaneous boys' wealth" (61). But only Jacob Dodson is singled out. Jacob, "in floods of tears," presses on him "with spluttering earnestness his lame pet hedgehog," which Tom is obliged to turn down (61). The cognitively disabled boy is important as an emotional register. Tom and the other boys suppress their tears at parting, but Jacob is allowed to be emotionally effusive.

Tom's individual friendships are part of the informal and formal friendship systems at Rugby, including the praepostor system, in which the Headmaster assigns exemplary older boys to be in charge of disciplining the younger boys, the fagging system, in which younger boys perform chores for sixth form boys, and the "small friend" system, in which a group of older boys make a pet of a younger boy and often corrupt him.[7] The friendship between Tom and Arthur exists in contradistinction to the informal "small friend" system but bears some similarity to the relationship between the praepostors and the fags. In the same chapter in which Arthur is introduced, we hear about the "small friend" system when a young boy demands that East and Tom fag for his friend on the playing field. The narrator explains, "He was one of the miserable little pretty white-handed curly-headed boys, petted and pampered by some of the big fellows, who wrote their verses for them, taught them to drink and use bad language, and did all they could to spoil them for everything in this world and the next" (233).[8] By contrast, the difference between Tom and Arthur is a physical difference, not a stark age difference (they are only two years apart), and is thus distanced from the implicit pederasty of the "small friend" system, although it shares its emotional charge. Tom and Arthur physically and morally improve each other.

Tom's pattern of making friends with the emotionally expressive odd man out continues at Rugby. One such boy, Diggs the Mucker, is "a very queer specimen of boyhood" (174), "a big loose-made fellow, with huge limbs which had grown too far through his jacket and trousers" (174–75). Diggs is big for his age, and also too clever, having risen almost to the top of the fifth form well before he should have. But he is not old enough in years to fit his body or his standing in the school, and the other boys generally ostracize him, the older boys being "warned off by his oddness, for he was a very queer fellow" (175). Diggs appears as if out of nowhere at the end of the hall, where he has been "lying unobserved" on a bench, and he advises Tom and his young friends to fag only for the sixth form, and stop fagging for the fifth form, who are not yet entitled to the service of younger boys, rather than peaching (173). "Don't you go to anybody at all," he tells them, for "you just stand out; say you won't fag—they'll soon get tired of licking you. I've tried it years ago on their forerunners" (174). The boys succeed in stopping illegal fagging with Diggs's advice. Because of his oddities, he is a much more accessible mentor than a paragon of virtue like Old Brooke.

The novel gains much of its color and liveliness through characters like Diggs or, later, Madman Martin, a boy philosopher who occupies a small study apart from all the other boys. Martin actually starts as Arthur's friend rather than Tom's. He is known for kicking up "precious stinks" in his study, or "den" (247), as he is an "experimental chemist on a small scale" (250), as well as a bird fancier and naturalist. The narrator describes him as "one of those unfortunates who were at that time of day (and are, I fear, still) quite out of their places at a public school" (250). Tom is able to participate in the bird fancying while distancing himself from Martin's oddities. To be sure, Tom has his ordinary friends at Rugby. But companions like East (or Scud) and the Tadpole (Hall) seem to be there to show that Tom is not getting into mischief on his own. East is not as memorable as the odd boys. He is mainly distinguishable from Tom in having been at Rugby a term longer (and being full of importance initially because of it) and in the doctor's assessment that he is the follower rather than the leader in the scrapes he and Tom get into.

Tom Brown's friendships with these odd boys and men pave the way for his most important friendship, that with the invalid George Arthur, who teaches Tom moral piety. Arthur, "a new boy" who is thirteen years old but does not look it, is "very delicate, and has never been from home before," and he needs someone to fight for him (217). As headmaster and chaplain of Rugby, Dr. Arnold brings the two boys together so that the pious but sickly Arthur will have a good spiritual influence on the young scapegrace Tom and the popular and energetic Tom will ease the timid Arthur's transition from a coddled home life with his widowed mother and sisters to the rough world of boys and men at public school. The opening of the second book is also the opening of a new life for Tom. As the narrator explains, "[I]n his new character of bear-leader to a gentle little boy straight from home," Tom "seemed to himself to have become a new boy again, without any of the long-suffering and meekness indispensable for supporting that character with moderate success. From morning till night he had the feeling of responsibility on his mind; and, even if he left Arthur in their study or in the close for an hour, was never at ease till he had him in sight again" (230–31). Tom's friendship with Arthur, then, both delineates Tom's normalcy by force of contrast and moves his moral progress forward.

While many of Tom's friends seem to be there solely to aid and abet his boyish games, Arthur aids his moral progress so that he is no longer a scapegrace but on his way to becoming an upright, honest man. In Hughes's novel, the sickroom scene actually brings out the antagonistic side of Tom and Arthur's relationship. Hughes first underscores the physical difference between the two boys in an intensely homoerotic scene. Tom finds Arthur "lying on the sofa by the open window, through which the rays of the western sun stole gently, lighting up his white face and golden hair" and is reminded of "a German picture of an angel" he knows (307). The sickroom scene is the scene of a moral transformation for Tom.

> Never till that moment had he felt how his little chum had twined himself round his heartstrings; and as he stole gently across the room and knelt down, and put his arm round Arthur's head on the pillow, felt ashamed and half angry at his own red and brown face, and the bounding sense of health and power which filled every fibre of his body, and made every movement of mere living a joy to him. (308)

The scene ends with a shift to Tom and Arthur's moral differences as they are embodied by their physical differences. Arthur makes Tom promise to give up his cribs and vulgus books, but he also acknowledges what Tom has done for him. He confesses to Tom, "My mother brought our old medical man, who attended me when I was a poor sickly child; he said my constitution was quite changed, and that I'm fit for anything now. If it hadn't, I couldn't have stood three days of this illness. That's all thanks to you, and the games you've made me fond of" (315). The significance of the sickroom scene is twofold: first, it brings the antagonism between Tom and Arthur's opposite sensibilities to the fore; and, second, it resolves this antagonism by showing how shared physical and spiritual pain can bridge these differences. As in Kingsley and Yonge, this capacity for moral suffering is that of a Christian gentleman.[9]

The Mill on the Floss

It is perhaps this capacity for suffering and sympathy that is lacking in Tom Tulliver. If muscular Christian novelists present their hero as an admirable everyman (or boy), at first Eliot seems to follow suit in her representation of Tom's normalcy and exemplarity. If Kingsley's Tom Thurnall exemplifies that "bull-terrier type so common in England" (3), Tom Tulliver is "one of those lads that grow everywhere in England, and at twelve or thirteen years of age look as much alike as goslings,—a lad with light-brown hair, cheeks of cream and roses, full lips, indeterminate nose and eyebrows,—a physiognomy in which it seems impossible to discern anything but the generic character of boyhood" (36). But Eliot's Tom Tulliver, far from malleable, carries the muscular Christian hero's propensity for stubbornness to an extreme. The narrator warns readers against interpreting Tom's "average boyish" physiognomy as indicative of his malleability. "Under these average boyish physiognomies that she seems to turn off by the gross," she writes, nature "conceals some of her most rigid, inflexible purposes, some of her most unmodifiable characters" (36–37). Tom becomes even more entrenched in his ways when circumstances are not working in his favor. Losing an opportunity to go rat catching with Bob Jakins, Tom feels himself in the right nonetheless: "[I]f Tom had told his strongest feeling at that moment," the narrator observes, "he would have said, 'I'd do just the same again.' That was his usual mode of viewing his past actions; whereas Maggie was always wishing she had done something different" (57). Eliot links Tom's moral rigidity to his physical rigidity and opposes it to Maggie's feminine flexibility. Tom is as morally rigid as his deportment, and Philip has been made sensitive by that "perpetually recurring mental ailment—half of it nervous irritability, half of it the heart-bitterness produced by the sense of his deformity" (175). Tom's ordinariness comes out most fully in contradistinction to his companion Philip's queerness, as Philip's weakness makes his friend's strength more arrestingly visible. Set against Philip's sensitive nature, Tom's blundering insensitivity gives rise to the early conflicts between the two boys.

Eliot links the susceptibility of Philip's nervous organization with his noncongenital hunchback, although, significantly, it is "the sense of his deformity," and not the deformity itself, that causes his "nervous irritability" (175). Physical "deformity" gives rise to the susceptibility that causes both morbidity and a wider range of feeling. Philip's hunchback, already partly the source of "a life in which the mental and bodily constitution had made pain predominate" (343), heightens his sensitivity. Because disability is associated with emotional as well as physical susceptibility, Philip becomes an affective center in the text, understanding emotions and their consequences more fully than any other character in the novel does.

Philip's physiology also feminizes him. His nerves, the narrator observes, are "as sensitive as a woman's" (444). Having been "kept aloof from all practical life" and being "by nature half feminine in sensitiveness," Philip has also developed "some of the woman's intolerant repulsion towards worldliness and the deliberate pursuit of sensual enjoyment" (344). As far as Maggie's uncle Deane is concerned, Wakem "has brought up Philip like a girl," failing to prepare him for a profession (438). Emphasizing the emotional responsiveness that nineteenth-century physiologists such as Marshall Hall sourced to the spine, the narrator links Philip's spinal deformity to his effeminacy, which in turn links him to Maggie.[10] Indeed, Maggie and Philip's kinship is formed through a shared sense of shame in their bodies, which have made them outsiders in St. Ogg's. Maggie's "keen sensitiveness and experience under family criticism," much of which is directed at her unruly hair and brown skin, suffice to teach her to behave "as if she were quite unconscious of Philip's deformity . . . as well as if she had been directed by the most finished breeding" (193). Maggie and Philip's ability to sympathize with one another, and with others, stems from their shared experience as outsiders. Philip shares some of the narrator's capacity for sympathy partly because he is so often an object of sympathy. While Maggie identifies with Philip as an outsider, Philip sympathizes with Maggie in part because his disability feminizes him.

Despite Philip's exceptional observational and emotional abilities, Eliot remains doubtful that personal disabilities or disadvantages are likely to make one more virtuous. Her wry observation that, although Philip's deformity was "the result of an accident in infancy . . . you do not expect from Tom any acquaintance with such distinctions: to him, Philip was simply a humpback" (170) can be read as a caution against overreading what is a chance deformity. When Tom begins to "have a puzzled suspicion that Philip's crooked back might be the source of [his] remarkable faculties" in sketching donkeys and panniers (171), Eliot makes it clear that he is misguided. As the narrator cautions, "Ugly and deformed people have great need of unusual virtues, because they are likely to be extremely uncomfortable without them: but the theory that unusual virtues spring by a direct consequence out of personal disadvantages, as animals get thicker wool in severe climates, is perhaps a little overstrained" (343–44). Sally Shuttleworth argues that this phrase refutes the implications of the Lamarckian theory of direct adaptation for human life, since Philip does not necessarily gain great virtues as a result of his hunchback (60).[11] Despite these qualifications, Eliot also makes it clear that the difficult experience of being disabled has widened Philip's sympathies. His disability may not give rise to great or unusual virtues, but it has resulted in some virtues nonetheless. These virtues, however, are not likely to result in a friendship with a boy so temperamentally unsuited to him. Robert Colby comments that "It must have been something of a jolt to readers to turn from the David-Jonathan friendship of *John Halifax, Gentleman* and the crippled Phineas Fletcher to Tom's thoughtless, even at times sadistic, treatment of the hunchbacked Philip Wakem" (219).

Laming Tom Tulliver

Tom's education disproves the popular view that the cultivation of an upright deportment will promote moral uprightness. Instead, Eliot suggests that Tom can only gain sympathy with Philip and Maggie when he lames his foot. Yet physical uprightness remains a focus of Tom's schooling. In her enumeration of the physical qualities of a gentleman of the 1830s, Mrs. Tulliver says, "'so far as talking proper and knowing everything, and walking with a bend in his back and setting his hair up, I shouldn't mind the lad being brought up to that" (14). Mrs. Tulliver associates intellectual knowledge with a specific kind of deportment: walking with a curve in the lumbar spine to throw the shoulders forward and accentuate one's uprightness is a sign of making one's living through professional, intellectual labor rather than the slouching associated with a peddler like Bob Jakin or a miller like Luke. This posture was associated with the good horsemanship that Tom so prides himself on later in the novel. G. J. Whyte-Melville wrote that "there is no better position for a rider than that which brings shoulder, hip, knee, and heel into one perpendicular line. A man thus placed on his horse cannot but sit well down with a bend in his back" (102). The Tullivers have high hopes for the way in which Tom will bear himself in the world. However, given Mr. Stelling's shortcomings as a teacher, it is not surprising that the cultivation of an upright deportment for Tom has been halfhearted from the start. Mr. Stelling makes some effort at molding Tom's deportment, but when Mrs. Stelling has Tom mind "the little cherub Laura," Mr. Stelling's priorities become apparent: "[I]t was certainly not the best thing in the world for young Tulliver's gait, to carry a heavy child, but he had plenty of exercise in long walks by himself" (151). Stelling resolves, nevertheless, to hire a drilling master in the next half year in order to develop Tom's comportment along with his mind.

The drilling master marks a shift from the dancing master who would have been employed even a decade earlier, in the early 1820s. As late as 1830, Lord Chesterfield's advice on manners in letters to his son (1774) were still being reprinted as the epitome of politeness, but Chesterfield's valuation of a "graceful carriage," acquired through a dancing master—since "no one can either sit, stand, or walk well, unless he dances well" (Stanhope 22)—was rapidly giving way by 1830 to a preference for a more military deportment. Instead of a dancing master, schools with middle-class pupils such as Mr. Stelling's were likely to hire a drilling master, who would emphasize not the grace of the old, enervated nobility but a modern and muscular gentlemanliness. The exercises he taught would "brace the muscles, increase the vigorous action of the frame, and promote a healthy constitution" (59). Samuel Gribble, a retired sergeant-cum-drilling master published his method in 1829 complete with instructions on riding and military formations. One of the purposes of these exercises was to straighten out deformities. "The succeeding Practices," Gribble writes,

> will be found of great utility to the human frame, by opening the chest and affording the lungs ample space and power for a full respiration. They tend to square the shoulders and strengthen the muscles, and have often proved effectual in removing deformities, whether occa-

sioned by natural weakness, or infirmity, or otherwise; as in the cases of crooked arms, knees bending inwards or outwards and a variety of other instances; in the cure of which, these exercises tend considerably to assist nature. (67)

The influence of a drilling master was meant to counteract any tendency toward physical irregularity or unmanly feebleness. Unfortunately, Mr. Stelling's drilling master, Mr. Poulter, is a parody of the conduct manual models. For all his own "martial erectness" (179), he succeeds only in enabling Tom to injure his foot. Tom conceives the idea of borrowing Mr. Poulter's sword as a way to impress Maggie with the idea that "he was going to be a soldier": "There was nobody but Maggie who would be silly enough to believe him, or whom he dared allow to know that he had a sword" (185). Tom pulls Maggie's thoughts away from "the poor deformed boy who was so clever" with the military spectacle of himself as a great warrior, wrapped in a red comforter, his face blackened with burnt cork, wielding Mr. Poulter's phallic sword (188). Of course, Tom only ends up injuring his foot with the sword. True to the Sedgwickian triangle, instead of impressing Maggie, the rivalry only brings Tom closer to Philip.

As it turns out, Tom's laming is one of the most important incidents in the "School-time" section of the book, for it is the only moment when the two boys can come together in the intimacy expected of the schoolboy novel. In other words, the two boys only experience fellow feeling when both are disabled rather than when one is weak and the other healthy. Philip is the only one in Mr. Stelling's household to anticipate that Tom might be worried about being permanently lamed after the accident: "It had been Philip's first thought when he had heard of the accident—'Will Tulliver be lame? It will be very hard for him if he is'— and Tom's hitherto unforgiven offences were washed out by that pity" (191). After ascertaining that Tom will recover, Philip tells him the good news and puts out "his small delicate hand, which Tom clasped immediately in his more substantial fingers" (191). This emblematic moment in the schoolboy friendship works differently in *The Mill on the Floss* than it does in other novels. Rather than signifying a lasting friendship, Tom and Philip's sympathy for one another does not long outlast their brief handshake.

In earlier novels, such as *John Halifax, Gentleman*, the homoerotic relationship between the strong man and the weak man is unmediated by a female rival. Phineas Fletcher takes up house with John and his wife

Ursula almost seamlessly. The helplessness of the disabled man offers myriad opportunities for tenderness and physical contact between the pair without the need for a woman to bring them together. In *The Mill on the Floss,* this dyad of the weak man and the strong man becomes a love triangle, and Philip and Tom do need Maggie as an axis in their evolving relationship. When Maggie first thinks of Philip, it is in terms of taking a brother's place in the triangle. She wishes to be "brother and sister in secret" (349). Later she laments, "'What a dear, good brother you would have been Philip,' . . . 'I think you would have made as much fuss about me, and been as pleased for me to love you, as would have satisfied even me. You would have loved me well enough to bear with me, and forgive me everything. That was what I always longed that Tom should do'" (341). There is a significant class difference between Philip Wakem, the son of a successful lawyer brought up to no profession, and Tom Tulliver, the son of a superior miller and maltster trying to rise in the world. But the triangle shared by Tom, Philip, and Maggie is primarily organized around physical rather than class difference that Sedgwick suggests differentiates pairings of men in the love triangle (*Between Men* 1). The relationships between men in the novel are of interest not only for their homoerotic charge but also because this homosocial rivalry has consequences for Eliot's vision of sympathy as the goal of all artistic production. The physical differences between Tom and Philip come into focus as the two vie for Maggie's affections at school, with Tom trying to impress her with his physical skill with the sword and Philip with his intellectual knowledge of classics and talent for drawing.

For Eliot a schoolboy friendship is more likely between two disabled boys than between one healthy boy and one sick boy, and the fellowship between Tom and Philip is only as lasting as Tom's convalescence. Furthermore, Maggie, who is visiting when Tom is lamed, is necessary to mediate this fleeting friendship. After the accident, Philip feels that they are "being drawn into a common current of suffering and sad privation. His imagination did not dwell on the outward calamity and its future effect on Tom's life, but it made vividly present to him the probable state of Tom's feeling: he had only lived fourteen years, but those years had, most of them, been steeped in the sense of a lot irremediably hard" (191). Philip spends all of Tom's convalescence with his schoolfellow and Maggie, telling the story of the lamed warrior Philoctetes—a fit emblem for Tom's battle scars—and commiserating with the pair. Maggie pleads with Tom to have some sympathy for Philip: "She was pained to hear Tom say in the holidays that Philip was as queer as ever again, and often cross: they were no longer very good friends, she perceived, and when she reminded Tom that he ought always to love Philip for being so good to him when his foot was bad, he answered, 'Well, it isn't my fault: *I* don't do anything to him'" (195). Even Maggie can no longer intercede on Philip's behalf, and the short-lived friendship between the two men becomes a rivalry, for, "when Tom by and by began to walk about as usual, the friendly warmth that had been kindled by pity and gratitude died out by degrees."

> Philip was often peevish and contemptuous; and Tom's more specific and kindly impressions gradually melted into the old background of suspicion and dislike toward him as a queer fellow, a humpback, and the son of a rogue. If boys and men are to be welded together in the glow of transient feeling, they must be made of metal that will mix, else they inevitably fall asunder when the heat dies out. (194–95)

Tom Tulliver as Self-Made Man

Eliot's use of the industrial metaphor "metal that will mix" to describe the Tom-Philip relationship points to a larger concern of the novel: the effect of industry on men's bodies and feelings. The same pairing of strength and weakness that characterizes the schoolboy friendship in mid-Victorian fiction extends to the adult friendship of the robust industrialist and the disabled man, as in the case of John Halifax and Phineas Fletcher. But Tom and Philip's schoolboy tiffs ripen into a full-fledged adult rivalry rather than a lifelong friendship. Instead of learning sympathy from Philip, Tom grows more taciturn and discontent as he climbs the industrial ladder. Nor does Tom draw Philip out into the larger world, as his tendency to become introverted and peevish grows more pronounced in adulthood. Eliot's critique of school reforms extends to a critique of the self-made man: both the ideal schoolboy and the ideal businessman are taciturn, stubborn characters who may be too inflexible to feel for their fellow men. While Kingsley and Craik hold the self-made man up as a moral exemplar, Eliot questions the moral stature of the businessman as hero.

Tom's status as a businessman-gentleman is dependent on his upright bearing and common sense rather than his consideration for those weaker than himself. He wins the admiration of the partners of Guest & Co by, as Stephen puts it, "riding home in some marvellous way, like Turpin, to bring them news about the stoppage of a bank" and thereby saving them from "a considerable loss" (381). Stephen's comparison of Tom to the famed highwayman and Newgate criminal Dick Turpin is hardly flattering. But Tom's physical prowess wins him favor nonetheless, and his success depends not on the elegance of his bearing but on a rigidity that is at once physical and moral. Mr. Tulliver makes his son's straight back a metaphor for his straightforward approach to duty when he pays off his father's debts: "They'll see I'm honest at last, and ha' got an honest son. Ah! Wakem 'ud be fine and glad to have a son like mine—a fine straight fellow—i'stead o' that poor crooked creatur!" (365–66). The men assembled at the dinner announcing the payment of the Tulliver debts similarly remark that Tom looks "gentlemanly as well as tall and straight" (368). Mr. Tulliver attributes this gentlemanly deportment to his son's education, but the straightness of Tom's physique is also an index of his rigid sense of duty. These analogies between Tom's sense of duty and his straight back invite comparison with Philip Wakem's humpback and his father's crooked dealings with the law. Tom Tulliver, with his stubborn narrow-mindedness, is a critique of this ideal, as Eliot aims to show that the inflexible morals associated with a muscular frame often lack the saving grace of sympathy. Eliot's novel marks a transition from the earlier schoolboy novels and stories of the self-made man in which physical difference leads to a redemptive sympathy between men that does not wholly undermine the masculinity of either man. In *The Mill on the Floss*, physical disability and sympathy are cast as feminizing more explicitly than they are in the earlier works of novelists like Hughes and Craik.

The health of the businessman was also potentially at risk. As Maria Frawley notes, the middle-class man's health was threatened by the workplace and the demands of overwork (97). Tom Tulliver's body looks quite different cramped up in the schoolroom than it does in the odiferous warehouses of Guest & Co, where he is at once more at ease and potentially more physically vulnerable to an industrial accident. In Eliot's worldview, the industrial demand for physical uprightness leads to moral rigidity. Industrial metaphors capture Tom's psychological state. His schooldays after the first two halves go on "with mill-like monotony, his mind continuing to move with a slow, half-stifled pulse in a medium of uninteresting or unintelligible ideas" (196). The trope of "mill-like monotony" suggests that industry, rather than ennobling Tom and bringing out his finer morals, as it does for John Halifax, blunts his sensibilities. Water is most commonly read in terms of female desire in *The Mill on the Floss*. But it is also a metaphor for the emotional restraint required of men: the successful businessman must harness the waters that run the mill. A failure to direct and contain these liquids is tantamount to a failure to contain one's emotions, as is the case with Tulliver's irrigation difficulties. Herbert Sussman writes that the "innate, distinctively male energy" that defined masculinity for the Victorians "was consistently imagined or fantasized in a metaphorics of fluid, suggestively seminal, and in an imagery of flame" (10). Tom Tulliver tamps down emotions that threaten to burst like hot water or steam from an iron boiler: Bob Jakin tells Maggie that he's "as close as an iron biler" at home after work (406). The industrial metaphor of the iron boiler brings together flame and liquid in a threatening equilibrium: it is difficult for the businessman to put aside the stresses of the workday at home, and he may explode at any minute. John Halifax's blood may reach "a boiling heat" (209), but it is never allowed to boil over. With Tom, the reader is not so sure if this will be the case.

It is assuredly not the case for the elder Tulliver, known as a particularly "confident and hot-tempered" man (205). Tulliver's general temperament and eventual nervous breakdown are described in terms of liquidity. When Tulliver loses a suit to control the waterpower of the mill to a neighbor, who has diverted it as steam power for his own purposes, "all the obstinacy and defiance of his nature" are "driven out of their old channel," just as the channel of his river has been diverted (205). As Tulliver tries to contain himself and sort out his affairs, a clerk in town is struck with his "glistening, excited glance" (208). The droplets of sweat wetting Tulliver's glance are somatic evidence that he is failing to keep his temper under control in the same way that he has failed with his irrigation difficulties.

The narrator describes Tulliver as a "superior miller and maltster," whose self-importance is nonetheless as high as if he were "a very lofty personage" (207). Tulliver's mill operates on a smaller, more provincial scale than John Halifax's Edenic cotton mill. It is noteworthy that Tulliver mills wheat into flour and barley into malt for beer rather than the more sober product, cotton, which John Halifax (and later Caspar Goodwood in Henry James's *The Portrait of a Lady*) deal in.[12] Eliot uses Tulliver's alcohol tolerance as a measure of and metaphor for his self-restraint, or lack thereof. She remarks, "Mr Tulliver was an essentially sober man—able to take his glass and not averse to it, but never exceeding the bounds of moderation. He had naturally an active Hotspur temperament, which did not crave liquid fire to set it aglow; his impetuosity was usually equal to an exciting occasion" (367). However, when Tulliver finds out his son has cleared his debts after four years of "gloom and hard fare: he desires brandy and water," seated at the table with his creditors, "his eye kindling and his cheek flushed with the consciousness that he was about to make an honourable figure once more" (367). Here Tulliver's liquidity is kept in check; he is the "warm-hearted and warm-tempered" (367) Tulliver of old rather than the beleaguered man whose blood has boiled over. But this is not always the case. As he is riding home after this visit to town, thinking over his business affairs and "simmering in this way," he arrives at Dorlcote Mill only to see Wakem on his "fine black horse" (369). At the sight of his old enemy, his blood begins "suddenly boiling up" (369). Wakem misinterprets this as inebriation, "really believing that this was the meaning of Tulliver's flushed face and sparkling eyes," but it is merely the liquidity of his hot temperament rising to a boil (369). Tulliver beats Wakem with his cane and dies soon after—his fiery temperament not helping him to manage his business relations.

Tom Tulliver shows a greater aptitude for the management of steam than his father does. Tom proposes, along with his Uncle Deane, to bring steam power to the family mill in the manner of John Halifax. This difference, Deane suggests, is partly generational, as the younger generation is better able to manage such technological innovations. Deane suggests that young men are moving up faster in the world than when he was a young fellow, and steam power is to blame. "Why, forty years ago, when I was much such a strapping youngster as you, a man expected to pull between the shafts the best part of his life, before he got the whip in his hand. The looms went slowish." He continues, "It's this steam, you see, that has made the difference—it drives on every wheel double pace and the wheel of Fortune along with 'em" (412). Tom is confident in his ability to handle steam power, and later in the same conversation he reminds his uncle, "If you remember, at the time my father's property was sold, there was some thought of your firm buying the Mill: I know you thought it would be a very good investment, especially if steam were applied" (414). Tom's determination helps him succeed in business, but there is also evidence to suggest that he may have too much of a one-track mind, to borrow another industrial metaphor.

Although Tom succeeds in business, Eliot worries about its effect in blunting his feelings. *The Mill on the Floss* shares the industrial novel's preoccupation with the tension between a man's public work and his private feelings. In his study of middle-class masculinity and domesticity in mid-Victorian England, John Tosh shows that the emergence of the strong, self-made man who was head of his home as well as his business was fraught with tension. "Domesticity supposedly allowed workhorses and calculating machines to become men again, by exposing them to human rhythms and human affections," writes Tosh (6). But this is clearly not the case for Tom Tulliver, who grows more taciturn at home than he is in the warehouse: "Tom's strong will bound together his integrity, his pride, his family regrets and his personal ambition, and made them one force, concentrating his efforts and surmounting discouragements" (321). Thomas Tegg, whose 1834 conduct book was aimed at lower-middle-class men who hoped to rise in the world, saw sureness of character, or rigidity, as one of the most important characteristics of the self-made man. Tegg wrote, "The surest guarantee of success in every great and laudable enterprise, is decision of character; and no one ever attained this enviable characteristic without acquiring the habit of acting upon fixed principles" (37). Tom's Uncle Deane has similar views. He declares to Tom, "Ours is a fine business—a splendid concern, sir—and there's no reason why it shouldn't go on growing." What is wanted to run the business are "men of right habits, none of your flashy fellows, but such as are to be depended on" (413).

Tom Tulliver could be a model of the self-made man, as well as a cautionary figure of the dangers of industry in blunting men's sensibilities. He is determined to cut a fine figure in the world eventually, "but his practical shrewdness told him that the means to such achievements could only lie for him in present abstinence and self-denial. . . . Having made up his mind to that point, he strode along without swerving, contracting some rather saturnine sternness, as a young man is likely to do who has a premature call upon him for self-reliance" (321–22). Unfortunately, Tom's self-reliance does not build up his moral character, and his silence is less than admirable when his "usual incommunicativeness at home" prevents his quarrel with Maggie from being noticed by their parents (363). Maggie fails as Tom's expressive and emotional foil, just as Philip does earlier in the novel. There is no rescuing the self-made man from his self-imposed taciturnity and glumness.

Eliot presents a skeptical view of the self-made man and the Smilesean ethic of self-help.[13] The Victorian cult of chivalry and gentlemanliness humanized business relations for many Victorian thinkers, particularly Samuel Smiles. But for Eliot chivalry and industry are uneasy bedfellows. Tom has little compassion for weaker men. Eliot's portrait of Tom suggests that these ideals of tenderness are not easily reconciled with the strict moral conduct of the businessman-gentleman as Craik would suggest.

Tom's rigidity is one reason why he cannot see the romance in the potential Philip-Maggie pairing. The novel encourages readers to see the pairing in terms of the conventions of romance and fairy story, in which Tom's education has been sorely lacking. Philip and Maggie's very first meeting takes place before Maggie has passed "the golden gates" (195) of childhood, at a time not so far off from when she half believed that she might really meet a "blinking dwarf in yellow" (114) on her journey across the commons. When Maggie kisses Philip as a child, it is with the same innocence and earnestness with which she kisses her brother (194), and, in a reference to the animal-bride cycle, her "dark eyes" remind Philip in turn of "the stories about princesses being turned into animals" (187). The prelapsarian state of this childhood romance is partly reinstated in the Red Deeps, the forest where Philip lends Maggie the romances of Sir Walter Scott and Madame de Stäel, and where he longs to paint Maggie as a mythical Hamadryad among the firs (339). After Maggie tells her cousin of her romance with Philip in the Red Deeps, Lucy uses her familiarity with fairy stories and romance to read the situation: "There is something romantic in it—out of the common way—just what everything that happens to you ought to be. And Philip will adore you like a husband in a fairy tale" (403). Although, in witnessing Maggie and Philip's first meeting after four years, Lucy cannot "resist the impression that her cousin Tom had some excuse for feeling shocked at the physical incongruity between the two," she concludes that it is Tom's lack of engagement with "poetry and fairy tales" that prevents him from seeing their romantic potential (428). Thus, it is as a reader of poetry and fairy tale that Lucy is able to envision Maggie and Philip living happily ever after. Philip, unlike Tom, reads the right books, or at least the books that are most favorable to his relationship with Maggie.

This emphasis on a rigid morality belongs to the lower middle classes in Eliot's novel: Bob Jakins and Stephen Guest are both more free to express their emotions because of their respectively lower and higher class statuses. As Tom's childhood friend and business partner, Bob shadows and doubles Tom in a comic vein. Bob, like Tom, is a successful self-made man who adores Maggie. He raises himself up in the world to support a small wife and child by the end of the novel, and it is his investment opportunity that allows Tom to make the money that pays his father's debts. But his status a few rungs down on the class ladder from Tom also allows him more self-expression, albeit in dialect. He is the first one to recognize the danger of Tom's taciturnity, and he asks Maggie to help. A self-described "'cute chap," Bob finds a "soft place" in

Tom—his love for his cousin Lucy. "But since then summat's come over him as he's set his teeth again things more nor iver," Bob tells Maggie, "for all he's had such good luck. . . . He's a deal too lonely—an' doesn't go into company enough" (406). Bob recognizes and articulates a problem with the self-made man's incredible self-discipline, which can easily harden into an inflexible rigidity. The portrait of Bob's fireside, with his comically small wife and large mother, his baby, and his dog Mumps is an almost Dickensian portrait of the warmth of the lower classes, which stands in stark contrast to the way master Tom "sits lookin' into the fire and frownin' as if he as watchin' folks at work in it" (406).

Stephen and Philip form a much more successful pairing of the strong man and the weak man than Philip and Tom do. Compared to Tom, Stephen's class status as the privileged son of a self-made man allows him a wider range of feeling: he has developed some of the sympathies, intellectual interests, and artistic tastes of Philip Wakem, which forms the basis of a friendship with the hunchback that Tom cannot enter into. When we first see them together, they sing several duets in the Deanes' drawing room at Lucy's request: "Let us have some music. We ought to take advantage of Philip and you together" (432–33). The focus in the chapter is on Maggie's response to the music and the men: "She looked very beautiful when her soul was being played on in this way by the inexorable power of song" (434). But we can imagine from Stephen's compliment to Philip on his playing—"there you are an enviable fellow. I can do nothing with my hands" (433)—that this "inspiring duet" (434) is only one of many the two happily performed together.

Stephen has most often been read in terms of Maggie's desire—he is the acceptable, nonincestuous replacement for Tom in the love triangle that occupies the last third of the novel. However, reading Stephen through Maggie's desire has led to a critical stalemate, in which readers find that Stephen Guest is an implausible match for Maggie, largely because of his effeminacy. Most famously, Leslie Stephen pronounced that George Eliot did not realize what a "hairdresser's block" she had created in Guest (104). As the narrator archly tells us, Stephen's "diamond ring, attar of roses, and air of nonchalant leisure at twelve o'clock in the day are the graceful and odoriferous result of the largest oil-mill and most extensive wharf in St Ogg's" (377). This quotation has often been taken as evidence of Stephen's effeminacy. But it seems more of a jab at the source of his wealth—the ungentlemanly milling of flaxseed into linseed oil and shipbuilding on the wharves—than it is at the masculine strength of a man who rows the well-built heroine down the river for the better part of a day. The reviewer for *Dublin University* magazine complained, "Surely, no woman of Maggie's sort would have let herself be wholly drawn away from her love for the deformed and suffering Philip by a mere outside fancy for the good looking, sweet-voiced coxcomb, Stephen Guest" (quoted in Carroll 150).

Yet the question of whether Stephen Guest has a full emotional range has importance beyond determining whether or not he is good enough for Maggie. Stephen's capacity (or lack thereof) for sympathetic friendship is part of a sustained critique of male fellowship throughout the novel. Stephen is friendlier toward Philip than was his predecessor Tom, but his feelings are at times shallow. Although Stephen's class position affords him greater latitude for self-expression than Tom has, his sympathies are not as well developed as Philip's. Philip writes of Stephen to Maggie, "I have felt the vibration of chords in your nature that I have continually felt the want of in his" (522). The supposed effeminacy that endows Stephen with some capacity for sympathy has the potential to be seen as shallow and foppish in an able-bodied man. The Stephen-Philip relationship is perhaps also a partly missed opportunity for a lifelong friendship of the strong man and the weak man sort. The narrator is specific that Maggie's grave is visited "at different moments by two men who both felt that their keenest joy and keenest sorrow were for ever buried there" (543). Rather than Maggie's death bringing the two friends together at her grave, it seems to permanently divide them.

On Sympathy and the Body

The schoolboy friendship turned adult rivalry between the strong man and the weak man is significant because it is Eliot's clearest example of the relationship between the body and the capacity for sympathy, the extension of which she sees as the goal of all art. Eliot famously declares that the goal of the artist is "the expansion of our sympathies. Appeals founded on generalizations and statistics require a sympathy ready-made, a moral sentiment already in activity; but a picture of human life such as a great artist can give, surprises even the trivial and the selfish into that attention to what is apart from themselves, which may be called the raw material of moral sentiment" ("Natural History of German Life" 111). In other words, Eliot defines sympathy as being taken out of ourselves to understand the feelings of others and argues that art can give us the distance (what is "apart" from ourselves) and perspective that will facilitate this understanding.

The relationship between weakness and disability and the capacity for sympathy in the Victorian novel has received little critical attention. Instead, the critical debate on the relationship between the capacity for sympathy and the body in Eliot in particular has tended to focus on race and gender. For example, in *Scenes of Sympathy*, Audrey Jaffe draws a parallel between the diffusiveness of any physical traits that would mark Daniel Deronda as Jewish and the diffusiveness of his "capacious and mobile sensibility," which "obscures his culture's investment in identities defined in more specific terms" (13, see also 122–25). Focusing mainly on gender in the Maggie-Stephen relationship, Rachel Ablow writes that for Eliot sympathy constitutes "a dangerous potentially irresponsible way for women to lose themselves in those they love" (15). In *The Mill on the Floss*, the critical focus on femininity has obscured a broad analysis of a midcentury trend that tied the capacity for sympathy to disabled, often masculine bodies.

Eliot's well-known defense of her realist aesthetic in *Adam Bede* also contains a defense of these kinds of physical imperfections. The narrator protests, "But, bless us, things may be lovable that are not altogether handsome, I hope?" (179).

> But let us love that other beauty too, which lies in no secret of proportion, but in the secret of deep human sympathy. . . . [D]o not impose on us any aesthetic rules which shall banish from the region of Art those old women scraping carrots with their work-worn hands, those heavy clowns taking holiday in a dingy pot-house, those rounded backs and stupid weather-beaten faces that have bent over the spade and done the rough work of the world—those homes with their tin pans, their brown pitchers, their rough curs, and their clusters of onions. In this world there are so many of these common, coarse people, who have no picturesque sentimental wretchedness! . . . I can't afford to give all my love and reverence to such rarities: I want a great deal of those feelings for my everyday fellow-men. (180)

In this passage, Eliot dwells on unattractive bodies as most needing our sympathy. Eliot asks not only who is most deserving of our readerly sympathy but also what kind of body is best equipped to extend that sympathy.

In Eliot's worldview, often a less than perfect body, like Philip

Wakem's, is most suited to both bequeath and be an object of sympathy.[14] In her *Scenes of Clerical Life* (1857), another physically unattractive character, the Reverend Amos Barton, who has "a narrow face of no particular complexion—even the small-pox that has attacked it seems to have been of a mongrel, indefinite kind—with features of no particular shape, and an eye of no particular expression, is surmounted by a slope of baldness gently rising from brow to crown," is seen through the "tender, short-sighted eyes" of his wife Milly.[15] The narrator meditates on "the loving light of her unreproaching eyes" as best suited for companionship with an imperfect man (15–16). The narrator remarks, "I, for one, do not grudge Amos Barton this sweet wife. I have all my life had a sympathy for mongrel ungainly dogs, who are nobody's pets; and I would rather surprise one of them with a pat and a pleasant morsel, than meet the condescending advances of the loveliest Skye-terrier who has his cushion by my lady's chair" (16). This passage recalls one from *The Mill on the Floss* in which the narrator tells us that Maggie delighted in petting the "wry-necked lambs, because it seemed to her that the lambs which were quite strong and well made wouldn't mind so much about being petted, and she was especially fond of petting objects that would think it very delightful to be petted by her" (186). Maggie's childhood emotions are often described in terms of her relationships with animals (she lets Tom's rabbits die, she is like a little Skye terrier following Tom, or like a Shetland pony shaking her wild mane).[16] The narrator's, and Maggie's, sympathy for unattractive or deformed animals early on in the narrative is eventually extended to human beings.

Philip's peevishness, in particular as it is expressed in his relationship with Tom, undermines the idea that physical weakness led to an unmixed capacity for fellow feeling. Philip, whose capacity for sympathy is rooted in his sense of exclusion, is at crucial moments in the plot unable to move outside himself to extend his sympathy to Maggie. In identifying Philip as a character who possesses a large capacity for sympathy, critics rely on (but do not always make explicit) the Victorian assumption that there is a natural connection between physical weakness and emotional susceptibility. But, while Philip's disability nurtures his capacity for sympathy, it also disrupts his sympathetic response, leading to peevishness and inertia. Barbara Hardy points out that Philip is in many ways akin to the narrator: he "warns and prepares the reader. He sees it all—or nearly all. He recognizes her [Maggie's] need, her clamping control of the need, and all the consequent dangers" (54). Like her contemporaries, Eliot links a weak constitution to intellectual superiority and sympathy, and a robust constitution to business acumen and blunt sensibilities. Yet she also explores the somatic limits of sympathy.

Philip reaches this limit when his nervous constitution and sympathies are overextended to the point of inefficacy. Most disastrously, his sympathetic anxiety over Maggie and a nervous headache literally cause him to miss the boat. After witnessing Stephen and Maggie shamefully avoiding each other, Philip goes home "in a state of hideous doubt mingled with wretched certainty" (481). Having guessed the truth, that there is "some mutual consciousness between Stephen and Maggie," Philip's "irritable, susceptible nerves" are "pressed upon almost to frenzy" for half the night (481). Seeing and sympathizing with all sides of the situation, the "possibilities that would not be driven out of sight" (482), he is unable to act: "When the morning came, Philip was too ill to think of keeping his engagement to go in the boat. In his present agitation he could decide on nothing; he could only alternate between contradictory intentions" (482). Philip delays action, waiting until the point when he can be sure he is acting from "pure anxiety for her, and not from egoistic irritation" (482). That point comes too late. Caught between feelings of sympathy for Maggie and his own pain, Philip asks Stephen Guest to replace him on the ill-fated trip down the river. Philip's sympathy manifests itself in the physical symptoms of nervous headaches and irritability. But these physical weaknesses, on which Eliot and her contemporaries predicate the capacity for sympathy, also prevent one from acting on sympathetic impulses. Maggie similarly experiences her indecision in physical symptoms—blushing, trembling, headaches, pain, and fatigue—that both signal her sympathy for others and hamper her ability to act. Feminine and weak constitutions in Eliot's novel are most receptive to sympathy, and also most likely to be undone by it.

Tom, by contrast, acts all too decisively, banishing Maggie without fully considering the situation. His physical response to Maggie's return quickly passes from a moment in which he is "trembling and white with disgust and indignation" (503) to the "cold inflexibility" that characterizes most of his actions (504). Tom enjoys the most robust and upright demeanor of any character in *The Mill on the Floss*, and his sympathies are similarly unbending. He is perhaps the character in Eliot's entire oeuvre most lacking the saving grace of sympathy. If anyone in the novel is a man of maxims, it is Tom, and, as the narrator remarks,

> All people of broad, strong sense have an instinctive repugnance to the men of maxims; because such people early discern that the mys-

terious complexity of our life is not to be embraced by maxims, and that to lace ourselves up in formulas of that sort is to repress all the divine promptings and inspirations that spring from growing insight and sympathy. (518)

Although the narrator censures Tom's lack of sympathy, she shares his love of maxims. The passage above is in fact a maxim condemning men of maxims. Tom is able to see the unornamented truth of certain situations more clearly than other characters in part because of his blunted sensibilities. When Tom says he can't be certain about anything Maggie does when it comes to Philip Wakem, the narrator remarks, "There was a terrible cutting truth in Tom's words—that hard rind of truth which is discerned by unimaginative, unsympathetic minds" (409). Maggie acknowledges that Tom is able to see the basic situation but lacks the sympathy to appreciate its subtleties. In these scenes, Maggie supplements Tom's laconism, accusing him of lacking sympathy. After Tom discovers Maggie's secret meetings with Philip in the Red Deeps, she taunts him, "You never do wrong, Tom," and he responds, "with proud sincerity": "Not if I know it" (355). Tom has little ability to feel regret and self-doubt, and these qualities are essential to Eliot's understanding of sympathy. As Maggie accuses Tom, "You have been reproaching other people all your life—you have been always sure you yourself are right: it is because you have not a mind large enough to see that there is anything better than your own conduct and your own petty aims" (360). Tom is the limit case of Eliot's meditation on the bounds of sympathy, with a body too coarse to allow him to feel for others.

No other Eliot novel links a capacity for sympathy to disabled and feminized bodies as clearly as *The Mill on the Floss*. In the later novels, sympathy is a more diffuse quality, often possessed by men like Will Laidislaw and Daniel Deronda, whose sheer capacity for sympathetic response hinders them from finding a direction in life. Sympathy is tied so closely to a particular physiognomy in *The Mill on the Floss* in part because of the novel's engagement with a specific motif from the novels of the 1850s: the homoerotic friendship of the strong man and the weak man that extends each man's ability to feel and act. In Eliot's rewriting of the male friendship, sympathy is still the property of the weak man, but he is unable to draw out his strong friend's feelings to meet his own. Because Eliot's portrait of the relations between men is so nuanced, she imagines friction arising from physical and psychological differences that sympathy cannot transcend. The weak or disabled man is no longer the moral center of the novel as he is in *Tom Brown's Schooldays* or *John Halifax, Gentleman*. Rather, he is at times unsympathetic, both for the reader and toward other characters in the novel.

Can an unsympathetic character extend the reader's sympathies? Many of Eliot's first readers were disappointed that she had not presented them with the idealized and edifying characters of a Thomas Hughes or a Dinah Mulock Craik. In the sharpest of these critiques, published after Eliot's death in December 1880, John Ruskin wrote that Maggie was pitiable and Tom a "lout," while the rest of the characters in *The Mill on the Floss* were no more than "the sweepings out of a Pentonville omnibus" (337). The failed schoolboy friendship is emblematic of Eliot's approach to sympathy: the possibilities for sympathy within the novel fall apart under the narrator's acute gaze as she considers the psychological and physiological differences that separate the two men. Yet, despite the feeling of many Victorian readers that their sympathies would be better served by exemplary characters, there is no reason to think that Eliot's portrait of the failure of sympathy between men would not serve to extend the reader's sympathies equally well. Simply put, readers are not bound to act as Tom and Philip do but can learn from their example. Despite her critique of the pairing of the strong man and the weak man, Eliot continues to link emotional susceptibility to effeminate weakness. Philip, rendered oversensitive by his disability but able to sympathize with Maggie when Tom cannot, models Eliot's vision of sympathy as a complex but identity-forming relation. Philip's sometimes incapacitating oversympathizing is parallel to the narrator's overly acute analysis of the physical and psychological differences that engender sympathy. Like Philip, the narrator at times becomes so absorbed in all the possible outcomes for her characters, "possibilities that would not be driven out of sight" (482), that she can no longer imagine sympathy smoothing the way entirely. While both these modes of overreading cast doubt on the possibility of an idealized sympathy, they retain a faith in the necessity of sympathy, even under the most difficult of circumstances. Not all fiction was to retain this faith in sympathy, or even in the possibility of a connection between the strong man and the weak man. As the century progressed, these two figures moved farther apart, such that an author like Henry James was able to reconfigure the pair as two types independent of one another.

CHAPTER 4

The Portrait of Two Gentlemen
Henry James's Invalids and Self-Made Men

By all rights, Caspar Goodwood and Ralph Touchett should have been friends. Goodwood, the hearty industrialist, and Touchett, the sympathetic invalid, are a pair that would have seemed familiar to Victorian readers. They are around the same age and both matriculated at Harvard, and it takes little stretch of the imagination to picture Ralph enjoying the scene of Caspar, a strong oarsmen, rowing along the Charles on a sunny day. But James rejects this possibility—the two men cannot even be bothered to be rivals—even while he retains the building blocks of the pairing of the strong man and the weak man. All the elements of the friendship of the strong man and his disabled companion and admirer exist in *The Portrait of a Lady* (1881),[1] but James does not bring them together, suggesting instead that the American industrialist's mode of masculinity is outdated and has been superseded by a new mode of masculinity, which privileges observation and consumption (both in the sense of material consumption and illness), over action, creation, and robust health. In this worldview, the invalid need not be called into action through friendship with the strong man. So widely valued is the invalid's ability to observe quietly that his lifestyle is adopted even by able-bodied men. The new men in the novel, from Osmond to Ned Rosier, adopt the invalid's pose of quiet self-restraint and restricted mobility.[2] James sees invalidism as a potential career or a kind of self-fashioning, suggesting a collapse between the self-made man and the aesthete-invalid, who are now one and the same person.

While most criticism of *The Portrait of a Lady* has naturally focused on Isabel, James's contemporaries were also quite taken with his portrait of masculinity in the novel. "If Mr. Henry James had called this book 'The Portrait of Two Gentlemen,'" wrote R. H. Hutton in his review for *The Spectator*, "we might have admitted the aptness of the description, for the real power of the book consists in the wonderful pictures given of Ralph Touchett and Mr. Osmond, which have rarely been equalled in fiction for the skill and delicacy of the painting" (Gard 93). Hutton found it hard to remember "that Phineas is of the male sex" in his review of *John Halifax, Gentleman* (475), but he was captivated with James's ability to flesh out the inner life of the invalid and the aesthete. Hutton's comments indicate James's intense engagement with issues of masculinity in the novel.

James borrows the figure of the invalid-observer figure and the strong self-made man from the mid-Victorian novel, although in his version, both figures are increasingly isolated. For James the position of the invalid-observer has become painful and ineffective. Much of the pathos of James's novel comes from the spectacle of masculine suffering as the reader watches Ralph Touchett barred from almost every pleasure except those of observation. In *The Portrait of a Lady*, James heightens the pathos of midcentury invalids like Charles Edmonstone by recasting the invalid as an alienated American and a dying man who cannot be brought into the world of business or politics through friendship with a strong man like Caspar Goodwood or Lord Warburton. On the one hand, Ralph is allowed untrammeled powers of observation without any sense that there need be anything beyond the pleasures and pains of observation in themselves. On the other hand, these powers of observation turn out to be completely ineffective, if not destructive. As an alienated American and an aesthete,[3] the tone of Ralph's observation is distanced, humorous, and ironic, and the novel valorizes this form of observation in making it the basis of the plot and allowing it to set the tone of the narrative. Ralph's actions motivate the plot, his death closes it, and his sensibilities train the reader to react to Isabel's situation first with delight and then with melancholy. In this way, the novel is deeply mid-Victorian in its use of the spectacle of suffering masculinity to frame the narrative and heighten the emotional content of the plot.

Henry James and British Women's Fiction

Consider the following mise-en-scène: an invalid confined to his family's country house finds himself restless. Just when he thinks he will positively die of ennui, an interesting cousin, naive and unused to English society, descends upon the family manse. This, thinks the invalid as he wanders about the expansive lawn, trailed by his small dog Bunchie, is promising material. Watching as society polishes the rough edges off his cousin will be quite as interesting as a novel. And it is. This scene might sound like an account of the opening chapters of *The Portrait of a Lady*, but if you were to rename the small dog Bustle instead of Bunchie, you would have a scene from Charlotte Yonge's *The Heir of Redclyffe*. The main difference in Yonge's opening scene is that the cousin is a naive young man brought up in a Gothic castle apart from society rather than a wide-eyed young American girl from Albany.

James's debt to canonical nineteenth-century novelists such as George Eliot and to popular American women's fiction is well documented.[4] Yet as a young man he was reading not only Eliot and Flaubert but also Charlotte Mary Yonge and Mary Elizabeth Braddon. Indeed, as his 1866 review of *A Noble Life* makes clear, James was steeped in the novels of Dinah Mulock Craik. Henry James was at once critical of and quite taken with the domestic realist novels he reviewed as a young man for *The Nation* and *The Atlantic Monthly*.[5] His reviews of midcentury authors like Craik, Yonge, and Charles Kingsley are often backhanded compliments: these are authors who have something of genius but are limited by their choice of genre. Of Craik he wrote in *The Nation* (1 March 1866), "[W]e gladly commend Miss Mulock as fairly successful.... If she has not much philosophy or much style, she has at least feeling and taste. If she does not savor of the classics, neither does she savor of the newspapers. If, in short, she is not George Eliot on the one hand, neither is she Miss Braddon on the other" (*Literary Criticism* 847). In his obituary for Kingsley, also published in *The Nation* (28 January 1875), he wrote that, although his "influence in many ways was for great good," he was "a striking example of a man who had a certain limited message to deliver—whose cup was filled, at the most, but halfway up to the brim" (*Literary Criticism* 1102). Of all these authors, Yonge was James's favorite. He characterizes her work as "Sunday reading" of the highest order. "It would be unjust to deny that these semi-developed novels are often very charming," he writes. "Occasionally, like the 'Heir of Redclyffe,' they almost legitimate themselves by the force of genius. But this is only when a first-rate mind takes the matter in hand" (*Literary Criticism* 826); the article appeared in *The Nation* on 1 February 1866).[6]

Despite his sometimes derisive tone, James was clearly struck by the emotional power of these midcentury novels. In his review of Craik's *A Noble Life*, he appreciates the affective power of her ideal hero with a popular audience, even while he mocks the response. *John Halifax, Gentleman*, he wrote, is "an attempt to tell the story of a life perfect in every particular, and to relate, moreover, every particular of it" (*Literary Criticism* 845). Of this "model gentleman" James writes, "We know of no scales that will hold him, and of no unit of length with which to compare him. He is infinite; he outlasts time; he is enshrined in a million innocent breasts; and before his awful perfection and his eternal durability we respectfully lower our lance" (845). James recognized the emotional sway that the tropes of midcentury domestic and sentimental fiction held over a popular audience. He recognized the readers of this sentimental fiction as a type. The heroine of his first novel, *The Watch and the Ward*, grows from a "little girl who slept with the 'Child's Own Book' under her pillow and dreamed of the Prince Avenant, into a lofty maiden who reperused the 'Heir of Redcliffe,' [*sic*] and mused upon the loves of the clergy" (87). In *The Portrait of a Lady*, he draws on the midcentury masculine types of the self-made man and the invalid to great effect, even while his more distanced and detached tone ironizes his appropriation.

The more obvious example of a British woman writer whose work influenced Henry James is George Eliot. James's debt to Eliot's portrait of Grandcourt in *Daniel Deronda* for his portrait of male masochism in Osmond is well documented, and the tubercular Ralph Touchett is also indebted to Eliot's portrait of the consumptive Jewish mystic Mordecai. Daniel himself is in some ways a strong man. He rescues Mirah while he is out rowing, and early in the novel he tenderly nurses his Cambridge friend Hans Meyrick, who suffers from a "severe inflammation of the eyes" just when he most needs to study. This does seem to establish him as a strong man and a tender friend. Daniel makes "every other occupation secondary to that of being companion and eyes to Hans" as he helps his friend cram in the Classics (154). As a result, he fails his mathematics exam while Hans wins his much-needed scholarship. This early pairing of the strong man and the weak man is repeated when Daniel becomes captivated by Mordecai, a "consumptive-looking Jew" who has "been conscious of an ebbing physical life, and a widening spiritual loneliness" for "many winters" (404). His dying wish is to have "some young ear into which he could pour his mind as a testament" (404), and Daniel, young and robust, becomes his pupil. Yet Daniel is too sensitive and intellectual to be cast completely as a strong man along the lines of John Halifax and Tom Tulliver. We might recall that Eliot compares his state of mind, when he suspects he may be Sir Hugo's illegitimate son, to that of a person who is morbidly susceptible about an orthopedic deformity. Eliot writes that Daniel's "silent consciousness of a grief within" might "be compared in some ways with Byron's susceptibility about his deformed foot" (147). Daniel, then, has the susceptibility and sensitivity of a Philip Wakem despite his healthy frame. James's portrait of the strong man and the weak man arguably has more in common with the pairings of the strong man and the weak man in the novels of the 1850s, with Ralph Touchett owing more to Charles Edmonstone or Phineas Fletcher than Mordecai, and Caspar Goodwood owing more to John Halifax than Daniel Deronda.

American Self-Made Men Abroad

James's novel, like Craik's, explores the place of the self-made man in contemporary culture. Where Craik's tone is celebratory, however, James's narrative tends to shunt aside the self-made man, who is as materially successful and inventive as ever but whose type of success is not emblematic of a desirable type of masculinity. The self-made man is nonetheless a persistent presence in the novel, from Daniel Touchett to Caspar Goodwood. Although his presence may be subdued, the self-made man is still a necessary counterpoint to the invalids and aesthetes who offer what Dana Luciano has called the "imaginative energies of dissident masculinity" (197).

James's concern with the place of the American self-made man in late-nineteenth-century England is evident from the first page of the novel, which opens with three gentlemen having afternoon tea. Ralph's father, Daniel Touchett, is a self-made man who has lived long enough to become an invalid. Ralph's relationship with his father, perhaps the only true self-made man in the novel (Caspar Goodwood inherits his mills) echoes the midcentury pairing of the strong man and the weak man, only to affirm that the self-made man is out of date and out of place across the Atlantic.[7] Daniel Touchett is an elderly self-made man whose distinguishing features are his "American physiognomy" and a look of "placid acuteness" on his face, the remains of his successful years in banking (21). Daniel is a reminder that the strong man will inevitably become weak, with age, which is perhaps one reason why John Halifax does not live to old age. When Daniel Touchett claims that his son is a very good nurse, Lord Warburton, the third member of the party, asks, "Isn't he a bit clumsy?" (23). Touchett, who is just as quick-witted as his son and his lordship, responds, "Oh no, he's not clumsy—considering that he's an invalid himself. He's a very good nurse—for a sick-nurse. I call him my sick-nurse because he's sick himself" (24). Touchett's comments gesture toward a new pairing—the tender care of a weak man by a man who is weaker than himself.

An American self-made man par excellence, Daniel Touchett lays out the problems with the young men of his son's generation that will characterize James's portrait of masculinity throughout the rest of the novel. Daniel identifies a new type of idleness in the young men of the next generation, be they strong, like Lord Warburton, or weak, like his son. Bounderby-like, Daniel advises his son and neighbor to avoid the idleness and boredom that characterize their lives: "When I was twenty years old I was very highly developed indeed. I was working tooth and nail. You wouldn't be bored if you had something to do; but all you young men are too idle. You think too much of your pleasure. You're too fastidious, and too indolent, and too rich" (25). James characterizes the men who have spent their formative years in the United States, like Daniel Touchett, who hails from Vermont, and Caspar Goodwood, from Massachusetts, as the most industrious workers, while the lifelong expatriates in the novel are idle. Pleasure seeking and idleness characterize the new mode of English masculinity in the novel, so Daniel's fond denouncement of his son and neighbor also functions as an announcement of a mode of masculinity that belongs to the past and is more geographically at home in the United States.

Daniel Touchett sees part of the problem with his son as his uncertain status as an alienated American. He is a "beautiful specimen" of the "alienated American" to borrow Henrietta Stackpole's phrase (105). For James, Ralph's rootlessness, along with his invalidism, seems to fit him for the position of the detached observer. Daniel, a native of Vermont who sees before him a "life-long residence in his adopted country" and graciously accepts his fate, though with no intention of "disamericanising" himself, has no "desire to teach his only son any such subtle art" (54).[8] He hopes that Ralph will live in England "assimilated yet unconverted," as he has, but finds this a more difficult task than he expected for the second generation (55). Ralph spends several terms at Harvard but strikes his father on his return as "redundantly native," at which point he places his son for three years residence at Oxford (55). Finally, "Oxford swallowed up Harvard, and Ralph became English enough at last" (55). Instead of Amercanizing him and giving him an English polish, Ralph's education deracinates him and gives him a taste for the pleasures of observation and contemplation. On his return Ralph enjoys "the opportunity of observing" his father and the "fine ivory surface, polished as by the English air," that the old man has "opposed to the possibilities of penetration" in the true style of the silent self-made man (55). "Daniel Touchett had been neither at Harvard nor Oxford, and it was his own fault if he had placed in his son's hands the key to modern criticism," explains the narrator (55). Ralph's transatlantic education aids his observation, but he has not been prepared for the worldly success that his father enjoys.

James's opening scene thus prepares the reader for a novel about man's place in the modern world. Even Lord Warburton, who is more of a conventional strong man, shares Ralph Touchett's ennui. Warburton's friendship with Ralph represents the midcentury pairing of the strong man and the weak man most closely, drawing on the familiar trope of contrasting the physiques of the strong man and the weak man to bring each into relief. James compares Ralph and Warburton as they take tea on the lawn at Gardencourt in the first scene. Warburton is a "remarkably well-made man of five-and thirty" with a "noticeably handsome face, fresh-coloured, fair and frank, with firm, straight features, a lively grey eye and the rich adornment of a chestnut beard" (21–22). By contrast, his companion is "Tall, lean, loosely and feebly put together" with an "ugly, sickly, witty, charming face, furnished, but by no means decorated, with a straggling moustache and whisker" (22). While Lord Warburton's beard adorns his face, which is as fair as the muscular Christian's, Ralph's merely straggles along his chin. James aestheticizes the muscular man as a the perfect type of the Englishman.

Lord Warburton shares the fair complexion and the well-built frame of the mid-nineteenth-century muscular Christian, traits that immediately identify him as an Englishman in a cosmopolitan world where it is important to pin down nationality. When he appears at the Palazzo Roccanera to court Pansy, Ned Rosier perceives the stranger immediately by his nationality, noting that "the visitor had a handsome face and a large, fair beard, and was evidently an Englishman" (408). One might argue that Lord Warburton's national affiliations are complicated when he returns from travel considerably bronzed by the sun, but he is still unmistakably English, and his adventuring in Turkey, Asia Minor (314), and earlier the Persian Gulf (24) can be read in the tradition of muscular Christian adventurers such as Tom Thurnall or perhaps, even more pertinently, the adventure stories that gained popularity a few years after *The Portrait of a Lady*.[9] After he returns from his travels in Turkey and Asia Minor, Warburton runs into Isabel on the streets of Rome near the foundations of the Capitol by the Forum: "He was splendidly sunburnt; even his multitudinous beard had been burnished by the fire of Asia." Yet Warburton retains his national identity even abroad. With "his manly figure, his minimising manner and his general air of being a gentleman and an explorer, he was such a representative of the British race as need not in any clime have been disavowed by those who have a kindness for it" (315). As "a gentleman and an explorer," Warburton is a recognizable heroic type. But he has not been traveling merely for adventure, as the heroes of Charles Kingsley and H. Rider Haggard often are. Instead, he has been traveling in an unsuccessful attempt to forget Isabel.

James redirects the focus of the pairing of the strong man and the weak man away from their feelings for each other and toward his heroine so that she preoccupies the men's minds even as the strong man tenderly escorts his dying companion to Rome to see his cousin one last time. Seeing that Ralph is determined to go to Rome despite the risk to his health, Lord Warburton accompanies his invalid friend. He explains to Isabel that they were ostensibly traveling to Sicily for Ralph's health, but traveling for health was only a pretext to go to Rome: "I wanted him at least to go by sea, to save fatigue; but he said he hated the sea and wished to stop at Rome. After that, though I thought it all rubbish, I made up my mind to come with him. I'm acting as—what do you call it in America?—a kind of moderator. Poor Ralph's very moderate now" (412). Warburton's assessment of himself as a kind of "moderator" rather than a tender friend suggests some distance in their relationship. Indeed, as the reader finds out, the two men have been keeping up "a sort of parliamentary debate all the way from London" with Ralph teasing Warburton that he is "the King of the Goths" and Warburton holding that Ralph is "the last of the Tories" (413). Neither man makes an allusion to the real reason for the journey: Isabel. James writes, "These two were gentleman of a race which is not distinguished by the absence of reserve, and they had travelled together from London to Rome without an allusion to matters that were uppermost in the mind of each," instead keeping a "half-diffident, half-confident silence" (427). In an earlier version of the pairing of the strong man and the weak man, Ralph would have been able to divine all of Warburton's thoughts without his speaking a word, and he would have relayed them to the reader. James's narrative instead shares the reserve of these men, relying on a similar understanding that the reader knows the reason why both men have come to Rome without a direct statement. Ralph's humorous relationship with Warburton, who needs no drawing out, serves to insulate him from a closer friendship.

While Lord Warburton does share a friendship with Ralph, James further rewrites the pairing of the strong man and the weak man by presenting the archetypal self-made able-bodied man, Caspar Goodwood, in isolation from friendship with other men. Goodwood, an active industrialist and Bostonian, does not fit into the world of contemplative illness and idleness at Gardencourt or on the Continent. The critical reception of *The Portrait of a Lady* has not always been kind to Goodwood; he is seen as at best monotonously masculine and at worst a kind of rapist at the end of the novel with his "white lightning" kiss (627).[10] Reading Goodwood in the literary tradition of the self-made man shows him in a gentler light. If this "perpendicular Bostonian" (527) has been made "a selfish as iron" (359) through his involvement in industry, perhaps an invalid friend or a wife would have had a softening influence. Goodwood, owner of a successful cotton mill, could be another John Halifax, and Ralph Touchett, with his consumption, his adoring Phineas Fletcher. The novel lays all the groundwork for a tender friendship or at least a rivalry between the two. Goodwood fits the mid-Victorian pattern of the earnest athleticism and practical insight of the self-made man. The narrator describes him as Isabel sees him for the first time in London: "He was tall, strong and somewhat stiff; he was also lean and brown" (52). Goodwood's physiognomy is similarly unbending, for it "had an air of requesting your attention, which it rewarded according to the charm you find in blue eyes of remarkable fixedness, the eyes of a complexion other than his own and a jaw of the somewhat angular mould which is supposed to bespeak resolution" (52). During his college years, Goodwood gains "renown rather as a gymnast and an oarsman than as a gleaner of more dispersed knowledge" (136).

Goodwood's pursuits of rowing and gymnastics are exactly in line with American ideals of masculine health and able-bodiedness in the second half of the nineteenth century. These sports were thought to instill physical qualities that would translate directly into moral qualities: pluck, determination, and bravery. Gymnastics, now often seen as a feminine sport emphasizing flexibility and graceful movement, was part of an effort to build a limber masculine frame in the mid–nineteenth century.

The practice of gymnastics was thought to be a scientific method for preventing or correcting deformities. Dio Lewis, the author of *The New Gymnastics for Men, Women, and Children* (1862), claimed that the "system of exercise will correct drooping or distorted shoulders, malposition of the head, and many other common defects" (5). Lewis protested that leaving these deformities to correct themselves was bound to fail: "A boy has round or stooping shoulders: hereby the organs of the chest and abdomen are all displaced. Give him the freedom of the yard and street—give him marbles, a ball, the skates! Does any body suppose he will become straight? Must he not, for this, and a hundred other defects have special, scientific training? There can be no doubt of it!" (11–12). Gymnastics was brought to the United States by German immigrants in the early nineteenth century and took a particular hold in Massachusetts, with two prominent early proponents going on to hold professorships at Harvard.[11] Goodwood's renown as a Harvard gymnast in the mid–nineteenth century thus makes perfect geographical and temporal sense.

Rowing also took hold in American and British universities in the early to mid–nineteenth century, with the first Oxford and Cambridge boat race established in 1829 and the first Harvard-Yale Regatta in 1852. The author of "On Rowing" suggests that "courage is intimately connected with a vigorous condition of the body. It is physically possible to go through efforts after a few weeks' regular living which would have knocked you up at the beginning of the period" ("On Rowing" 236). Training, he argues, "should raise a man's courage, not only by diminishing the painful obstacles arising from excessive fat and other evils that the flesh is heir to, but by more directly raising the morale of the subject" (237).

Like contemporary Ivy League athletes rumored to be in demand with top firms on the grounds that they are accustomed to grueling training schedules and teamwork, Caspar Goodwood's college athleticism leads directly to a successful career in business. James continues, then, in the tradition of muscular Christian theories that link able-bodiedness to the ability to think clearly and vigorously and succeed in business. It is only after he has completed his formal education that Goodwood realizes that there are feats of intellect quite as satisfying as those of athleticism, and he promptly invents and patents an improvement to the cotton-spinning process. He is as successful at managing men as that other cotton mill owner, inventor, and self-made man, John Halifax, and finds he has a gift for making people "work his will, believe in him, march before him and justify him" (136). Goodwood's almost military gifts for making his employees march before him could well have been learned from his time rowing at Harvard. The British author of "On Rowing" wrote:

> To be a Captain of a University Eight requires qualities which would go some way to make a successful general, though not perhaps to enable their possessor to grapple with the theory of the Absolute and the Infinite. He ought to be a refined diplomatist, to have a rapid and decisive judgment, and the power of enforcing discipline. He should have the courage to hold firmly to his own opinion, and the rarer courage to make changes when it is necessary. A captain requires as much skill in composing a crew as a minister in forming his cabinet. (239–40)

Rowing may not require a grasp of advanced metaphysics, but it shapes not only a muscular physique but also the ability to take decisive action and lead a team.

However, in the moral universe of James's novel, simply expanding business for business's sake is no longer a sign that one is a good man. Straightforwardness and honesty are not the moral virtues they were in Craik's novel, or even in Eliot's; rather, they are part of the industrialist's unbending personality. Isabel finds Goodwood too straightforward, too honest, too "deficient in the social drapery commonly muffling" (518), an odd metaphorical deficiency for a man who makes his living dealing in fiber as a cotton miller. "But she couldn't call him stupid; he was not that in the least; he was only extraordinarily honest. To be as honest as that made a man very different from most people; one had to be almost equally honest with *him*" (527 emphasis original). Goodwood is unsettled when he turns his attention to Isabel: "He showed his appetites and his designs too simply and artlessly; when one was alone with him he talked too much about the same subject, and when other people were present he talked too little about anything. And yet he was of supremely strong, clean make" (137). Goodwood is physically appealing, but the taciturnity of the self-made man has worn thin. When he declares, "I'm as selfish as iron," echoing the industrial metaphors of earlier Victorian novels, Isabel protests that "Even iron sometimes melts" (359).

Quite unlike the mid-century novel, however, few characters are interested in melting the iron heart of the self-made man. Almost no one will take the trouble to draw out this relic of an older age, or to encourage him to express his feelings. For Henrietta, Goodwood is "the most reserved, the least colloquial of men, and this enquiring authoress was constantly flashing her lantern into the quiet darkness of his soul. He wished she didn't care so much; he even wished, though it might seem rather brutal of him, that she would leave him alone" (493). Isabel simply sits out one silent interview after another with him: "He was open to a little conversation on general topics; it came back to her what she had said of him once, years before, 'Mr Goodwood speaks a good deal, but he doesn't talk.' He spoke a good deal now, but he talked perhaps as little as ever" (526–27). Those who interact with Goodwood do not take his silence as a sign that he is concealing mysterious depths of character; rather, his lack of conversation is seen as a sign that he has little interest beyond his cotton mills.

The Pains and Pleasures of Observation

In contrast to Caspar Goodwood's taciturnity, Ralph Touchett's loquacity continues the midcentury pattern of linking masculine physical weakness with a heightened capacity to observe, and with authorship. While scholars are generally agreed that Ralph's invalidism gives him a heightened ability to observe and articulate his observations, and that he is a stand-in for Henry James as author in this respect, there is a critical divide over the extent to which this is a positive position; those working in gender studies and queer theory tend to find in Ralph a laudable form of dissident masculinity, while those working in disability studies and the history of medicine agree that he is privileged as an observer but sometimes find the limitations of his life as an invalid more troubling.[12] Katherine Snyder locates Ralph Touchett in a tradition of bachelor-invalid narrators, including Lockwood in *Wuthering Heights* and Miles Coverdale in *The Blithedale Romance*. Ralph Touchett, she argues, is a reflector character through whom we understand the action of the novel, a position that is not without its benefits. While "his illness may foreclose on certain privileges and pleasures of normative masculinity," she argues, "it opens up others" (86). In her reading of the novel through queer theory, Dana Luciano finds that Ralph's invalidism allows him to corral the "imaginative energies of dissident masculinity" (197), which also determine the sense that Isabel makes of her own gender position. If Ralph is free not to marry, Isabel reasons at the beginning of the novel, there might be more possibilities for her in taking up the queer position of single woman as well. While Katherine Byrne, in her recent work on tuberculosis in

Victorian literature, agrees that "for certain men and particularly for the artist, invalidism has its own benefits and advantages, and they are worth some sacrifice of conventional masculine roles" (9), she takes a bleaker view of the significance of tuberculosis for modern masculinity, arguing that illness is a metaphor for "modern masculinity as intrinsically weakened, feminised and diseased" in the novel, an anxiety that James shares about his position as a male author (151).[13] I would argue that James takes too much pleasure in the refined sensibilities of the invalid for the role to be wholly oppressive or a metaphor for a diseased masculinity, but there are also, I would suggest, limitations to the invalid's sensibility of connoisseurship when unaccompanied by action.

James frames the major incidents of the novel through Ralph's perspective, suggesting that the pains and pleasures of observation could make up a career, not only for one to whom nothing else is left, but for any person of wit and taste.[14] For Ralph "the state of his health had seemed not a limitation, but a kind of intellectual advantage; it absolved him from all professional and official emotions and left him the luxury of being exclusively personal" (364). The reader sees Isabel's arrival in England almost entirely through Ralph's point of view and expects, along with Ralph, that something exciting is about to happen when she enters the scene. "I had never been more blue, more bored, than for a week before she came," Ralph muses, and "I had never expected less that anything pleasant would happen" (81). Ralph famously goes on to aestheticize Isabel and compare her to a work of art, a "Titian," a "Greek bas-relief" to hang over his chimney piece (81). But Isabel is a human being, not a work of art, and the entertainment she provides proves much more difficult to manage than the pleasure to be derived from a painting. Ralph arranges Isabel's bequest for the pleasure of seeing what she might do with it. He is understandably annoyed when he cannot watch the spectacle that he has anticipated so eagerly. When Isabel refuses to tell him the state of her affairs with Lord Warburton, he exclaims,

> Of course you mean that I'm meddling in what doesn't concern me. But why shouldn't I speak to you of this matter without annoying you or embarrassing myself? What's the use of being your cousin if I can't have a few privileges? What's the use of adoring you without hope of a reward if I can't have a few compensations? What's the use of being ill and disabled and restricted to mere spectatorship at the game of life if I really can't see the show when I've paid so much for my ticket? (169)

Ralph claims that his invalidism is reason enough for him to be privy to what is going on—if he has suffered enough to be painfully excluded from the courtship plot, he has at least won a seat as a privileged observer. The only pleasure that Ralph hopes for in life, he claims, is to observe Isabel. "I don't pretend to advise you," he confides to her, "I content myself with watching you—with the deepest interest" (170). Ralph expects nothing less than a splendid amusement. "If his cousin were to be nothing more than an entertainment to him, Ralph was conscious that she was an entertainment of a high order" (81). He is delighted with the thought that "in these few months of his knowing her he should observe a fresh suitor at her gate. She had wanted to see life, and fortune was serving her to her taste; a succession of fine gentlemen going down on their knees to her would do as well as anything else. Ralph looked forward to a fourth, a fifth, a tenth besieger; he had no conviction she would stop at a third" (299). Ralph hopes not to interfere but to observe. This is not to say that observation is not a form of involvement; one could hardly be more involved than Ralph is when he asks his father to divide his fortune with Isabel. But Ralph is not motivated to action on his own behalf. For him the pleasures and pains of observation are a reason for living in and of themselves.

Ralph's painful position as an observer-invalid is enough to constitute a career in a fin de siècle culture that prizes observation and inaction. Early in the novel, Madame Merle quizzes Isabel, "Look at poor Ralph Touchett: what sort of a figure do you call that? Fortunately he has a consumption; I say fortunately, because it gives him something to do. His consumption's his *carrière*, it's a kind of position" (218). In the same passage, Madame Merle makes a grammatically and thematically parallel statement about Gilbert Osmond: "Fortunately he's very indolent, so indolent that it amounts to a sort of position. He can say, 'Oh, I do nothing; I'm too deadly lazy. You can do nothing to-day unless you get up at five o'clock in the morning.' In that way he becomes a sort of exception; you feel he might do something if only he'd rise early" (219). The basis of the connoisseurship shared by Osmond and Ralph, I would argue, is an invalid lifestyle—a life of physical restraint, restricted mobility, and intense observation—that is shared by all the new men in the novel. Madame Merle's flip assessment that invalidism could be a career, or even that indolence could amount to a kind of position, indicates a shift in modes of masculinity at the end of the century. If Ralph's consumption—in the sense of both his tuberculosis and his consumerism—suffices as a career, a view that James seems to endorse along with Madame Merle, it is possible to read Ralph as a self-made man in his own right. This view makes sense of his lack of friendship with Goodwood, since Ralph would have no need of a vicarious claim to action through the industrialist. Ralph thus collapses the figure of the self-made man and the weak man.

Invalid Aesthetes

In making invalidism a career, Ralph Touchett's character foregrounds the inactive state of modern masculinity in the novel. The characters in the *The Portrait of a Lady* are happy to claim all sorts of nonactivities as occupations. Isabel and Gilbert Osmond both claim that being married is an occupation (536, 542). "Ah you see, being married's in itself an occupation," explains Osmond. "It isn't always active; it's often passive; but that takes even more attention" (542). Ralph's consumption, which confines his physical actions to some extent, seems to make him the ultimate figure of physical inaction and inner reflection. Striving to be as content and quiet and still as possible, almost as invalid-like as possible, requires the most strenuous self-making.[15] Osmond actively decides to do what Ralph's health forces him to do when he resolves to renounce the honors of the world. He tells Isabel during their courtship that he made a plan years ago "to be as quiet as possible" (288).

Ralph's life of stasis and ennui is shared by many of the minor male characters in the novel, whose lives of leisure mirror the lifestyle of the chronically ill invalid. To be able to do nothing is a kind of self-making for them. The main difference between these characters and the male invalid is that the able-bodied men living a restricted life are happy in their lot, and thus lacking in the tone of "passionate, inspired resistance" that James argues characterizes the invalid's struggle. Mr Luce, who divides his time between the American banker's and, in good weather, "a chair in the Champs Elysées," and is revered for his skill in ordering a dinner, arguably does less than Ralph, who at least travels the Continent for his health. "These were his only known pastimes," notes the narrator of Mr Luce, "but they had beguiled his hours for upwards of half a century, and they doubtless justified his frequent declaration that there was no place like Paris. In no other place, on these terms, could Mr Luce flatter himself that he was enjoying life" (234). Ned Rosier, "a very gentle and gracious youth, with what are called cultivated tastes," can "order a dinner almost as well as Mr Luce," which makes it "probable that as his experience accumulated he would be a worthy successor to that gentleman" (236). Compared to Mr Luce or even the slightly more active Ned Rosier, Ralph actually seems remarkably active, especially when one takes into consideration the strenuous travel itineraries he undertakes for the sake of his health.

Although invalidism is most often seen as confining, it is also an excuse for travel much more demanding than that which Mr Luce undertakes. Ralph, though seemingly inactive, winters abroad in Mediterranean climes like San Remo and Nice for the sake of his health. The invalid author of *San Remo as a Winter Residence* is convinced that the destination will be "ere long the great winter sanatorium for diseases of the chest" (Aspinall 13). Far from convincing his tubercular audience to while away the winter under a white umbrella, as Ralph does, Aspinall recommends bathing and donkey rides and gives routes for several scenic walks among the picturesque lemon and olive groves. This contradictory combination of strict confinement and robust travel characterized the invalid lifestyle more generally in the nineteenth century. Maria Frawley writes of this contradiction, "The emphasis placed on the revivifying power of motion provides a fascinating counterpoint to the association of invalidism with stasis" (114).

One common thread in the assumption of a passive, invalidlike lifestyle for men and women is James's insistence on how difficult it is to maintain this absolute stillness. To be still is a more strenuous kind of self-fashioning than to be original and have initiative. When she is first learning about Osmond's quiet character, Isabel asks if giving up things has been negative for him: "Call it affirmative if you like. Only it has affirmed my indifference. Mind you, not my natural indifference—I *had* none. But my studied, my wilful renunciation" (289 emphasis original). Osmond's character suggests that James is ambivalent about the results of the invalid lifestyle adopted by many of the new men in the novel—expatriate Americans who live a life of quiet and restraint abroad, not because their health forces them to but because they enjoy it.

For a man in good health, to be a connoisseur with a tremendous capacity for appreciation and no capacity for action is frightening. Jonathan Freedman has noted that the "numerous troubling similarities" between Gilbert Osmond and Ralph Touchett might lead one to ask which man ultimately does Isabel more harm. Freedman argues that their "common connoisseurship" is at the center of these troubling similarities (153).[16] Although Osmond and Ralph have their position as connoisseurs in common, one key difference between them is their humors—both in terms of health and in terms of their sense of fun. "He had consulted his taste in everything—his taste alone perhaps, as a sick man consciously incurable consults at last only his lawyer: that was what made him so different from everyone else," the narrator tells us of Osmond. James himself acknowledges the troubling similarities between Osmond and Ralph when he tells his reader, "Ralph had something of this same quality, this appearance of thinking that life was a matter of connoisseurship; but in Ralph it was an anomaly, a kind of humorous excrescence, whereas in Mr Osmond it was the keynote, and everything was in harmony with it" (286). These male characters take the invalid's passivity and passion for observation to such an extreme that it becomes a kind of self-making, suggesting that an invalid like Ralph or a man who appears to do nothing like Osmond could be a self-made man in terms of his sense of connoisseurship.

The Strong Woman

With the men in the novel too hard, like Caspar Goodwood, the character who fills the position of friend and companion to the weak man most fully is a woman. Henrietta Stackpole takes up the position of the strong man when she becomes sick nurse to Ralph on his journey home, a duty that Goodwood undertakes grudgingly and fulfills sulkily at Isabel's request. Unlike Goodwood, Isabel does not need to ask Henrietta to visit her sick cousin. Henrietta, "on hearing that he was too ill to come out had immediately gone of her own motion. After that she paid him a daily visit—always under the conviction that they were great enemies" (528). Henrietta ends up wondering "that she should never have liked him before," while Ralph likes her "exactly as much as he had always done" having "never doubted for a moment that she was an excellent fellow" (529). Their friendship ends with Henrietta volunteering to escort Ralph home, a task that Isabel had imagined Goodwood fulfilling. In a role reversal from their banter early in their friendship, Henrietta is the one to maintain the humorous distance in their friendship, while Ralph becomes uncharacteristically earnest if only for a moment.

> "Yes, I know you don't like me, but I'll go with you all the same. It would be better for your health to lie down again."
> Ralph looked at her a little; then he slowly relapsed. "I like you very much," he said in a moment. (531–32)

Although his claim that Henrietta is a good woman and he likes her very much are uncharacteristically earnest, Ralph sees the humor in Henrietta taking up the position of the strong man and escorting him home, and when she leaves he bursts "into a loud fit of laughter" (532). There is something ridiculous for Ralph in a woman taking him home: "It seemed to him so inconsequent, such a conclusive proof of his having abdicated all functions and renounced all exercise, that he should start on a journey across Europe under the supervision of Miss Stackpole" (532). Ralph's surrender to Henrietta's care at the end of the novel recalls a humorous remark he makes to Isabel on hearing of her plan to go to London with the woman journalist, unchaperoned by any male. "Ah then," said Ralph, "let me take advantage of her protection to go up to town as well. I may never have a chance to travel so safely!" (146). Yet for all the humor in Ralph's reduced situation at the end of the novel, he feels "gratefully, luxuriously passive" at the thought of being under her care (532). Henrietta must give up her patient to another strong woman, Mrs. Touchett, as she ends her journey, but she is the one who fills the position of strong friend in Ralph's last journey.

Under circumstances in which the strong industrialist has broken down, then, the best strong man in the novel is actually a woman. Like earlier strong, self-made men, Henrietta, bristling with sharp edges, is softened and feminized through friendship with two weak men, Ralph and Mr Bantling. Henrietta's earnest and straightforward nature and eagerness to do her national duty are reminiscent of the strong man's, as is her lack of quick-wittedness early on. Ralph's observation combines ennui and humor, and he is constantly toying with his more earnest companions, who fail to catch on to his dry sense of humor. For example, Ralph pretends to misunderstand Henrietta's deeply held belief that it is the national duty of every citizen to marry. He takes the joke a step further, pretending that she must want to marry him and accepting her kind offer of marriage. When Henrietta, frustrated, exclaims that she is only trying to draw out his opinions on an important subject, Ralph counters, feigning excitement, "Ah, do draw me out! . . . So few people will take the trouble" (107). When Henrietta accuses him of having no "regular occupation," Ralph is all too ready to agree. "I'm the idlest man living," he admits, much to Henrietta's chagrin (108). Henrietta is trying to draw him into a serious conversation about matters of national importance, and Ralph confounds her earnest attempts at every turn.

In contrast to Henrietta, Caspar Goodwood, who also accompanies Ralph on his final journey home, is hardly a friend. Isabel actually attempts to orchestrate a friendship between the strong man and the weak man in order to dispense with Goodwood's too persistent attentions and Ralph's prying eyes. Her vision of Goodwood tenderly taking care of her cousin on the train echoes the edifying friendships of the mid-century novel. In asking her rejected suitor to visit her ailing cousin, she gives him an occupation, and converts him "into a caretaker of Ralph" (529). As if in a nod to the multiple potential pairings of the strong man and the weak man that structure the novel, Isabel reflects, "Lord Warburton had brought Ralph to Rome and Mr Goodwood should take him away. There seemed a happy symmetry in this" (529). Despite the highly structured narrative laid out for him by Isabel, Goodwood does not feel the requisite sympathy toward the invalid necessary to soften his own iron constitution. Instead of feeling tenderness, he feels "sorry for that unclassable personage; he couldn't bear to see a pleasant man, so pleasant for all his queerness, so beyond anything to be done. There was always something to be done, for Goodwood, and he did it in this case by repeating several times his visit" (529). Yet, as he tells Isabel, even these visits have prompted little fellow feeling in him, and he escorts her cousin home only for her sake. "I tell you I don't care a straw for your cousin, but I don't mean that I don't like him. I mean that it isn't because I like him that I go away with him. I'd go if he were an idiot and you should have asked me. If you should ask me I'd go to Siberia tomorrow" (545). Goodwood is not particularly polite to Ralph when he offers to escort that dying gentleman back to England with Henrietta but frankly admits that it is not for his sake: "The kindness on my part is to her; it's hardly to you" (532). Ralph equally tries to excuse Goodwood from accompanying him on the journey with the plea that "Henrietta's extraordinarily efficient" (532), but for a man supposed to be of little imagination, Goodwood correctly discerns that Isabel's motive is for him to leave Rome (532). Henrietta sums up the journey to Isabel as a matter of having two weak men to deal with: "[S]he had really two patients on her hands instead of one, inasmuch as Mr Goodwood, who had been of no earthly use, was quite as ailing, in a different way, as Mr Touchett" (568). James rewrites the position of strong man so that Caspar Goodwood stands in need of as much help as any invalid.

Henrietta not only has the requisite strength of the traditional self-made man, but she also has his capacity for tenderness. At Ralph's funeral, Isabel notes that Goodwood lifts "his head higher than the rest—bowing it rather less" while "Henrietta had been crying" (616–17). Henrietta has the proper feeling for the invalid, while Goodwood remains iron hearted. Ralph's aesthetic and moral value lies in the quiet activity of his impassioned, inspired resistance to passivity, and to death. When her aunt declares that Ralph's "has not been a successful life," Isabel contradicts her: "No—it has only been a beautiful one" (605–6). James seems to endorse this view that Ralph's life has been beautiful, and worthwhile because it was so.

Given the novel's emphasis on the aesthetic and moral beauty of a quiet life of observation, accompanied by genuine feelings of tenderness and interest in others, it seems peculiar that James ends the novel with Caspar Goodwood. Goodwood's determined pursuit of Isabel has not diminished. Nor, despite the seeming self-sufficiency of the invalid as self-made man in his own right, has his presence as man of industry diminished. As he stands on the doorstep of Henrietta's lodgings in Wimpole Street, he explains that he has already been to Gardencourt that morning in search of Isabel. On receiving the news from Henrietta that she has already left for Rome, he is immovable: "Oh, she started—? He stammered. And without finishing his phrase or looking up he stiffly averted himself. But he couldn't otherwise move" (628). Seeing his disappointment, Henrietta tells him, "just you wait!" (628). And he does. "She stood shining at him with that cheap comfort, and it added, on the spot, thirty years to his life. She walked him away with her, however, as if she had given him now the key to patience" (628). Goodwood remains rooted in the novel even when the novel seems to be done with him. His stubborn presence on Henrietta's doorstop in London, at the Osmonds' soirées in Rome, and at the end of a novel that has wanted little to do with him gestures to the persistence of the pairing of the strong man and the weak man, long beyond the thirty years added to his life.

Conclusion
Modern Men

Henry James's portrait of a lonely Caspar Goodwood, unacknowledged on Isabel Archer's doorstep and unmoved by Ralph Touchett's funeral, would seem to suggest that there is little place for the strong industrialist in the fiction of the 1880s. The innovative owner of a cotton mill and former oarsman and gymnast seems no more than a relic of the mid-century strong man. The novels I have examined in this study suggest a trajectory from an uncomplicated and improving friendship between the strong man and the weak man to a rivalry to almost no relationship at all between the pair. Writers as diverse as Charles Kingsley and Charlotte Yonge suggest that this friendship is essential to the development of Christian character. Tom Brown has been in one too many scrapes and is only pulled in line when he is given the charge of a weak new boy, George Arthur. In turn Tom instills a love of a healthy romp through the woods in Arthur and ultimately saves his life by strengthening his constitution to the point where he can survive a life-threatening illness. Phineas Fletcher is given a new interest in life when John Halifax enters Norton Bury, and it is John's tender care of the invalid that proves his mettle more than any feat of athleticism could, paving the way for him to become a successful patriarch and captain of industry. George Eliot, ever skeptical and engaged with the literary trends of the times, turns the tender friendship between the strong man and his disabled companion into a bitter enmity, suggesting that the athletic and intellectual temperaments presumed to accompany the strong and weak body are not likely to be in sympathy with each other. Henry James, himself steeped in the novels of both Dinah Mulock Craik and George Eliot, takes up the pairing of the strong man and the weak man, but his strong man is not up to the task of caring for the invalid and is replaced by a strong woman instead as Henrietta Stackpole nurses Ralph through his final journey home.

This trajectory would seem to signal the end of the pairing of the strong man and the weak man with Ralph Touchett's lonely death, and that perhaps in some ways it was a narrative trope that begged to be dissected at the hands of a James or an Eliot. Yet I wish to suggest in this conclusion that the narrative consequences of the pairing of the strong man and the weak man continued to be provocative for novelists throughout the nineteenth century and beyond, and that the trope continues to hold affective power to this day. Even as they critique the idea that the strong man and the weak man would naturally develop a sympathetic friendship, authors like George Eliot and Henry James shored up the idea that a strong frame was ideal for a captain of industry like Tom Tulliver or Caspar Goodwood, and that a weaker frame would lead to a more sensitive and intellectual temperament in Philip Wakem or Ralph Touchett. Furthermore, those writers, like Thomas Hughes and Craik, who idealized the friendship were not simply too obtuse to see that a friendship across physical and cognitive abilities could never work. Rather, they tapped into a powerful emotional trope that remains a distinctly Victorian feature of the literary and filmic landscape today.

The pairing of the strong man and the weak man thus continued to be a powerful trope throughout the Victorian period and beyond, with writers experimenting with the moral valences and narrative consequences of the pairing. Immediately following the domestic novels of the midcentury, sensation fiction, by authors like Wilkie Collins, and detective fiction often reconceived the admirable strong man as a villain. Fiction of the fin de siècle collapses the strong man and the weak man into one character, à la Jekyll and Hyde. In modern fiction, such as E. M. Forster's *The Longest Journey* (1907) and Somerset Maugham's *Of Human Bondage* (1915), the pairing of the strong man and the weak man moves the focus of the pairing to the interiority of the disabled protagonist rather than humanizing his stronger counterparts. The pairing of the strong man and the weak man is also part of the landscape of twentieth- and twenty-first-century popular culture, as the ideal of friendship between a George Arthur and a Tom Brown remains a persistent feature of narrative today, perhaps particularly in children's film and literature. The more recent pairings of the strong-weak dyad, such as John Irving's *A Prayer for Owen Meany* (1989), culminate in a narrative twist wherein the strong, able-bodied boy becomes sensitive and literary enough to replace the introspective weak or disabled boy as narrator.

In this study, I have focused on domestic realist fiction as a genre that tends to promote a normative function in the pairing of the strong man and the weak man, delineating the characteristics of the idealized strong hero through the eyes of his weaker admirer. Yet this narrative dyad was contested and reformulated not only in the fiction of Eliot and James but also in several popular novelistic genres, including sensation and detective fiction, boys' adventure stories, and the decadent novels of the fin de siècle. The sensation novels of the 1860s that immediately followed mid-century domestic and adventure fiction often portray the strong man as downright villainous rather than just a scapegrace, while the weak man continues to hold the moral high ground. Wilkie Collins in particular was engaged with the pairing of the strong man and the weak man in his sensation fiction. Collins's fiction questions the midcentury expectation that strong muscles will inevitably lead to strong morals, and his novels often reverse this expectation, casting the muscular Christian as the villain and the weak man as the hero. The real thief in Collins's *The Moonstone* (1868), Godfrey Ablewhite, is as flaxen haired, strong, and tall as his last name (a compound of *able* and *white*) would suggest. Duplicitous, he turns out to be a kind of parody of the muscular Christian. By contrast, Collins's true heroes, like Franklin Blake in the same novel and Walter Hartwright in *The Woman in White* (1860), are more slight and sensitive men. Perhaps the most memorable masculine pairing to structure a sensation novel is found in *Armadale* (1866). Instead of a fair-haired woman and her darker-haired counterpart, Collins's novel explicitly contrasts a dark man and a fair man, both named Allan Armadale. The dark Armadale serves as narrator for much of the novel, and if he is not outright weak he is undersized and un-English, while the fair Armadale is superior in size and strength but inferior in intellect. In these novels, the weaker man always has the stronger morals. Collins continued this pairing of strong villain and weak hero throughout the 1870s, when, as Tamara S. Wagner notes, "the contrast between muscular men of the world and sentimental heroes recurs endlessly" (489).

Wilkie Collins's parody of muscular Christianity, *Man and Wife* (1870), establishes the importance of the odd or weak man in delineating the contours of the strong man's normalcy, and it critiques the idea that a healthy body is an uncomplicated indicator of a healthy frame of mind. Collins calls into question the idea that the influence of a weak man will lead to moral growth for the strong hero, suggesting that the weak man may have more insight and courtesy.[1] As Wagner notes, Collins resurrects the eighteenth-century man of feeling, in the character of the clubfooted Sir Patrick Lundie, in order to critique the new muscular Christian.[2] This character also calls to mind the polite and pious weak men of midcentury fiction. Sir Patrick, the lame hero of *Man and Wife*, and Geoffrey Delamayne, its muscular villain, are introduced side by side, with the young man as "a striking representative of the school that is among us—as Sir Patrick was a striking representative of the school that has passed away" (61). Geoffrey is "young and florid, tall and strong" with "curly Saxon locks" and features "as perfectly regular and as perfectly unintelligent as human features can be" (61). By contrast, Sir Patrick is "little and wiry and slim" with a "wry twist of humour curling sharply at the corners of his lips" (58). The narrator remarks, "He carried his lameness, as he carried his years, gaily" (58). Although athleticism may help a young man win a physical victory, it will not help him win a moral victory. As it turns out, Geoffrey Delamayne has seduced and deserted the novel's heroine, Anne Silvester. Unlike Kingsley's heroes, he lacks the self-restraint necessary to elevate his baser nature with chivalry. Furthermore, his athleticism proves dangerous to himself. His doctor declares that "of the young men who are now putting themselves to violent athletic tests of strength and endurance," many "are taking that course to the serious and permanent injury of their own health" (217). Geoffrey is not so lucky: he collapses and dies after a footrace. Despite his clubfoot, Sir Patrick is able to offer the most chivalrous protection to the women in the novel. He is so charmed by Anne's womanly strength and modesty under adverse circumstances that he ends his long bachelorhood to marry her. This ending suggests that the kindness and courteousness of Sir Patrick's more sensitive organization is what is needed to make amends for the damage inflicted by brute force.

Authors at the end of the century continue to play with the idea of pairing masculine strength and weakness, sometimes collapsing the two figures in novels like Robert Louis Stevenson's *The Strange Case of Dr. Jekyll and Mr. Hyde* (1886) and Oscar Wilde's *The Picture of Dorian Grey* (1891). Detective figures continue the midcentury trope of exceptional observation being linked to weakness and disability.[3] In Collins's *The Moonstone* (1868) Ezra Jennings's experience as an opium addict gives him the key to the mystery. In Arthur Conan Doyle's Sherlock Holmes stories, Watson, who suffered a war injury in Afghanistan, narrates the successes of Holmes, whose nervous temperament and cocaine use is linked to his ability to solve mysteries (3). H. Rider Haggard makes use of the well-established pairing of a Saxon strong man and a darker deformed man gifted with observational powers. Horace Holly, the narrator of the best-selling *She*, and his ward Leo Vincey are first observed walking down the street together by another pair of university men, one of whom appreciatively exclaims of Leo, "[W]hy, that fellow looks like a statue of Apollo come to life. What a splendid man he is" (10). Holly, by contrast, describes himself as "Short, thick-set, and deep-chested almost to deformity," with a "low brow half overgrown with a mop of thick black hair, like a deserted clearing on which the forest had once more begun to encroach" (20). These physical characteristics, darkness and unusual features bordering on deformity, quickly establish Holly as a brooding type, well suited to the narration of his adventures with his well-built ward. This pairing of masculine strength and disability or weakness, with the dark, weak man often serving as narrator, is firmly entrenched in the fiction of the second half of the nineteenth century. Nor did it disappear in modernist fiction.

The Longest Journey

Recognizing the pairing of the strong man and the weak man as a persistent literary trope helps us to reread the significance of disability in early-twentieth-century novels. Novels such as E. M. Forster's *The Longest Journey* and Somerset Maugham's *Of Human Bondage* follow in the Victorian tradition of the pairing of the strong man and the weak man, with the significant difference that the focus is almost entirely on the interiority of the disabled protagonist rather than on fleshing out the interiority of his strong counterpart. In Maugham's and Forster's novels, the protagonists's clubfeet have been traditionally read autobiographically as a code for the author's homosexuality. "Rickie's club foot" the editor to the Penguin edition of *The Longest Journey* declares, "has been universally interpreted as a covert metaphor for Forster's publicly repressed homosexuality" (Adair xiv). Gore Vidal makes light of this interpretation in an essay on Maugham, writing, "It is the common view of Maugham biographers that the true tragic flaw was homosexuality, disguised as a club foot in *Of Human Bondage*—or was that the stammer?" (xii). Despite this critical view of the reading of the clubfoot as a straightforward signal of the author's sexuality, the one-to-one equation between the author's homosexuality and his protagonist's clubfoot persists to the present day. A recent biographer of Somerset Maugham writes, "Philip's clubfoot stands for Maugham's stammer but, as Francis King has pointed out, it was also (as in Forster) 'a metaphor for a graver disability'" (Meyers 108). The interpretation of a disability as a symbol of the novelist's deep-seated anxieties about authorship, gender, and sexuality echoes second-wave feminist arguments about mid-nineteenth-century women writers' use of disabled protagonists as representative of women's position in a patriarchal society. Placing these modern novels in the context of their Victorian predecessors allows them instead to be read as part of a sixty-year tradition of schoolboy fiction in which an introverted disabled boy is paired with a strong friend or tormentor.

The Longest Journey (1907), Forster's second novel, continues the pairing of the strong boy and the weak boy in two iterations: the first pairing is a familiar schoolboy rivalry, while the second is a less familiar fraternal plot in which one brother is lame and the other, illegitimate brother is strong and athletic. The first follows the familiar pattern of schoolboy rivalry, reintroduced after public schooldays are over and the former bully and his victim meet again in the home of a mutual friend. The protagonist, Rickie, who has a hereditary congenital clubfoot, finds that the boy who bullied him in his schooldays, the athletic but simpleminded Gerald Dawson, is now engaged to his friend Agnes Pembroke. The physical differences between the two men are introduced through her point of view. Agnes finds Rickie's orthopedic shoes in the hallway: "Rickie was slightly deformed, and so the shoes were not the same size, and one of them had a thick heel to help him towards an even walk. 'Ugh!' she exclaimed, and removed them gingerly to the bedroom. There she saw other shoes and boots and pumps, a whole row of them, all deformed. 'Ugh! Poor boy! It is too bad. Why shouldn't he be like other people? This hereditary business is too awful'" (9). Agnes banishes this unpleasant image of deformity by recalling "the perfect form of Gerald, his athletic walk, the poise of his shoulders, his arms stretched forward to receive her. Gradually she was comforted" (9).

Forster uses the pairing of the strong man and the weak man, unexpectedly, to flesh out Rickie's consciousness rather than the strong, taciturn Gerald's. Rickie remembers his old friend with horror when Agnes first introduces him. As the narrator remarks of their late Victorian schooldays, "An apple-pie bed is nothing; pinches, kicks, boxed ears, twisted arms, pulled hair, ghosts at night, inky books, befouled photographs, amount to very little by themselves. But let them be united and continuous, and you have a hell that no grown-up devil can devise" (37). Rickie remembers being bullied at school but nonetheless magnanimously offers his former tormentor the money he needs to marry. Gerald, however, is unwilling to accept the gift. He is missing the strong man's tenderness. Agnes accuses him playfully, "You don't know what it is to pity the weak," and he responds that it is "Woman's job" and if lending them money to marry is "Mr. Rickety Elliot's idea of a soldier and an Englishman, it isn't mine, and I wish I'd had a horsewhip" (49). Agnes, although she scolds him for his former bullying of the weak boy, experiences a masochistic "thrill of joy when she thought of the weak boy in the clutches of the strong one" (50). Here Forster renders the potential masochism that underlies the early friendships of the strong man and the weak man overt, as Agnes dwells pleasurably on Gerald's physical power.

Forster, however, drives home the point that physical strength is not as reliable as it seems, shifting the focus to the interiority of his disabled protagonist. In a scene that echoes the untimely demise of Collins's Geoffrey Delamayne in a footrace, Forster satirically kills off Gerald in the next chapter. Gerald dies on the playing field, "broken up in the football match." Forster writes, "It was no good torturing him by a drive to the hospital, and he was merely carried to the little pavilion and laid upon the floor. A doctor came, and so did a clergyman, but it seemed better to leave him for the last few minutes with Agnes" (51). In a twist that recalls Maggie's oscillation between the deformed Philip and the strong Stephen Guest, Agnes marries Rickie once she has lost her strong lover. Perhaps unexpectedly, Forster's fraught pairing of the strong man and the weak man continues past the hero's schooldays, when he finds out that he has an illegitimate brother, his mother's son, who is as well-made as he is weak. Stephen is "a powerful boy of twenty, admirably muscular, but rather too broad for his height" (87). That the weak man and the strong man are brothers in the novel's second iteration of the pairing suggests the intimacy of the bond.

Yet Forster's novel, with a weak man as its protagonist, casts suspicion on the strong man's silence. When Rickie's philosophical friend Stuart Ansell warns him against marrying Agnes, partly because of his hereditary deformity, a eugenicist strain creeps into the novel: "You are not a person who ought to marry at all. You are unfitted in body: that we once discussed. You are also unfitted in soul: you want and you need to like many people, and a man of that sort ought not to marry" (81).[4] Rickie writes in reply, "Up to now I think we have been too much like the strong heroes in books who feel so much and say so little, and feel all the more for saying so little. Now that's over and we shall never be that kind of an ass again" (82–83). Rickie's aunt, Emily Failing, similarly declares of Stephen, her ward, "Let him thank his stars he isn't a silent strong man, or I'd turn him into the gutter" (90). Rickie eventually sacrifices himself to save his brother Stephen in a railway accident. Rickie's stories become a success posthumously, solidifying the connection between disability and authorship.

Of Human Bondage

Of Human Bondage pushes the focus on the interiority of the disabled protagonist even further, so that the strong bullies and friends who make their inevitable appearance in the novel appear mainly as aids to Philip's character development. Maugham thus takes an idea that has its roots in nineteenth-century orthopedic medicine to an extreme: a man is liable to become peevish and introspective when he feels that a physical deformity sets him apart. Maugham's novel can be read as a fictionalization of mid-Victorian surgeon William John Little's claim that historians "have described the influence of deformity in alternately stimulating the cultivation of the worst and of the best passions and instincts" (18). Like Rickie's clubfoot, Philip's clubfoot is congenital, a fact Maugham uses to suggest that it is an integral part of the shaping of his character. The congenital nature of this disability, the novel seems to suggest, is significantly different from the potentially heroic disabilities that were becoming prominent with the beginning of World War I.[5] Philip is so humiliated by his congenital clubfoot that he is unable to reach out to other boys in friendship, much less act as a morally improving force. He does, however, share the intellectual prowess of the weak boy, and he wins "a collection of prizes, worthless books on bad paper, but in gorgeous bindings decorated with the arms of the school." His position "freed him from bullying," and his "fellows forgave him his success because of his deformity" (44). Philip's ideas about school life as he enters the King's School at Tercanbury are Victorian: "He knew little of school life but what he had read in the stories of *The Boy's Own Paper*. He had also read *Eric, or Little by Little*" (33). A scene of torture in the schoolyard echoes the grim opening scene of another Victorian schoolboy novel, G. A. Lawrence's *Guy Livingstone* (1857): "Then one of them had the brilliant idea of imitating Philip's clumsy run. Other boys saw it and began to laugh; then they all copied the first; and they ran round Philip, limping grotesquely, screaming in their treble voices with shrill laughter" (38).

Maugham analyzes and rejects the Christian view of disability as a God-given burden supported by earlier novelists like Charlotte Yonge, exploring instead the secular introversion of his protagonist. Philip's headmaster acknowledges the difficulty of school life for the exceptional boy: "Of course schools are made for the average. The holes are all round, and whatever shape the pegs are they must wedge in somehow" (84). He offers Philip a Christian reading of his clubfoot that could come directly from a Yonge novel: "As long as you accept it rebelliously it can only cause you shame. But if you looked upon it as a cross that was given you to bear only because your shoulders were strong enough to bear it, a sign of God's favour, then it would be a source of happiness to you instead of misery" (66). Philip rejects this reading and struggles with the psychological effects of his deformity throughout his adolescence and young adulthood. The narrator writes:

> Philip had few friends. His habit of reading isolated him . . . and he had not the skill to hide his contempt for his companions' stupidity. . . . He was developing a sense of humour, and found that he had a knack of saying bitter things, which caught people on the raw; he said them because they amused him, hardly realizing how much they hurt, and was much offended when he found that his victims regarded him with active dislike. The humiliations he suffered when he first went to school had caused in him a shrinking from his fellows which he could never entirely overcome; he remained shy and silent. (67)

Interestingly, Philip develops the introspective nature of the weak boy but not his loquacious nature. Instead, his shyness causes him to conceal first his feelings of shame at his deformity and eventually all his feelings under an imperturbable reserve. "Philip desired popularity but he could bring himself to make no advances to others. A fear of rebuff prevented him from affability, and he concealed his shyness, which was still intense, under a frigid taciturnity" (266).

An early friendship with an ordinary popular boy who excels at sport, à la Tom Brown and George Arthur, serves only to render Philip increasingly introspective and peevish. Rose is a familiar type: "He was neither clever nor stupid, but good enough at his work and better at games. He was a favourite with masters and boys, and he in his turn liked everyone"

(68). Philip is at first "too grateful for Rose's friendship to make any demands on him," but "presently he began to resent Rose's universal amiability; he wanted a more exclusive attachment" (70). Philip oscillates between nursing ill-humors and returning to Rose with renewed passion for their friendship: "But the best was over, and Philip could see that Rose often walked with him merely from old habit or from fear of his anger; they had not so much to say to one another as at first, and Rose was often bored. Philip felt that his lameness began to irritate him" (71). Philip is stricken during an outbreak of scarlet fever at the school, and, although Rose sends him "a couple of little notes," each ending with the words "Hurry up and come back," there is no tender sickroom scene of reconciliation between the two boys (71). Philip's friendship with Rose is not lifelong or edifying but instead sets a pattern of masochism, jealousy, pain, and humiliation that persists in his infatuation with Mildred Rogers in his adulthood.[6]

Maugham's representation of Philip's clubfoot has shades of eugenics: in order to compensate for his disability Philip must marry a healthy, normal woman rather than the physically and morally deviant type to which he is most attracted. Marriage with a strong woman, according to this line of thought, promises the moral and physical corrective that Philip has not received in his friendships with men. The pairing of the weak type and the strong type, rather than being embodied in Philip's male friendships, is thus transposed to the women in the novel, the anemic Mildred versus the robust Sally. Mildred, with her boyish, androgynous figure and her anemic constitution, begins as a waitress but, through a love of finery and lack of moral fiber, eventually descends into prostitution and contracts syphilis. Philip, a medical student, sees her as a physically degenerate type from the beginning of his relationship with her but loves her nonetheless: "He did not think her pretty; he hated the thinness of her, only that evening he had noticed how the bones of her chest stood out in the evening dress" and "the unhealthiness of her colour vaguely repelled him" (277). In the grip of a slavish passion for Mildred, Philip feels "just as he had felt sometimes in the hands of a bigger boy at school" (285). Maugham's parallel between the bullying relationship of the strong boy and the weak boy and Philip's masochistic pursuit of the waitress is telling: neither male friendship nor a weak woman is right for Philip.

Philip's choice of wife reflects the eugenicist concerns of Maugham's novel. The healthy lower-class Sally is apprenticed to a dressmaker in Regent's street, but Philip sees that she belongs in the country. "Sally had frank blue eyes, a broad brow, and plentiful shining hair; she was buxom, with broad hips and full breasts" (572). Sally resists the class type of the frail seamstress: "[S]he was healthy, strong and normal; it must be odd to see her among the other girls in the shop with their flat chests and anaemic faces" Philip reflects. "Mildred suffered from anaemia" (573). Philip dwells on Sally's physical perfections at length: "[H]e admired her magnificent healthiness. She was a splendid animal, without defect; and physical perfection filled him always with admiring awe. She made him feel unworthy" (603). He explicitly imagines that marrying and reproducing with Sally will wipe out the congenital taint of his deformity. Philip imagines "putting his hands over" the "little perfect limbs" of his child with Sally, and "he knew he would be beautiful" (607). Reading early-twentieth-century fiction through the literary tradition of the pairing of the strong man and the weak man suggests the persistent and evolving representation of weak or disabled men as author figures, whose deviance is defined against the presence of a stronger friend.

The Late-Twentieth-Century Schoolboy Story

The Victorian plot of a schoolboy friendship between a disabled boy and a strong boy persists in contemporary young adult fiction, suggesting that the pairing is seen as an emotionally useful tool for teaching children that the value of friendship can transcend, or even be reinforced by, physical difference.[7] This trope continues to the present day, but, perhaps because the pairing of the strong adult man and the weak adult man has come to be coded as queer, it is often a pairing of a strong boy and a weak boy. The contemporary critical reception of the Victorian plot of the strong boy and his disabled friend has taken its strongest hold in schoolboy stories such as John Irving's *A Prayer for Owen Meany* (1989) and Rodman Philbrick's *Freak the Mighty* (1993), which are often part of middle and high school curriculums, a trend that suggests that the pairing of the strong boy and the weak boy is now seen as a pedagogical tool. Like Forster's and Maugham's novels, *A Prayer for Owen Meany* and *Freak the Mighty* are read as largely autobiographical novels that draw on the authors' schooldays, and both feature a disabled male protagonist. These novels have a twist on the traditional schoolboy pairing of strength and weakness, although the strong man becomes literate and sensitive enough through friendship to serve as the narrator.

Compared to the novels of Maugham and Forster, which only flirt with the friendship of the strong boy and the weak boy, Irving's bestselling *A Prayer for Owen Meany* marks a return to a Victorian ideal. Surprisingly, some of the narratives that most closely follow the mid-nineteenth-century structure of pairing a strong man and a weak man have been published or filmed in the last twenty years. This physical difference is not necessarily pathologized, as it is in Maugham in particular, but instead is redeemed through friendship. There is a twist in these narratives in that the weak boy usually teaches his stronger friend an appreciation for literature to the extent that he is able to narrate the story himself rather than the weak or disabled boy acting as the narrator or the narrator figure.

A Prayer for Owen Meany follows the pattern of the weak boy humanizing his school friend and is a direct literary descendant of *Tom Brown's Schooldays*. Owen is small enough to play the baby Jesus in an elementary school play and has a "permanently fixed larynx" that causes him to shout every time he speaks, which Irving represents through capital lettering in Owen's dialogue and writing (359). The narrator, John, like Tom Brown, gains faith and begins to apply himself in school through his friendship with Owen Meany. He learns to appreciate Thomas Hardy and eventually becomes an English teacher at a private girl's school in Toronto, where he records the story of his friendship with Owen. Owen's disability thus facilitates John's authorship. Most important in terms of the parallels between the Victorian schoolboy novel and Irving's contemporary work, John becomes a Christian through his friend. The novel begins, "I am doomed to remember a boy with a wrecked voice—not because of his voice, or because he was the smallest person I ever knew, or even because he was the instrument of my mother's death, but because he is the reason I believe in God; I am a Christian because of Owen Meany" (3). Although Owen and John may seem like a perfect Victorian pairing of the strong man and the weak man, at the end of the novel John is more the typical weak man, shattered and literally mutilated through his friendship with Owen, while Owen is a strong war hero.

The young adult novel *Freak the Mighty*, by Rodman Philbrick, takes the pairing of the strong boy and the weak boy to such an extreme that both boys are seen as disabled. This is in some ways the logical extension of midcentury claims about the exemplarity and normalcy of the strong hero: pushed just a little further, the strong man comes to seem cognitively disabled in his taciturnity, his large body a burden.[8] Max's large body is a source of shame to him—the readers see him struggling with his physical presence in the world even more so than his small friend—from buying sneakers at the mall in a size so large the clerk does not believe that it exists to the cruelty of constant teasing at school. Kevin Avery, the "freak" of the title, has a rare form of dwarfism, Morquio syndrome. Max, watching him move in next door, describes him as a "crippled-up yellow-haired midget kid" who struts around giving orders to the movers (7). Philbrick pairs the strong boy and the weak boy with extreme versions of the cognitive abilities associated with these physical types; Max, like the Scarecrow in the *Wizard of Oz*, claims to have no brain. Max's disabilities are at least partially the result of the psychological trauma of seeing his father kill his mother at age four. Max's cognitive capabilities are represented as improvable, especially through friendship, just as Tom Brown's moral fiber is improved through his friendship with George Arthur. Max ends the novel by claiming that he has so far advanced that he was not only to narrate the novel but to write it down. After Kevin dies, he ends the novel, "So I wrote the unvanquished truth stuff down and then kept on going, for months and months, until it was spring again, and the world was really and truly green all over. By the time we got here, which I guess should be the end, I'm feeling okay about remembering things. And now that I've written a book who knows, I might even read a few" (160).

The film versions of *Freak the Mighty* and *A Prayer for Owen Meany*, retitled *The Mighty* and *Simon Birch* (both 1998), are often taught in middle schools, while Irving's novel continues to make high school reading lists.[9] The critical appropriation of stories of the pairing of the strong boy and the weak boy as pedagogical tools suggests that friendships along the lines of *Tom Brown's Schooldays* are now seen as suitable for children and adolescents, perhaps because the bond between the two, which often involves the strong boy literally carrying the weak boy through their many scrapes, feels too sentimental for adult films. In a recent article on the two films as a pedagogical tool in the middle school classroom, the authors find the representation of the disabled adolescent boy protagonists problematic in their message that disability is a pitiable condition that can be overcome through the heroism that the disabled boy learns in his long suffering. They write that, although the "films are usually presented as positive and empowering representations of disability, as models to nondisabled students or 'normates,' about overcoming adversity, leading selfless lives, and heroism" they are "mired in the presentation of these boys as both selfless heroes and pitiable individuals, whose heroism and sacrifice emanate directly from their 'afflictions'" (Arndt, White, and Chervenak). They suggest that a more critical pedagogy could provide students with "the power to question the status quo and hold multiple viewpoints that resist the dominant constructions presented in film." Part of this critical pedagogy would need to be a recognition of the historical arc of the friendship of an able-bodied and a disabled boy, in which each has something to learn and something to teach.

The plot of a schoolboy friendship between a stronger boy and a weaker boy has retained much of its emotional currency over the last 150 years. These recent novels show that there is a persistent cultural connection between physical weakness and the humanizing function of literature. Literature is seen as teaching the strong to protect the weak and teaching the strong, in effect, to become fully human through their tenderness and care for others and their newfound literacy and ability to articulate these feelings. This pairing is not always felicitous, but its very persistence suggests the role of such narrative dyads in defining a normative type of strong masculinity in contradistinction to masculine weakness and disability. At the same time that masculine strength came to be defined as taciturn and controlled, masculine weakness came to be seen as loquacious and emotive. This is one reason why it is so easy for contemporary critics to continue to relate characters with disabilities directly to the author's biography. It has come to seem natural that the position of the disabled man parallels the position of the author: both are marginal figures, primed by their suffering as marginal figures to observe, and both have the artistic temperament necessary to turn their observations to good aesthetic account. Yet the logic that has made it so easy to equate the author with the disabled protagonist has a history. The pairing of a strong man and his disabled friend may seem too queer for mainstream culture today, but it persists in popular culture through alternate routes, in the racialized and physically and cognitively different dyads. The supposition that the strong man and the weak man embody two cognitively and emotionally disparate yet complementary forms of masculinity is our inheritance from the Victorians, an inheritance that remains current to this day.

Notes

Introduction

1. Orthopedic medicine, which today treats conditions of the musculoskeletal system ranging from sporting injuries to spinal curvature, began as a general practice of child rearing in France with Nicolas Andry's *Orthopaedia* (1741) and became a specialized and highly innovative branch of medicine from the 1830s to the 1860s. In the eighteenth and early nineteenth centuries, these kinds of deformities were treated mechanically through the use of massage and machines that stretched the limbs. For example, Byron's clubfoot was treated variously with machines and bandages administered by his nurse, and by a "quack" named Lavender from Nottingham who took to "rubbing the foot over, for a considerable time, with handfuls of oil, and then twisting the limb forcibly round, and screwing it up in a wooden machine." Thomas Moore, *Letters and Journals of Lord Byron, with Notices of His Life* (London: J. Murray, 1830), 9, 27. In contrast to these mechanical methods, early orthopedic medicine made deformity a surgical problem and generally treated asymmetries in the human frame through subcutaneous splitting of the tendons of the affected muscles, or tenotomy. Essentially, surgeons attempted to make as small an incision as possible and operate underneath the skin to reduce the chance of infection. This type of surgery has a famously disastrous outcome in *Madame Bovary*, when Charles Bovary operates on the clubfooted stableboy Hippolyte, only to have the limb turn gangrenous and have to be amputated. For a history of orthopedic medicine aimed at medical professionals, see Leslie Klenerman, *The Evolution of Orthopaedic Surgery* (London: Royal Society of Medicine, 2002).

2. The most important document for exploring the psychology of deformity in the eighteenth century is William Hay's (1754), which argues for the sympathetic treatment of those with visible disabilities. See Hay, *Deformity: An Essay*, ed. Kathleen James-Cavan. (Victoria, BC: U of Victoria, 2004). Helen Deutsch writes that Hay is "arguably the first writer in the history of English literature to conceptualize and articulate physical disability as a personal identity." See Deutsch, "The Body's Moments:

Visible Disability, the Essay, and the Limits of Sympathy," *Prose Studies* 27.1–2 (2005): 11. While characters with deformities certainly appeared in literature before the nineteenth century, the Victorian treatment of deformity was new in the idea that a deformed man was worthy of sympathy rather than ridicule and that he must have cultivated a deep inner self through years of suffering.

3. Examples of characters named Tom include Kingsley's Tom Thurnall, Eliot's Tom Tulliver, and Hughes's Tom Brown; Guys include Yonge's Guy Morville, Lawrence's Guy Livingstone, and Craik's Guy Halifax. For weak men, Franks include Kingsley's Frank Leigh and Frank Headley and Lawrence's Frank Hammond, while Philips include Eliot's Philip Wakem and Maugham's Philip Carey.

4. For an analysis of the role of male friendship in ideals of Victorian government and citizenship, see Richard Dellamora, *Friendship's Bonds: Democracy and the Novel in Victorian England* (Philadelphia: U of Pennsylvania P, 2004).

5. Two examples of the use of disability to mark a villain in the nineteenth-century novel include Charles Dickens's Daniel Quilp in *The Old Curiosity Shop* (1841) and Wilkie Collins's Misserimus Dexter in *The Law and the Lady* (1875). See Martha Stoddard Holmes, *Fictions of Affliction*, 17–18; and Garland-Thomson 36, for analyses of these negative connotations.

6. A significant literary progenitor of the weak man of the mid–nineteenth century was the man of feeling of the late-eighteenth-century sentimental novel. Men of feeling, like Henry Mackenzie's Harley or Laurence Sterne's Yorick, were possessed of susceptible nervous systems that were easily moved to tears. On their sentimental journeys, they encountered beggars, prostitutes, and widows—sentimental figures who elicited their fellow feeling and sympathy. Harley and Yorick are tongue-tied at the tableaux they encounter, but they show their sentimental feeling for the scenes before them through somatic responses, including tears, sighs, and blushes. Their primary purpose is to observe, and to give the reader a sentimental education in the proper emotional response to all they see. They are articulate insofar as they are the narrators of their own tales—though Harley's tale is told through scraps of letters collected by an editor figure after the world proves too exhausting for his nerves. But the man of feeling lacks the agency to shape his own story—part of its affective power derives from its fragmentary state. The weak man of the mid–nineteenth century shares the man of feeling's nervous constitution, but not his inarticulate nature. He is able not only to observe but also to give narrative shape to what he sees, usually without expiring in the effort. Moreover, his object of observation is not the prostitute or the beggar but rather a person of his own class and gender, a man who differs from him only in his physical strength and emotional taciturnity. In recent work on eighteenth-century masculinity and the feeling body, Mike Goode has argued that in the work of eighteenth-century historians such as Edmund Burke, part of manliness was the ability of "their bodies' constitutional power to feel" (22). In other words, an eighteenth century gentleman was authoritative by virtue of his body's susceptibility to feeling. See Goode, *Sentimental Masculinity and the Rise of History, 1790–1890* (New York: Cambridge UP, 2009). See also Markman Ellis, *Race, Gender, and Commerce in the Sentimental Novel* (Cambridge: Cambridge UP, 1996), for a description of the role of somatic "emblem[s] of sensitivity" in the sentimental novel (19) and for a broader argument about the politics of sentimentality in the eighteenth-century novel.

7. Increasing industrialization took a high toll on workers' bodies, and incidences of injuries were high. In his work on the factory worker's body, Mike Sanders

suggests that after the agitation of the Factory Debates of the 1830s and 1840s, from the 1850s onward there was a "veritable sea-change in judicial opinion concerning employer liability," which culminated in the Employer's Liability Act of 1880 and the Workmen's Compensation Act of 1897 (320). Sanders, "Manufacturing Accident: Industrialism and the Worker's Body in Early Victorian Fiction," *Victorian Literature and Culture* 28.2 (2000): 313–29. See also Maria Frawley's account of working class invalids, such as the author of the *Narrative of the Experience and Sufferings of William Dodd, a Factory Cripple*, in her *Invalidism and Identity in Nineteenth-Century Britain* (Chicago: U of Chicago P, 2004), 42.

8. Christopher Oldstone-Moore has challenged the idea that Crimean soldiers popularized the beard, dating the trend in facial hair earlier, in the 1850s. See Oldstone-Moore, "The Beard Movement in Victorian Britain," *Victorian Studies* 48.1 (2005): 7–34. Nonetheless, the Crimean War seems emblematic of the tension between the rugged, strong masculinity of the soldier going to war and the maimed soldier returning home on crutches. See Stefanie Markovits, *The Crimean War in the British Imagination* (New York: Cambridge UP, 2009).

9. For an analysis of the development of the relationship between physical hygiene and fitness and fitness for citizenship, see Pamela Gilbert, *The Citizen's Body: Desire, Health, and the Social in Victorian England* (Columbus: Ohio State UP, 2007). Gilbert writes, "As the citizen came to be defined against the pauper, and by a particular kind of domestic practice, the pauper was coming to be defined chiefly in terms of a threat to the physical as well as moral health of the social body. The rhetoric of sanitary reform and of franchise reform dovetail early on in the 1830s formulation of the fitness problem, and the morally desirable practices of domesticity that are urged on the pauper are sanctioned by the mandates of public health" (47).

10. For more on the Victorian cult of the healthy body, see Bruce Haley's classic study *The Healthy Body and Victorian Culture* (Cambridge, MA: Harvard UP, 1978); or, more recently, Mary Wilson Carpenter's study of the role of illness and disease in Victorian culture, *Health, Medicine, and Society in Victorian England* (Santa Barbara, CA: Praeger, 2010), which includes a disability studies perspective.

11. William John Little himself traveled to Germany to have an operation on his clubfoot and brought the latest techniques in orthopedic surgery back to England. See Klenerman 3.

12. The seminal work in disability studies is Lennard Davis's *Enforcing Normalcy: Disability, Deafness, and the Body* (New York: Verso, 1995), which argues that the nineteenth century saw the development of a concept of normal that in turn pathologized disability. The most important monograph in Victorian disability studies is Martha Stoddard Holmes's *Fictions of Affliction*. Mark Mossman has also published a book entitled *Disability, Representation, and the Body in Irish Writing, 1800–1922* (New York: Palgrave Macmillan, 2009). In nineteenth-century American studies, Rosemarie Garland-Thomson's *Extraordinary Bodies* examines the culture of freakery in the circus, as well as in the domestic and sentimental novel. Although few monographs have yet been written in Victorian disability studies, there are, increasingly, excellent articles and special collections of journals on Victorian disability. For a history of the relationship between disability studies and Victorian studies, see Jennifer Esmail and Christopher Keep, "Victorian Disability," *Victorian Review* 25.2 (Fall 2009): 45–51; and Mark Mossman and Martha Stoddard Holmes, "Critical Transformations: Disability and the Body in Nineteenth-Century Britain," *Nineteenth-Century Gender Studies* 4.2

(Summer 2008), online at http://ncgsjournal.com/issue42/introduction.htm. For essays on the place of freakery in Victorian culture, see Marlene Tromp, ed., *Victorian Freaks: The Social Context of Freakery in Britain* (Columbus: Ohio State UP, 2008).

13. As Susan Wendell and others point out, we tend to conceive of disability as permanent and absolute, but in reality most people who live long enough will experience some form of disablement in their lives. See Wendell, *The Rejected Body: Feminist Philosophical Reflections on Disability* (New York: Routledge, 1996). Lennard Davis writes, "In the process of disabling people with disabilities, ableist society creates the absolute category of disability. 'Normal' people tend to think of 'the disabled' as the deaf, the blind, the orthopedically impaired, the mentally retarded." *Enforcing Normalcy* 7–8. This is an established point in disability studies but worth making here since it suggests that resistance to including a chronically ill character such as Ralph Touchett in the category of "disabled" may be part of a larger stigmatizing of the disabled as "other." Including illness in the category of disability may make disability seem uncomfortably close to those who cannot imagine themselves developing an orthopedic deformity but can imagine themselves becoming ill.

14. I do not include sensory disabilities, such as deafness and blindness, in this study, as they do not seem to fit the paradigm of masculine strength and weakness in the novel.

15. There are several excellent studies of invalidism in Victorian literature and culture. I also take it as part of my task in this work to extend a disability studies perspective to the existing literature. See Miriam Bailin, *The Sickroom in Victorian Fiction: The Art of being Ill* (New York: Cambridge UP, 1994); Maria Frawley, *Invalidism and Identity in Nineteenth-Century Britain*; and Athena Vrettos, *Somatic Fictions: Imagining Illness in Victorian Culture* (Stanford, CA: Stanford UP, 1995). Erin O'Connor's *Raw Material: Producing Pathology in Victorian Culture* (Durham, NC: Duke UP, 2000) provides an interesting analysis of the role of prostheses in Victorian literature and culture.

16. Placing a similar emphasis on the relationship between oppositionally defined able-bodied and disabled characters, Julia Miele Rodas argues that representations of disability in the nineteenth-century novel can be characterized as a "satellite syndrome," in which the disabled act as ancillary characters to the able-bodied. See Rodas, "Tiny Tim, Blind Bertha, and the Resistance of Miss Mowcher: Charles Dickens and the Uses of Disability," *Dickens Studies Annual* 34 (2004): 51–97.

17. For readings of masculinity in Tennyson, Clough, Barrett Browning, and Robert Browning, especially in relation to the tension between civilization and a male propensity for violence, see Clinton Machann, *Masculinity in Four Victorian Epics: A Darwinist Reading* (Burlington, VT: Ashgate, 2010).

18. On degeneration, see Daniel Pick, *Faces of Degeneration: A European Disorder, c. 1848–c. 1918* (New York: Cambridge UP, 1989).

Chapter 1

1. It is interesting to note that Kingsley dedicated *Westward Ho!* to the same man to whom Yonge gave the profits from *The Heir of Redclyffe*, George Augustus Selwyn, the bishop of New Zealand, who was evidently held in high esteem by both writers. Kingsley deemed him to possess that "type of English virtue, at once manful and godly, practical and enthusiastic, prudent and self-sacrificing" (dedication in *Westward Ho!*). Yonge, who met Bishop Selwyn in the summer of 1854, donated the proceeds

from *The Heir of Redclyffe* to enable the schooner *Southern Cross* to be put into service on behalf of Selwyn. Yonge's and Kingsley's shared interest in Selwyn suggests similarities in their ideal of Christian manhood as both practical and self-sacrificing; the modern Christian knight with an opportunity to do active good in a threatening setting was a missionary. Susan Walton writes that summaries of Yonge's life often refer to her donations of money toward Melanesian missionary work, and "the superficial impression created is of a submissive daughter in thrall both to her family and to hazy idealistic dreams of converting South Seas people to Christianity: she is made to appear complicit with patriarchy and with imperialism. While there are elements of truth in this impression, the reality is far more multifaceted." Walton, *Imagining Soldiers and Fathers in the Mid-Victorian Era: Charlotte Yonge's Models of Manliness* (Burlington VT: Ashgate, 2010), 140.

2. As Amy Cruse points out, soldiers and statesmen, from William Gladstone to John Manners, were moved by Yonge's work. See *The Victorians and Their Books* (London: Allen & Unwin, 1935), 64. William Morris and Edward Burne-Jones were extraordinarily moved by the book, which was published in the same year that they came up to Exeter College, Oxford, 1853. Morris's biographer writes that he and his set took, "the young hero of the book," Guy Morville, with his "conscientiousness, his chivalrous courtesy, his intense earnestness, his eagerness for all such social reforms as might be effected from above downwards," and his "notions of love, friendship, and honour" as "a pattern for actual life," with Morris perhaps taking it more strongly than the rest, from "his own greater wealth and more aristocratic temper" (Mackail 48). Indeed, Canon Dixon (who, half a century later, maintained that Yonge's novel was "unquestionably one of the finest books in the world") describes his friend during his undergraduate days as "an aristocrat, and a High Churchman," with a "countenance" that was "beautiful in features and expression, particularly in the expression of purity," and which occasionally "had a melancholy look" (Mackail 54)—terms that could apply equally well to the novel's hero. See J. W. Mackail, *The Life of William Morris* (1899; London: Electric Book Co., 2001).

3. Kingsley writes "Young" for "Yonge" here. The novelist's spelling, as his biographer Susan Chitty writes, "was never perfect. He invariably spelt the name of *Fraser's Magazine* as Frazer's even though he was a regular contributor" (42). For a recent biography that extends Chitty's long standard *The Beast and the Monk: A Life of Charles Kingsley* (London: Hodder and Stoughton, 1974), see J. M. I. Klaver, *The Apostle of the Flesh: A Critical Life of Charles Kingsley* (Leiden: Brill, 2006).

4. Similarly, the critic for the *North American Review* proclaimed that Yonge's novel had found a large and tearful audience among both men and women and all classes in America: "The soldier, the divine, the seamstress, the lawyer, the grocer-boy, the belle, and the hair-dresser peeping over her shoulder," he wrote, "joined in full cry, according to their different modes of lacrymation." See Anon., "Review of the *Heir of Redclyffe* and *Heartsease*," *North American Review* 166 (April 1855): 443. Yonge's brother, Julian, wrote to say that nearly all the young men in his regiment had a copy of the novel. See Christabel R. Coleridge, *Charlotte Mary Yonge, Her Life and Letters* (New York: Macmillan, 1903), 183.

5. For an account of the revival of medieval notions of chivalry in the nineteenth century, see Mark Girouard, *The Return to Camelot: Chivalry and the English Gentleman* (New Haven, CT: Yale UP), 1981.

6. Cornelia D. J. Pearsall has recently questioned this standard reading of Simeon's direct plea to God as undermining his claim to sainthood, asking whether Sime-

on's tone is less earnest, and perhaps more comic, than it might initially appear. She asks, "What if Simeon is not the object or audience of the joke, but its performer? If the joke is not on him, but his, it would mean that the speaker is deliberately wielding an extreme comic language to some effect, the first of which might be laughter." Pearsall, *Tennyson's Rapture: Transformation in the Victorian Dramatic Monologue* (New York: Oxford UP, 2008), 56.

7. First published in 1823, Digby's manifesto went through several editions. I use the 1846 edition here as closest in date to Kingsley's and Yonge's novels.

8. As Elizabeth C. Juckett argues in her reading of *The Pillars of the House* (1873), Yonge is committed to making every Christian in her novels a docile member of the Anglican Church, often through physical suffering. She argues that for Yonge "a precondition of heroic Christianity is submission, subjection, physical limitation" (129). See Juckett, "Cross-Gendering the Underwoods: Christian Subjugation in Charlotte Yonge's *The Pillars of the House*," in *Antifeminism and the Victorian Novel: Rereading Nineteenth-Century Women Writers*, ed. Tamara S. Wagner (Amherst, NY: Cambria Press, 2009).

9. The plot of many of Yonge's novels consists of her characters finding their duties and fulfilling them. This struggle is perhaps most dramatic for her invalids, who must find their duty in a very narrow sphere indeed. Yonge's novelistic form imitates this struggle since, perhaps counter to our expectations of such a didactic novelist, her narrator offers little in the way of moral commentary or judgment. In his work on realism and typology in *The Heir of Redclyffe*, Gavin Budge notes that the third-person narrator of a Yonge novel is not omniscient. The result, he argues, is that "characters in the novel, the figure of the author and Yonge's reader are placed on a level in regard to interpretation of events. Yonge's novels thus come to exhibit a curious kind of self-reflexivity in which questions about interpretation debated by characters in the novel are also ones which readers themselves must address, and to which the narratorial voice can offer no answers." Budge, "Realism and Typology in Charlotte M. Yonge's *The Heir of Redclyffe*," *Victorian Literature and Culture* 31.1 (Spring 2003): 208. As Barbara Dennis points out, domestic realism is particularly suited to Yonge's religious affiliations with the Oxford movement, since the "general lessons of the movement are shown as revealed in the lives of the characters in her novels." Dennis, *Charlotte Yonge (1823–1901), Novelist of the Oxford Movement: A Literature of Victorian Culture and Society* (Lewiston, NY: Mellen, 1992), 56. Since the narratorial voice offers little guidance, readers must decide early on how trustworthy varying interpretations of events are, relying in part on the response of the characters to events to guide their own emotional and intellectual responses.

10. June Sturrock argues that the novel "shows Yonge's domestic vision embracing and engulfing the masculine through a fusion of 'realist' domestic novel and romance, as Sir Guy Morville of Redclyffe becomes the domesticated hero of romance" (99). Sturrock suggests that Yonge's high church novels are so deeply conservative that, in some ways, the demand that both men and women integrate themselves wholly into the home becomes a radical claim about the domestic nature of masculinity. She argues, "Rather than undercutting domestic ideology," Yonge "actually extends it far beyond its conventional limitations and represents the domestic—and by implication the feminine—as morally, spiritually and culturally central for the male as well as the female" (25). One of the reasons that the home becomes so central for men, I would argue, is that Yonge's emphasis on male suffering heightens the dramatic intensity of

the domestic sphere. See Sturrock, *"Heaven and Home": Charlotte M. Yonge's Domestic Fiction Victoria* (Victoria, BC: U of Victoria, 1995).

11. Brodie's *Pathological Researches Respecting the Diseases of the Joints* went through five editions between the time he first delivered a paper in 1813 to the end of his life in 1864, and the profits from the book greatly increased his income. See Benjamin Brodie, *Autobiography of the Late Sir Benjamin C. Brodie, Bart* (London: Longman, Green and Co., 1865), 99, 127.

12. Charlotte Yonge's letters have recently become available online. See Charlotte Mitchell, Ellen Jordan, and Helen Schinske, eds., *Letters of Charlotte Mary Yonge*, 13 September 2012, http://yongeletters.com.

13. Yonge's 1865 novel *The Clever Woman of the Family* (Peterborough, ON: Broadview Press, 2001) contains another iteration of the pairing of the strong man and the weak man in Colonel Colin Keith and his cousin Captain Alick Keith. Despite his past heroism in taking an explosive out of an invalid tent during the siege of Delhi, which has caused him to lose several fingers and scar his hand, as the novel opens Alick Keith is languorous and effeminate. "Very young indeed were both face and figure, fair and pale, and though there was a moustache, it was so light and silky as to be scarcely visible" (145). Alick seems so languid as to be an annoyance to Rachel, the clever woman of the title: "[T]he long limbs had in every movement something of weight and slowness, the very sight of which fretted Rachel, and made her long to shake him" (146). This languorous demeanor stands in contrast to that of his burly bearded cousin Colin. As Rachel sees it, "[O]ne was tall, bald, and bearded, not dangerously young, but on that very account the more dangerously good-looking; and the other was almost a boy, slim and light, just of the empty young officer type" (110). See Talia Schaffer, "Maiden Pairs: The Sororal Romance in *The Clever Woman of the Family*," in *Antifeminism and the Victorian Novel: Rereading Nineteenth-Century Women Writers,* ed. Tamara S. Wagner (Amherst, NY: Cambria Press, 2009), for a reading of both masculine and feminine pairings in the novel.

14. As Talia Schaffer argues, Yonge's novels often aim to raise dissidence only to tame it (247). She insists that "her characters learn to love their hampered lives" even while she makes the substance of the plot out of their struggles to tame their desires. Schaffer, "The Mysterious Magnum Bonum: Fighting to Read Charlotte Yonge," *Nineteenth-Century Literature* 55.2 (2000): 245.

15. Stefanie Markovits argues that *Westward Ho!* is Kingsley's attempt to "reinvigorate British manhood" at the start of the Crimean War (70). For an analysis of both Charles and his brother Henry Kingsley's fiction in relation to the war, see Markovits, *The Crimean War in the British Imagination* (New York: Cambridge UP, 2009).

16. Kaja Silverman argues that the Oedipus complex is the primary framework for thinking about masculinity, even those "non-phallic" masculinities that seem to fall on the margins of dominant Freudian readings (2). While it is provocative, this Freudian reading does not help us to think outside the paradigm of the castrating woman author and her feminized male protagonist. More helpful is Silverman's assertion that there is a narrow boundary separating moral masochism and exemplary maleness (9), which speaks to the importance of suffering for the muscular Christian. See Silverman, *Male Subjectivity at the Margins* (New York: Routledge, 1992).

17. Charles Barker has suggested that Frank, who was based on Kingsley's classmate from Cambridge Charles Mansfield, is a strong example of the same-sex desire in Kingsley's oeuvre that existed alongside his same-sex marital passion (179–80).

Barker argues that part of Kingsley's sense that marital sexuality was divine was, surprisingly, homosocial desire. He writes, "Kingsley sought to justify his desires by embedding them within a sanctifying framework, but this strategy often had the exorbitant effect of turning Christianity into a vehicle for Kingsley's erotic imaginary. This imaginary is notable for its violent scenarios, its interweaving of same-sex and cross-sex desire, and its supplementing of intercourse with alternative modes of consummation that forgo physical contact." See Barker, "Erotic Martyrdom: Kingsley's Sexuality beyond Sex," *Victorian Studies* 44.3 (Spring 2002): 465.

18. Kingsley's emphasis on chivalry persists in *Two Years Ago* in his portrait of Stangrave, who draws parallels between the mores and manners of the American South and those of England. For an analysis of Kingsley's treatment of race and slavery in *Two Years Ago*, particularly in the character of Marie Lavington as a racialized and sexually dangerous figure who must be contained in marriage to Stangrave, see Kimberly Snyder Manganelli, "The Tragic Mulatta Plays the Tragic Muse," *Victorian Literature and Culture* 37.2 (2009): 501–22.

19. The interpretation of blinding the hero as a form of symbolic castration is a familiar one. Mary Wilson Carpenter argues that Kingsley's blinding of Amyas Leigh represents "the restoration of the phallic mother to the man-child." See Carpenter, "Blinding the Hero," *Differences: A Journal of Feminist Cultural Studies* 17.3 (Fall 2006): 61. Similarly, Stanwood S. Walker reads Amyas's blinding as a moral chastisement. See Walker, "'Backwards and Backwards Ever': Charles Kingsley's Racial-Historical Allegory and the Liberal Anglican Revisioning of Britain," *Nineteenth-Century Literature* 62.3 (2007): 367.

20. Much has been written about Kingsley's own performances as a nervous but charismatic public speaker. For an analysis of Kingsley as mediator of science and religion in public lectures, see Caroline Rose, "Charles Kingsley Speaking in Public: Empowered or at Risk?," *Nineteenth-Century Prose* 29.1 (Spring 2002): 133–50.

21. Central figures included Sydney Dobell, Philip Bailey, and J. Stanyan Bigg. The term *Spasmodic* was also applied to poetry by Tennyson and Byron seen as exhibiting the characteristics of the school. According to Gerald Massey's "Poetry—the Spasmodists," *North British Review* 28 (February 1858), these characteristics were "'abstruse research' among morbid phenomena," seeking for that "which is rare and peculiar" and being "afraid of that which is common" and involuted thinking (129). The Spasmodic poet was characterized by a nervous, high-strung temperament given to physical illness. Yet his weakness depended on an ideal of physical strength. Massey asked, "[W]hat constitutes spasm, but weakness trying to be strong, and collapsing in the effort?" (129). Implicit in the idea of spasmodic poetry, then, is a normative claim about the strong masculine body. Kirstie Blair shows how the popular and much-parodied critical discourse around the Spasmodic poetry of the 1850s "exploited medical implications of weakness, effeminacy, nervousness, and lack of will in order to trope Spasmodic poetry as pathological" (473–74). Spasmodic poetry thus challenges mid-Victorian masculinity's increasing emphasis on physical hardiness. Spasmodic poems that "devote considerable space to describing their heroes' deliberate surrender to physical and emotional responses, frequently envisioned as spasms," argues Blair, "implicitly question the limits of British masculinity" (479). See Blair, "Spasmodic Affections: Poetry, Pathology, and the Spasmodic Hero," *Victorian Poetry* 42.4 (Winter 2004): 473–90.

22. In his critique of spasmodic poetry (ibid.), Massey also suggests that the subject of poetry should be Wordsworthian common life. He writes that "if a poet pos-

sesses his manhood in common with the rest of us, shares our thoughts and has feelings in tune, and has truly a genius for transmuting and translating these into poetic forms, he cannot keep too much on broad human grounds" (130).

Chapter 2

1. See Eve Kosofsky Sedgwick, "Tales of the Avunculate: Queer Tutelage in *The Importance of Being Earnest*," in *Tendencies* (Durham, NC: Duke UP, 1993).

2. This type is similar to the bachelor narrator examined by Katherine Snyder. Snyder argues that this untethered figure, who is often an invalid as well, is able to "delineate the thresholds of bourgeois domesticity and manhood, thereby enabling themselves and their authorial creators to mark the boundaries of normativity while simultaneously going out of bounds." Snyder, *Bachelors, Manhood, and the Novel, 1850–1925* (Cambridge UP, 1999), 17.

3. Craik was ill when she wrote *John Halifax*. She wrote to her brother Ben on 7 November c. 1854, "I am getting in thorough strong health as to walking—but walk any distance almost having nothing ailing me except a slight rustiness in my brains which I try to do 'John' but that is wearing off. You need not trouble about me in the least" (Dinah Mulock Craik, Letters to Benjamin Mulock, MS., Mulock Family Papers, Charles E. Young Research Library, University of California, Los Angeles). Rather than proving the difficulties of being a woman author in a patriarchal society, as Sandra Gilbert and Susan Gubar argue is the case with George Eliot's headaches (448), Craik's health problems can be seen as shoring up her claim to performing difficult and worthwhile labor as an author. See Gilbert and Gubar, *The Madwoman in the Attic: The Woman Writer and the Nineteenth-Century Literary Imagination*, 2nd ed. (1979; New Haven, CT: Yale UP, 2000).

4. Phineas, by contrast, has the dark coloring typical of the weak or disabled man. He self-deprecatingly proclaims "what a fine specimen of the noble genus homo" he is at twenty, and John playfully replies that, although he is a "slight, delicate person," he is no longer lame and possessed of "Big eyes, much given to observation" (which means staring at John) and "long hair, which, since the powder tax, has resumed its original blackness" and is, in John's words "exceedingly bewitching" (79). Dinah Mulock Craik, *John Halifax, Gentleman*, ed. Lynne M. Alexander (1856; Peterborough, ON: Broadview Press, 2005).

5. The Craiks' library contained inscribed editions of all of Charles Kingsley's major novels (see Dinah Mulock Craik, Catalogue of Dinah and George Craik's Library, MS., Morris L. Parrish Collection of Victorian Novelists, Princeton University, Princeton, NJ), and she and her husband, George Craik, shared a working friendship with the Kingsleys. To be fair, Craik was also a close friend of Sydney Dobell, the Spasmodic poet and brother of the Clarence Dobell, who was with her when she came up with the idea of *John Halifax*.

6. Craik reviewed Eliot's novel for *Macmillan's Magazine*. See Dinah Mulock Craik, "To Novelists—and a Novelist," *Macmillan's* 3 (1861): 441–48.

7. In his work on manly love in Victorian culture, Jeffrey Richards has shown that such relationships between men "surpassing the love of woman," to use the biblical language that Craik also borrows, were not uncommon at midcentury and were characterized as brotherhoods of a spiritual rather than a physical nature promoted by the ideals of chivalry and self-sacrifice that underpinned all-male institutions from the public school to the armed forces. These friendships, modeled on the heroic friend-

ships of Greek and Christian literature, were encouraged in the 1850s as cultivating virtues of duty, chivalry, and manliness (112). This does not diminish the homoerotic charge of the Phineas-John friendship; rather, it is part of the more capacious continuum of possible relationships between men in the 1850s.

8. Critics have been quick to note the homoeroticism of the John-Phineas relationship. Kiran Mascarenhas describes a "homoerotic tension so strong" that it feminizes Phineas. See Mascarenhas, "John Halifax, Gentleman: A Counter Story," in *Antifeminism and the Victorian Novel: Rereading Nineteenth-Century Women Writers*, ed. Tamara S. Wagner (Amherst, NY; Cambria Press, 2009), 260. Silvana Colella focuses mainly on the way that Phineas's admiration of John's body, which John appreciates only for the work it can do, makes John's body an aesthetic commodity "to be admired and loved for its beauty and intrinsic moral worth." Colella, "Gifts and Interests: *John Halifax, Gentleman* and the Purity of Business," *Victorian Literature and Culture* 35.2 (Fall 2007): 398.

9. In particular, Olive grows closer to her mother after her mother goes blind. The narrator writes, "[T]he more helpless she grew, the closer she was clasped by those supporting arms of filial love, which softened all pain, supplied all need, and were to her instead of strength, youth eyesight!" (140). Dinah Mulock Craik, *Olive*, ed. Cora Kaplan (1850; New York: Oxford UP, 1996).

10. For an analysis of the *John Halifax, Gentleman* as a precursor to Samuel Smiles's famous *Self-Help* (1859), see Ivan Melda, *The Captain of Industry in English Fiction, 1821-1871* (Albuquerque: U of New Mexico P, 1970), 397; and Robin Gilmour, "Dickens and the Self-Help Idea," in *The Victorians and Social Protest*, ed. J. Butt and I. F. Clarke (Newton Abbot: David and Charles, 1973), 77.

11. Gallagher shows that many nineteenth-century writers endowed their authorship with economic value by claiming the labor was painful. Gallagher draws a portrait of Dickens as the unhappy clown, the writer who must entertain but who is unhappy doing it, "relentless unhappiness is, after all, a sign of productive labor" in Benthamite logic. Catherine Gallagher, *The Body Economic: Life, Death, and Sensation in Political Economy and the Victorian Novel* (Princeton, NJ: Princeton UP, 2006), 80.

12. In her reassessment of the importance of Craik's work to the Victorian canon, Elaine Showalter claimed that the novelist "expressed her sense of freakishness and abnormality" through "the crippled Fletcher and other maimed male characters in her fiction" (19). Showalter, "Dinah Mulock Craik and the Tactics of Sentiment: A Case Study in Victorian Female Authorship," *Feminist Studies* 2.3 (1975): 5-23. Similarly, Sally Mitchell noted the importance of disability in Craik's oeuvre, writing that one "crucial feature" in her "map of interior territory is illness, disability, and the figure of the weak or damaged human." Mitchell, like Showalter, argued that the disabled man was a stand-in for the woman writer: "Certainly the ill or disabled male is an inevitable persona for the woman who sees herself as being in every way like a man except that she has less muscular strength. Physical incapacity codifies the pain of helplessness, the lack of power and social position and financial ability and legal right to control the circumstances of one's own life." Mitchell, *Dinah Mulock Craik* (Boston: Twayne Publishers, 1983), 112.

13. Katherine V. Snyder argues that bachelor narrators are "radically revisionary models of bourgeois manhood, as male figures whose susceptibility to the spheres of others enables them not simply to speak for those others, but to speak in a doubled voice one which is collaborative rather than prescriptive." Snyder, *Bachelors, Manhood, and the Novel, 1850-1925* (New York: Cambridge UP, 1999), 83.

14. It is tempting to read this passage in terms of Craik's own marriage to George Lillie Craik, who was eleven years her junior. Craik did not fall in love with her husband until around 1860, but she may have been predisposed or at least open-minded about these cross-age relationships.

15. Some readers recognized an alternative to the marriage plot in John and Phineas's friendship. The reviewer for *Athenaeum* wrote, "The friendship between John Halifax and Phineas Fletcher is well managed, and opens a source of interest and emotion which we wonder is not oftener and more efficiently used in novels:—friendship has capabilities of interest quite as deep and as universal as love, only it requires more knowledge to handle it nobly and adequately." Anon., "New Novels: *John Halifax, Gentleman*," *Athenaeum* (26 April 1856): 520.

16. *Chantry House* (1886) is a response to and a rewriting of *John Halifax, Gentleman*, and the wider muscular Christian ideals of an unreflective, vigorous manhood as the basis for success in life and business. Yonge's novel is also narrated from the point of view of a disabled bachelor uncle, Ned. A fall from the baluster on the second floor to the vestibule in toddlerhood cripples Ned, who has "a curved spine, a dwarfed stature, an elevated shoulder, and a shortened, nearly useless leg" (3). Ned compares and contrasts the temperaments of his two brothers, Clarence and Griffith, throughout the novel. Clarence, who is self-searching almost to the point of morbidity and suffers from a shameful dismissal from the navy early in life, actually turns out to be the better businessman later in life, due to these experiences, than his active, careless brother Griffith. Yonge writes, "At school Griffith was very happy, and brilliantly successful, alike in study and sport, though sports were not made prominent in those days, and triumphs in them were regarded by the elders with doubtful pride, lest they should denote a lack of attention to matters of greater importance" (17). Yonge is careful to set the action of her story "in those pre-Arnoldian times" when "no lofty code of honour was even ideal among schoolboys, or expected of them by masters; shuffling was thought natural, and allowances made for faults in indolent despair," and she describes the bullying that Clarence endures at Harrow (19). Griffith begins life well but goes downhill after Harrow. In short he trifles with a barmaid's affections while at Oxford, breaks an engagement with a family friend who dies of a broken heart, and marries a divorcée instead, ending his days gambling and dissolute in Baden. Yonge's novel highlights the danger that there truly is no deeper principle informing the actions of a man who acts without thinking about it. See Charlotte Yonge, *Chantry House* (1886; London: Macmillan, 1905).

17. Eliot made this snide remark on being compared to Craik by an impertinent French reviewer who referred to her as "Miss Evans" in passing and then devoted the whole review to Craik. Eliot wrote to a friend, "A very excellent woman she is, I believe—but we belong to an entirely different order of writers." George Eliot, *The George Eliot Letters*, ed. Gordon S. Haight, vol. 3 (New Haven, CT: Yale UP, 1954–78), 302. The review that incited Eliot's comment was E. D. Forgue's "Le roman de femme en Angleterre," *Revue des deux mondes* 25 (1860): 797–831.

The Craik novel that Henry James reviewed, *A Noble Life*, details the life of the Earl of Cairnforth, whose disabilities, cheerful temperament, and work ethic were based on those of her friend Frank Smedley. *A Noble Life* also concludes with a pairing of masculine strength and weakness, when the Earl of Cairnforth whisks away his godson, who has gotten into debt and other trouble at the University of Edinburgh, to a quieter life in Saint Andrews, where the pair soon becomes recognizable all about town. "A strange contrast they were—the small figure in the pony-chair, and the tall young man walking beside it in all the vigor, grace, and activity of his blooming youth. Two companions pathetically unlike, and yet always seen together, and evidently associating with one another from pure love" (228). Craik writes, "It was the sort of companionship, free and tender, cheerful and bright, yet with all the influence of the elder over the younger, which, occurring to a young man of Cardross's age and temperament, usually determines his character for life" (231). Dinah Mulock Craik, *A Noble Life* (New York: Harper and Brothers, 1866).

Chapter 3

1. John Tosh writes that "a middle class dignity could hardly be sustained . . . on an income of much lower than £300 per annum" around 1847. Tosh, *A Man's Place: Masculinity and the Middle-Class Home in Victorian England* (New Haven, CT: Yale UP, 1999), 12.

2. Robert Colby has argued that Eliot had John Halifax in mind when creating Tom Tulliver: "When George Eliot assured her readers that Tom was not "moulded on the spooney type of the Industrious Apprentice" (Book Fifth, Ch. II), she undoubtedly had Miss Mulock's Bible-reading young tanner in mind, for Tom's 'practical shrewdness' and calculated virtue effectively offset the sanctimoniousness of John Halifax." Colby, *Fiction with a Purpose: Major and Minor Nineteenth-Century Novels* (Bloomington: Indiana UP, 1967), 219. In her note to the Penguin edition, A. S. Byatt tells us that the reference is to Hogarth's progress paintings of industry and idleness. George Eliot, *The Mill on the Floss*, ed. A. S. Byatt (1860; New York: Penguin, 2003), 575. Regardless of which text is the referent, the extensive plot parallels between the two novels warrant the comparison with *John Halifax, Gentleman*.

3. For an analysis of the mid-nineteenth-century schoolboy novel, see Jenny Holt, *Public School Literature, Civic Education, and the Politics of Male Adolescence* (Burlington VT: Ashgate, 2008), 170–75. Holt analyzes the role of school stories in the formation of normative types of adolescence, emphasizing in particular "how public school stories tackled ideas of appropriate adolescent education in terms of training for citizenship and statesmanship" (4). Her study mines an impressive archive of school stories from the nineteenth century to the early twentieth century.

4. George Eliot was not the only author to critique the schoolboy friendship between a strong boy and a disabled boy. *Guy Livingstone* (1857), a bleak novel written by another Rugby alumnus, G. A. Lawrence, and published in the same year as *Tom Brown's Schooldays*, paints a picture of school life at Rugby quite different from the edifying friendship Hughes portrays. The novel opens up with the narrator, Frank Hammond, as a new, sickly boy, watching his first football match, and decidedly less enchanted with the spectacle than Tom Brown, which he describes as "a mob of two hundred lower boys, vicious with cold and the enforcement of keeping goal through the first football match of the season—in the midst, I, who speak to you, feeling myself in an eminently false position." George Alfred Lawrence, *Guy Livingstone; or, "Thorough"* (1857; Leipzig: Tauchnitz, 1860), 7. Hammond feels there is little room for sickly boys like him at Rugby. Rather than being an expression of healthy boyhood and school spirit, the violent energy of the football match is a mirror of the threatened violence of the "small persecutors" that surround Hammond just before the match begins. Fortunately, the novel's eponymous hero, Guy, sweeps in to rescue Hammond. "From that first day when he interfered in my favour," writes Frank, "Guy never ceased to accord me the aegis of his protection, and it served me well; for, then,

as now, I was strong neither in body nor nerve" (6–7). As a narrator, however, Frank does not temper Guy's potential sexual and physical brutality: he only chronicles it until Guy's rakish life ends in a riding accident. Eliot's version of the school story, transposed to a rural clergyman's house, is not as extreme in its brutality, but she taps into the strong potential for weaker boys to be tormented in her portrait of Philip and Tom. *Guy Livingstone* was an enormously popular book, going through six editions in ten years (Fleming 46). The relationship between Frank and Guy would also have been part of the pattern of the schoolboy friendship between the disabled boy and the strong boy in the Victorian imagination.

    5. Allen argues that Hughes's "erasure of the body seems, finally, designed to mystify" the tensions between Arthur's spirituality and Tom's animalism (117), and that their bodies are instead projected onto their respective landscapes, Tom's vale in the south of England and Arthur's northern moors. This displacement resolves the opposition between the two boys' bodies and ties their bodies to England in order to grapple with questions of nationalism. See Dennis W. Allen, "Young England: Muscular Christianity and the Politics of the Body in *Tom Brown's Schooldays*," in *Muscular Christianity: Embodying the Victorian Age*, ed. Donald E. Hall (Cambridge: Cambridge UP, 1994).

    6. All of Tom Brown's first friendships, that with Old Benjy included, cross class boundaries since he is the squire's son and the only gentleman in the neighborhood. We hear briefly about an exemplary village boy, Harry Winburn, "the quickest and best boy in the parish" in both mind and body, and about Job Rudkin, the "stolid" son of the "most bustling woman in the parish" (51). These are two of Tom's companions among the dozen or so undistinguished and undistinguishable village boys who play with him. Harry, like Old Brooke and Young Brooke later in the novel, is distinguished as an exemplar, while Job Rudkin is only distinguished by the difference in his temperament from his mother's. Throughout the novel, Hughes distinguishes normal boys by setting them against an even more minor character with the quality they lack, as in the energy of Job's mother compared to that of her son. Despite the reader's sense that Tom is spending most of his time playing games with Harry Winburn and Job Rudkin and a dozen other unnamed boys, Hughes spends very little time describing the boys or their games. Tom is soon "initiated into the delights" of "prisoner's base, rounders, high-cock-alorum, cricket and football," but we hear nothing of what these delights might be (57). Hughes's point is that they are typical games played by typical boys, and to devote any more time to narrating them would inevitably bring up peculiarities that would undermine the sense that nothing is out of the ordinary. Thomas Hughes, *Tom Brown's Schooldays*, ed. Andrew Sanders (1857; New York: Oxford UP, 1999).

    The crossing of class boundaries becomes even more pronounced in the 1861 sequel, *Tom Brown at Oxford* (1861; New York: H. M. Caldwell Co, n.d.), in which Tom's key friend is not a disabled man but a servitor, Hardy. Furthermore, Harry Winburn reappears in a class plot in which he gets in trouble with the law and Tom tries to help him.

    7. The praepostor system was already in place when Dr. Arnold came to Rugby in 1827, but he famously used it, in the words of his former student and biographer, Arthur Penhryn Stanley, "as the chief means of creating a respect for moral and intellectual excellence, and of diffusing his own influence through the mass of the school" (117). For more on Arnold's use of the praeposter system, see Stanley, *The Life and Correspondence of Thomas Arnold*, 3rd ed. (Boston: Ticknor and Fields, 1870).

8. The much-discussed footnote about the small friend system suggests that this relationship is sexual. Paul Puccio argues that Hughes sets the friendship of Tom Brown and George Arthur apart from this one as a Christian friendship. See Puccio, "At the Heart of *Tom Brown's Schooldays*: Thomas Arnold and Christian Friendship," *Modern Language Studies* 25.4 (Fall 1995): 57–74.

9. A similar example of an edifying deathbed scene occurs in F. W. Farrar's (headmaster of Marlborough, 1871–76) *Eric; or, Little by Little* (1858). The novel's hero, the fair-haired, blue-eyed Eric Williams, initially a promising scholar and a Christian, is contaminated by the evil influence of other boys at the fictional Roslyn school, and sinks into a life of drinking and dissipation. Worse, as a popular sportsman and captain of the eleven, he is a bad influence on the other boys, including his younger brother Vernon. Midway through the novel, Eric changes his ways for a brief period in time after his friend Edwin Russell dies. Eric heroically saves his friend from drowning but not before irreparable damage is done. Initially it seems that Russell's leg is only sprained, but Farrar amplifies the emotional response to the scene when the news breaks to the boys that it must be amputated. "Only think," says Eric, "isn't it hard, isn't it cruel? When we see our brave, bright Edwin again, he will be a cripple" (137). The narrator adds, "Eric hardly understood that he was railing at the providence of a merciful God" (137). As the headmaster explains, it is best that Edwin die soon, for not only is there loss of limb, but "the blow on the head would certainly affect the brain and the intellect if he lived" (143). The crippled boy himself concurs with this assessment, telling his friend, "There was nothing to be sorry for in this, so long as God gave me health and strength; but health went for ever into those waves at the Stack, where you saved my life, dear, gallant Eric; and what could I do now? It doesn't look so happy to *halt* through life. Oh Eric, Eric, I am young, but I am dying—dying Eric" (141). Schoolboy life, it seems, isn't worth living as a cripple. Farrar takes a bleaker view of the boys' nature than does Hughes or even Eliot, and Eric is only permanently reformed after his brother Vernon falls off a cliff and dies as well. Farrar, *Eric; or, Little by Little* (Edinburgh: Adam and Charles Black, 1858).

10. On Marshall Hall, see Peter Logan, *Nerves and Narratives: A Cultural History of Hysteria in Nineteenth-Century British Prose* (1858; Berkeley: U of California P, 1997), 168. George Henry Lewes also thought that nervous susceptibility, which he related to emotional susceptibility, originated in the spine. The brain, he argued, was only the most important organ in the nervous system, and previous research had overlooked the importance of the spine as part of that system. See Lewes, *The Physiology of Common Life*, vol. 2 (Leipzig: Tauchnitz, 1860), 4.

11. Readings of Eliot and evolutionary theories are numerous. Gillian Beer argues in her work on Darwin that Daniel Deronda tackles the question of whether one can "escape from one's genetic and cultural inheritance." Beer, *Darwin's Plots: Evolutionary Narrative in Darwin, George Eliot, and Nineteenth-Century Fiction*, 2nd ed. (Cambridge: Cambridge UP, 2000), 218. Nancy L. Paxton argues that Stephen Guest portrays his union with Maggie as her "biological destiny" (88) when he refers to "the natural law [that] surmounts every other." Paxton, *George Eliot and Herbert Spencer: Feminism, Evolutionism, and the Reconstruction of Gender* (Princeton, NJ: Princeton UP, 1991), 495. Although Paxton is not explicit on this point, her argument implies that if Stephen is the biologically sound choice, then Philip is the evolutionarily inappropriate mate for Maggie. For a reading of Philip Wakem in terms of nineteenth-century giants and dwarves, see James Diedrick, "The 'Grotesque Body': Physiology in *The Mill on the Floss*," *Mosaic* 21.4 (1998): 27–43.

12. Cotton is problematic as a product of the slave trade. As Elaine Freedgood notes in *The Ideas in Things: Fugitive Meaning in the Victorian Novel* (Chicago: U of Chicago P, 2006), the rhetoric of slavery was applied to the relations between factory workers and masters in novels such as *Mary Barton*. The novels I consider, in particular *John Halifax, Gentleman*, paint a considerably more idyllic portrait of the relationship between workers and masters than Elizabeth Gaskell does in *Mary Barton* or *North and South*. In Craik's treatment, cotton seems to be an appropriately manly and restrained product. Kathleen Blake points out that industry in St. Ogg's mixes foreign and domestic products and traditional and modern technologies. "St. Ogg's is an old market town with stepped-up current business. It exports wool and cheeses, imports fir, probably Baltic, and Russian Flaxseed. Mr. Tulliver mills presumably English wheat and malt, while the town has profitable oil-mills milling foreign flaxseed for linseed oil. No doubt this, like timber, serves shipbuilding and port and warehouse construction in support of commerce. There is coal on the ships, and Tom gets sent by Guest and Co on business to smoky Newcastle. Steam comes to St. Ogg's in the course of the novel. Tom shares with Mr. Deane the idea of bringing steam power to Dorlcote Mill, and Maggie and Stephen board a steamboat." Blake, "Between Economies in *The Mill on the Floss*: Loans versus Gifts, or Auditing Mr. Tulliver's Accounts," *Victorian Literature and Culture* 33.2 (Fall 2005): 232.

13. See David Malcolm, "*The Mill on the Floss* and Contemporary Social Values: Tom Tulliver and Samuel Smiles," *Cahiers Victoriens et Édouardiens* 26 (1987): 37–45.

14. Critics have often noted in passing that Philip, whose hunchback tends to marginalize him—or allow him to see that which is "apart" from himself—is perhaps the character who most closely embodies her theory of the aesthetic and ethical value of sympathy. George Levine notes that the "crippled aesthete of the midlands" who is "alienated from work and society by his hump back" and "too sensitive for the midland world," shares the narrator's sensibility because sensitivity bordering on the "incapacity to live" is "the enabling condition of the writer." Levine, *The Realistic Imagination: English Fiction from Frankenstein to Lady Chatterley* (Chicago: U of Chicago P, 1981), 303. Elaine Showalter argues that Philip, who is raised like a girl and like Maggie feels uncomfortable with his sexual role, shares many of the heroine's dilemmas and is "uniquely qualified to analyze them for her and for the reader." Showalter, *A Literature of Their Own: British Women Novelists from Brontë to Lessing* (1977; Princeton, NJ: Princeton UP, 1999), 127.

15. Shortsighted eyes can sometimes be indicative of a metaphorical shortsightedness in Eliot, as is the case with Dorothea Brooke and Silas Marner, but here shortsightedness leads to greater sympathy.

16. For an analysis of animal imagery in *The Mill on the Floss*, see Mary Jean Corbett, "'The Crossing o' Breeds' in *The Mill on the Floss*," in *Animal Dreams: Representations of Animals in Victorian Literature and Culture*, ed. Deborah Denenholze Morse and Martin A. Danahay (Burlington, VT: Ashgate, 2007). Corbett argues that Eliot draws on animal imagery in the "specialist discourse of breeding" as she attempts to identify where Tom and Maggie come from, or "how it is that these children came to be who they are, or, at least, appear to be" (122).

Chapter 4

1. Nicola Bradbury reprints the text of the 1907 New York edition of James's work in her edition for Oxford World's Classics, which does differ from the original

1881 edition, most notably according to Bradbury in the omission of two pages analyzing Osmond's reasons for marrying Isabel. She suggests that the "New York Ralph is distinguished by laughter and flowers: a 'luxury of laughter', and, accepting his illness, 'His serenity was but the array of wild flowers niched in his ruin.'" Bradbury, "Note on the Text," in *The Portrait of a Lady,* ed. Roger Luckhurst (New York: Oxford UP, 2009), xxvi. I use the New York edition as the more familiar text.

2. This preference for an invalid lifestyle is related to James's engagement with aestheticism in the novel. As Jonathan Freedman has noted in his influential work on James's aestheticism, the aesthete is "languid, weary, enervated, bored; he prefers inaction to action, passivity to assertion, all things decaying to those robust and healthy" (148). I follow Freedman's influential work in reading *The Portrait of a Lady* as an aesthetic novel and Ralph Touchett as a fin de siècle dandy figure. Freedman, *Professions of Taste: Henry James, British Aestheticism, and Commodity Culture* (Stanford, CA: Stanford UP, 1990).

3. For an analysis of the figure of the alienated American, see Alex Zwerdling, *Improvised Europeans: American Literary Expatriates and the Siege of London* (New York: Basic Books, 1998).

4. Critics have explored the connection between James and popular midcentury American women's fiction, but his relationship to popular British fiction has received much less attention. Marcia Jacobson argues that the image that James left us with is that of "James the Master," but his fiction is indebted to an "immense change in the literary market place" in the emergence of a mass market in the 1880s and 1890s. Jacobson, *Henry James and the Mass Market* (Tuscaloosa: U of Alabama P, 1983), 1, 3. Although the changes in the mass production and consumption of books at the fin de siècle certainly influenced James's work, I would locate his debt to the literary market much earlier, in the popular novels of the 1850s. James's debt to midcentury fiction, especially American women's fiction, has not gone unexplored. Several critics argue that the techniques and tropes of popular fiction inform his earlier work, ending with *Portrait,* but he abandons the practice in his later work. William Veeder, for example, in his study of James and the mass market, finds that popular style thwarts James in *The Watch and the Ward* (1870) and *Roderick Hudson* (1875), but he turns the exaggerations and plot points of the mass market into great art in *The Portrait of a Lady.* See Veeder, *Henry James: The Lessons of the Master—Popular Fiction and Personal Style in the Nineteenth Century* (Chicago: U of Chicago P, 1975), 8. Some of these plot points include the orphan heroine who falls in love with a father figure, a plot that Alfred Habegger argues underpins *Portrait* and American women's fiction of the 1850s, in particular *The Wide, Wide World* and *The Lamplighter.* He finds that James's early novels rest on an "appropriation, masterly and distorting, of women's fiction." Habegger, *Henry James and the "Woman Business"* (New York: Cambridge UP, 1989), 5. Sara B. Daugherty argues that *Portrait* evinces a deep engagement with a "mass feminine daydream" found in this American women's fiction, and she reads Isabel Archer's marriage to Gilbert Osmond as a version of the marriage plots of Susan Warner and Maria Cummins, in which the heroine's erotic desires center around a similar kind of father figure. Daugherty, *The Literary Criticism of Henry James* (Athens: Ohio UP, 1981), 26. *The Portrait of a Lady* clearly harks back to the conventions of the mid–nineteenth century, but what critics concentrating on his debt to American women's fiction miss is his engagement with the tropes of British women's fiction, particularly the pathos of his representation of male invalids and self-made men.

5. See Daugherty's *Literary Criticism of Henry James* for a review of James's early journalism and literary criticism.

6. James's criticism of English writers is reprinted in the first volume of Henry James, *Literary Criticism: Essays on Literature, American Writers, and English Writers*, ed. Leon Edel and Mark Wilson (New York: Penguin, 1984), which I use here.

7. For an analysis of Daniel Touchett's character, especially as it resonates with the biblical Daniel, see Sharon Baris, "Gender, Judgment, and Presumptuous Readers: The Role of Daniel in *The Portrait of a Lady*," *Henry James Review* 12.3 (Fall 1991): 212–30.

8. Alex Zwerdling argues that the degree of flatness in characters in *Portrait* corresponds to national stereotypes. He writes, "Isabel Archer's persistent suitors Lord Warburton and Caspar Goodwood are still conceived of as static national stereotypes," but "the characters who affect her life most deeply are not. They amalgamate different national traits. Her uncle Daniel Touchett has retained his American identity despite decades of living in England" and his "wife and son are similar hybrids" while Madame Merle and Gilbert Osmond are "the least easily placed characters" because their cosmopolitanism lends them complexity (150). Reading Caspar Goodwood and Lord Warburton as types familiar from British literature allows us to see them as richer and more dynamic characters than Zwerdling's assessment of them as national stereotypes suggests. See Zwerdling, *Improvised Europeans: American Literary Expatriates and the Siege of London* (New York: Basic Books, 1998).

9. Warburton's adventures abroad are unnarrated and receive scant attention compared to his somewhat contradictory position as a radical member of Parliament and nobleman. It would be interesting to compare Warburton to a hero like H. Rider Haggard's Leo Vincy in *King Solomon's Mines* (1885).

10. For an overview of the critical reception of Caspar Goodwood, ranging from Leon Edel's assessment of him as "monotonously masculine" to Carren Kaston's assessment of him as a "rapist lover," see Leland S. Person, *Henry James and the Suspense of Masculinity* (Philadelphia: U of Pennsylvania P, 2003), 88–89. Although Goodwood's mode of masculinity may seem outdated on English soil, the captain of industry may seem less dated from an American perspective. For an analysis of the persistence of the rags-to-riches story in US fiction, see James V. Catano, *Ragged Dicks: Masculinity, Steel, and the Rhetoric of the Self-Made Man* (Carbondale IL: Southern Illinois UP, 2001). Catano offers a psychoanalytic reading of Horatio Alger myths of the self-made man with a focus on the U.S. steel industry, beginning with the birth of Andrew Carnegie in 1835 through the collapse of the industry and its attempted revival in the late twentieth century.

11. Gymnastics was also seen as a suitable exercise for women and children, although some of the first gymnastic societies in Germany were developed to strengthen young men for the Napoleonic wars. In the United States, gymnastic societies flourished in the 1850s when a new wave of German immigrants came to North America as a result of the suppression of the revolutionary movement of 1848–49. See Henry Metzner, *A Brief History of the North American Gymnastic Union,* trans. Friedrich Ludwig John (Indianapolis, IN: National Executive Committee of the North American Gymnastic Union, 1911), 23.

12. I do not attempt to give a reading of Ralph Touchett's illness in terms of the medical history of tuberculosis in this chapter, partially because so much excellent work has already been done in the area. The most influential work is Susan Sontag's

Illness as Metaphor (New York: Farrar, Straus and Giroux, 1978). More recently Katherine Byrne has given sustained attention to Ralph Touchett in terms of the medical history of tuberculosis. See Byrne, *Tuberculosis and the Victorian Literary Imagination* (New York: Cambridge UP, 2011). For an overview of the history of tuberculosis in the nineteenth century, see Mary Wilson Carpenter, *Health, Medicine, and Society in Victorian England.* .

13. Byrne writes, "Consumption, a disease associated with capitalism and luxury, becomes in this novel symbolic of the moral and emotional sickness which manifests itself in the men in *Portrait* and which is presented as the inevitable consequence of the idleness and indulgence inherent in affluent middle- and upper-class existence" (9). Alexandra Tankard takes an even bleaker view, arguing that the physical disability that facilitates Ralph's "liberation from the oppressive confines of conventional masculinity also imprisons" him "in the equally oppressive role of impotent voyeur." Tankard, "Emasculation, Eugenics and the Consumptive Voyeur in *The Portrait of a Lady* (1881) and *The Story of a Nobody* (1893)," *Critical Survey* 20.3 (2008): 65.

14. For a brief reading of Ralph Touchett as an observer whose role closely resembles that of the author, see Carolyn Porter, *Seeing and Being: The Plight of the Participant Observer in Emerson, James, Adams, and Faulkner* (Middletown, CT: Wesleyan UP, 1981), 127–30. Porter writes, "Like James, Ralph wants to see what she [Isabel] will do if given the opportunity to live up to the limits of her imagination. He is at once the detached spectator of the dramatic unfolding of her doom, and an unwitting agent of that doom" (128). "Ralph's habit of keeping his hands in his pockets signals at once his impotence and the source of his power: the gesture reflects the passivity of a man who can only watch Isabel live while he dies, but who also can and does empty his pockets for her" (129).

15. For an analysis of the closely related quality of patience in James, see Michael Snediker "Stasis and Verve: Henry James and the Fictions of Patience," *Henry James Review* 27.1 (Winter 2006): 24–41. Snediker discusses the primacy of patience in the conclusion of *The Portrait of a Lady* and *Roderick Hudson* as a framework for his reading of *The Golden Bowl*, arguing that the way in which time is overdetermined such that it "seems nearly material" in that novel registers most clearly in its descriptions of waiting (25).

16. It has become a critical commonplace to note the threatening similarities between Ralph and Osmond, but this was not how the pair struck some of the novel's first readers. R. H. Hutton saw them not only as the characters of the most interest in the novel but also as foils to one another: "In scene after scene this character is developed, and always with some fresh touch of fastidious insolence or intense though petty pride, which makes of it a wonderful, and yet most repulsive, artistic achievement. As a set-off against this disagreeable picture is that of Ralph Touchett, the humorous, Anglo-American invalid,—who throughout the book is slowly dying of consumption,—and who fixed on the life about him, eliciting all its characteristic features, in love with Isabel himself, though without ever thinking of sacrificing her, and indeed generously forgetting his own future in the desire to add to his cousin Isabel's happiness" (Gard 95). Hutton continues with an aesthetic metaphor: "Ralph Touchett is a very powerful picture, and a fine pendant to that of Osmond, the delicately-enamelled idolator of his own tastes and dignity, for whom Ralph's improvident generosity to his cousin unfortunately set a trap. Such are the two leading characters of the book,—as powerfully drawn as Isabel's is feebly and faintly drawn,— companion pictures of niggardness of soul, on the one side, and magnanimity, of an

unpretending type, on the other" (Gard 95). Hutton's review of *The Portrait of a Lady*, published in *The Spectator* 54 (November 1881): 1504–6, is reprinted in Roger Gard, ed., *Henry James, The Critical Heritage* (London: Routledge and Kegan Paul, 1968).

Conclusion

1. In the late 1860s, Charles Dickens and Wilkie Collins were both writing novels that parodied the young, empty-headed sportsman. These novels dealt with the question of race much more explicitly than did the earlier novels of Kingsley, Hughes, and Lawrence. In reading the orientalism of the opening scenes of *The Mystery of Edwin Drood* (1870), it becomes apparent that the muscular Christians, from Tom Thurnall to Tom Tulliver, are all fair. Dickens's Reverend Crisparkle is no exception, and one of the first things we hear about him is how fair his complexion is. Unlike the fair-haired woman of the nineteenth-century novel, however, the fair man is not always perfectly good. "Mr. Crisparkle, Minor Canon, fair and rosy, and perpetually pitching himself head-foremost into all the deep running water in the surrounding country . . . early riser, musical, classical, cheerful, kind, good-natured, social, contented, boy-like" (14), is less of a moral influence than one would hope for from his muscles. In fact he does little more than assist "his circulation by boxing at a looking-glass with great science and prowess," "feinting and dodging with the utmost artfulness" (51). The Reverend Crisparkle's preening does little to solve the mystery of Edwin Drood's death, which suggests that a love of bathing in cold water and boxing may strengthen one's constitution but not one's morals.

2. Tamara S. Wagner suggests that Sir Patrick Lundie is an heir to the man of feeling. Collins continued this pairing of strong villain and weak hero throughout the 1870s, when, as Wagner notes, "the contrast between muscular men of the world and sentimental heroes recurs endlessly" (489). Wagner goes on to consider *Poor Miss Finch, The New Magdalene,* and *The Law and the Lady.* Wagner, "'Overpowering Vitality': Nostalgia and Men of Sensibility in the Fiction of Wilkie Collins," *Modern Language Quarterly: A Journal of Literary History*, 63.4 (December 2002): 471–500.

3. For more on disability in detective fiction, see Irving Zola, "Any Distinguishing Features? The Portrayal of Disability in the Crime-Mystery Genre," *Policy Studies Journal* 15.3 (March 1987): 485–513; and Sander Gilman, *Fat Boys: A Slim Book* (Lincoln: U of Nebraska P, 2004).

4. Ansell's warning that Rickie is "unfitted in soul" to marry is often taken as a reference to Forster's sexuality; it is worth noting here that Ansell takes Rickie's physical deformity as a related but separate issue and does not directly equate being "unfitted in body" to being "unfitted in soul."

5. Perhaps the most obvious place to analyze disability and masculinity in the early twentieth century is in the figure of the disabled World War I veteran. Historical studies of this figure include Joanna Bourke's *Dismembering the Male: Men's Bodies, Britain, and the Great War* (Chicago: U of Chicago P, 1996); Deborah Cohen's *The War Come Home: Disabled Veterans in Britain and Germany, 1914–1939* (Berkeley: U of California P, 2001); and Beth Linker's *War's Waste: Rehabilitation in World War I America* (Chicago: U of Chicago P, 2011).

6. A central incident in Philip's affair with Mildred is another missed friendship with a strong man, Philip's fellow medical student Harry Griffith, who absconds with Mildred even though he knows Philip is in love with her. In a tender Victorian sickroom scene, Griffith nurses Philip through a difficult bout of influenza: "He was

a thoughtful fellow, gentle and encouraging; but his greatest quality was a vitality which seemed to give health to everyone with whom he came in contact. Philip was unused to the petting which most people enjoy from mothers or sisters and he was deeply touched by the feminine tenderness of this strong young man" (327–28). The narrator remarks, "Philip worshipped him as at school he had worshipped boys who were tall and straight and high of spirits" (328). Their short-lived friendship gestures toward a happier pairing of masculine strength and weakness in earlier novels. Maugham details many more male friendships and affairs with women than I have the space to analyze here, including his protagonist's friendships with fellow student artists in Paris and his affair with the motherly Norah. Maugham, *Of Human Bondage* (1915; New York: Modern Library, 1999).

7. In the Harry Potter series, J. K. Rowling constructs her main friendship triangle of Harry, Ron, and Hermione primarily around gender rather than physical difference. Rather than a disabled boy, Hermione is the odd intellectual who proves that diligent scholarship can be useful, while Harry relies on his natural athletic abilities (he discovers an innate talent for the school sport of Quidditch in the first novel) and a prowess at sorcery that comes to him unbidden without his needing to overanalyze it. Harry's marriage to Ron's sister Ginny at the end of the series continues the schoolboy novel trope of marrying a school friend's sister as a means of solidifying one's connection with that friend. J. K. Rowling, *Harry Potter and the Deathly Hallows* (New York: Arthur A. Levine Books, 2007).

8. Max's narration undermines the claim that he has no brain from the start. He begins the novel, "I never had a brain until Freak came along and let me borrow his for a while" (1). Max's claim about borrowing his small friend's brain is significant because he is so large and ostensibly slow-witted as to be disabled himself. Readers learn early on that he is "LD" or part of the learning-disabled class at school. Max himself links his physical size to his cognitive abilities when he explains that he cannot write his thoughts because "writing the stuff down is not like talking, and my hand feels so huge and clumsy, it's like the pencil is a piece of spaghetti or something and it keeps slipping" (82). Through his friendship with Kevin, or Freak, he moves to a regular eighth-grade class and miraculously starts reading at grade level. The principal, Mrs. Addison, lets him know that "we're all very pleased with your progress. It's nothing short of miraculous, and it almost convinces me you knew how to read at your level all along and were for some reason keeping it a secret" (84). His reading skills tutor, Mr. Meehan, avers that "the tests have always shown that you're not dyslexic or disabled, and this proves it. As you know, heh heh, my personal opinion has always been that you're lazy and stubborn and you didn't want to learn" (81). The sympathetic reader infers that Max's disabilities are at least partially the result of the psychological trauma of seeing his father kill his mother at age four. See Rodman Philbrick, *Freak the Mighty* (1993; New York: Scholastic, 2001).

9. *A Prayer for Owen Meany* appears, for example, in an online Random House catalog for high school teachers. http://www.randomhouse.com/highschool/catalog/display.pperl?isbn=9780345361790&view=qa.

Bibliography

Ablow, Rachel. *The Marriage of Minds: Reading Sympathy in the Victorian Marriage Plot.* Stanford: Stanford UP, 2007. Print.
Acland, Henry W. *Biographical Sketch of Sir Benjamin Brodie, Late Sergeant-Surgeon to the Queen and President of the Royal Society.* London: Longman, Green and Co, 1864. Print.
Adair, Gilbert. Introduction to *The Longest Journey.* By E. M. Forster. Ed. Elizabeth Heine. New York: Penguin, 2006. Print.
Adams, James Eli. *Dandies and Desert Saints: Styles of Victorian Masculinity.* Ithaca, NY: Cornell UP, 1995. Print.
Adams, William. *Club-Foot, Its Causes, Pathology, and Treatment.* London: Churchill, 1866. Print.
Adams, William. *Lectures on the Pathology and Treatment of Lateral and Other of Forms of Curvature of the Spine.* London: Churchill, 1865. Print.
Allen, Dennis W. "Young England: Muscular Christianity and the Politics of the Body in *Tom Brown's Schooldays.*" In *Muscular Christianity: Embodying the Victorian Age.* Ed. Donald E. Hall. Cambridge: Cambridge UP, 1994. Print.
Andry, Nicolas. *Orthopaedia: Or, the Art of Correcting and Preventing Deformities in Children: By such means, as may easily be put in Practice by Parents themselves, and all such as are employed in Educating Children. To which is added, A Defence of the Orthopaedia, by way of Supplement, by the Author.* London: A. Millar, 1743. Print.
Anon. "The Author of *John Halifax.*" *British Quarterly Review* 44 (1866): 32–58. Print.
Anon. "New Novels: *John Halifax, Gentleman.*" *Athenaeum* (26 April 1856): 520. Print.
Anon. "Novels, Past and Present." *Saturday Review* 21 (1866): 438–40. Print.
Anon. "Review of *The Heir of Redclyffe* and *Heartsease.*" *North American Review* 166 (April 1855): 209–27. Web.
Arndt, Katrina, Julia M White, and Andrea Chervenak. "'Gotta Go Now': Rethinking the Use of *The Mighty* and *Simon Birch* in the Middle School Classroom." *Disability Studies Quarterly* 30.1 (2010). Web.

[Aspinall, W. B.] *San Remo as a Winter Residence, by an Invalid.* London: John Churchill and Sons, 1865. Web.

Auerbach, Nina. "The Power of Hunger: Demonism and Maggie Tulliver." *Nineteenth-Century Fiction* 30.2 (September 1975): 150–71. Web.

Bailin, Miriam. *The Sickroom in Victorian Fiction: The Art of Being Ill.* New York: Cambridge UP, 1994. Print.

Baris, Sharon. "Gender, Judgment, and Presumptuous Readers: The Role of Daniel in *The Portrait of a Lady*." *Henry James Review* 12.3 (Fall 1991): 212–30. Web.

Barker, Charles. "Erotic Martyrdom: Kingsley's Sexuality beyond Sex." *Victorian Studies* 44.3 (Spring 2002): 465–88. Web.

Beer, Gillian. *Darwin's Plots: Evolutionary Narrative in Darwin, George Eliot, and Nineteenth-Century Fiction.* 1983. 2nd ed. New York: Cambridge UP, 2000. Print.

Blair, Kirstie. "Spasmodic Affections: Poetry, Pathology, and the Spasmodic Hero." *Victorian Poetry* 42.4 (Winter 2004): 473–90. Web.

Blake, Kathleen. "Between Economies in *The Mill on the Floss*: Loans versus Gifts, or Auditing Mr. Tulliver's Accounts." *Victorian Literature and Culture* 33.2 (Fall 2005): 219–37. Web.

Bourke, Joanna. *Dismembering the Male: Men's Bodies, Britain, and the Great War.* Chicago: U of Chicago P, 1996. Print.

Bradbury, Nicola. "Note on the Text." In *The Portrait of a Lady*. By Henry James. 1881. Ed. Roger Luckhurst. New York: Oxford UP, 2009. Print.

Brantlinger, Patrick. *The Spirit of Reform: British Literature and Politics, 1832–1867.* Cambridge, MA: Harvard UP, 1977. Print.

Brodie, Benjamin. *Autobiography of the Late Sir Benjamin C. Brodie, Bart.* London: Longman, Green and Co. 1865. Print.

Brontë, Charlotte. *Jane Eyre.* 1847. Ed. Michael Mason. New York: Penguin, 2003. Print.

Brontë, Emily. *Wuthering Heights.* 1847. Ed. Ian Jack. New York: Oxford UP, 2008. Print.

Browning, Elizabeth Barrett. *Aurora Leigh.* 1856. Ed. Kerry McSweeney. New York: Oxford UP, 1998. Print.

Budge, Gavin. "Realism and Typology in Charlotte M. Yonge's *The Heir of Redclyffe*." *Victorian Literature and Culture* 31.1 (Spring 2003): 193–223. Web.

Byrne, Katherine. *Tuberculosis and the Victorian Literary Imagination.* New York: Cambridge UP, 2011. Print.

Carlyle, Thomas. *On Heroes, Hero-Worship, and the Heroic in History.* London: Chapman and Hall, 1840. Print.

Carlyle, Thomas. *Past and Present.* 1843. Ed. Richard D. Altick. New York: New York UP, 1965. Print.

Carpenter, Mary Wilson. "Blinding the Hero." *Differences: A Journal of Feminist Cultural Studies* 17.3 (Fall 2006): 52–68. Web.

Carpenter, Mary Wilson. *Health, Medicine, and Society in Victorian England.* Santa Barbara, CA: Praeger, 2010. Print.

Carroll, David J., ed. *George Eliot: The Critical Heritage.* London: Routledge and Kegan Paul, 1971. Print.

Catano, James V. *Ragged Dicks: Masculinity, Steel, and the Rhetoric of the Self-Made Man.* Carbondale: Southern Illinois UP, 2001. Print.

Chitty, Susan. *The Beast and the Monk: A Life of Charles Kingsley.* London: Hodder and Stoughton, 1974. Print.

Cleere, Eileen. *Avuncularism: Capitalism, Patriarchy, and Nineteenth-Century English Culture.* Stanford, CA: Stanford UP, 2004. Print.
Clough, Arthur. *The Poems of Arthur Hugh Clough.* Ed. A. L. P. Norrington. New York: Oxford UP, 1968. Print.
Cohen, Deborah. *The War Come Home: Disabled Veterans in Britain and Germany, 1914–1939.* Berkeley: U of California P, 2001. Print.
Colby, Robert. *Fiction with a Purpose: Major and Minor Nineteenth-Century Novels.* Bloomington: Indiana UP, 1967. Print.
Colella, Silvana. "Gifts and Interests: *John Halifax, Gentleman* and the Purity of Business." *Victorian Literature and Culture* 35.2 (Fall 2007): 397–415. Web.
Coleridge, Christabel R. *Charlotte Mary Yonge, Her Life and Letters.* New York: Macmillan, 1903. Print.
Collins, Wilkie. *Armadale.* 1866. Ed. Catharine Peters. New York: Oxford UP, 1999. Print.
Collins, Wilkie. *The Law and the Lady.* 1875. Ed. Jenny Bourne Taylor. New York: Oxford UP, 1999. Print.
Collins, Wilkie. *Man and Wife.* 1870. Ed. Norman Page. New York: Oxford UP, 1995. Print.
Collins, Wilkie. *The Moonstone.* 1868. Ed. John Sutherland. New York: Oxford UP, 1999. Print.
Collins, Wilkie. *The Woman in White.* 1860. Ed. John Sutherland. New York: Oxford UP, 1999. Print.
Conan Doyle, Arthur. *The Sign of the Four.* London: Spencer and Blackett, 1890. Print.
Corbett, Mary Jean. "'The Crossing o' Breeds' in *The Mill on the Floss.*" In *Animal Dreams: Representations of Animals in Victorian Literature and Culture.* Ed. Deborah Denenholze Morse and Martin A. Danahay. Burlington, VT: Ashgate, 2007. Print.
Craik, Dinah Mulock. Catalogue of Dinah and George Craik's Library. MS. Morris L. Parrish Collection of Victorian Novelists. Princeton University, Princeton, NJ.
Craik, Dinah Mulock. *John Halifax, Gentleman.* 1856. Ed. Lynne M. Alexander. Peterborough, ON: Broadview Press, 2005. Print.
Craik, Dinah Mulock. Letters to Benjamin Mulock. MS. Mulock Family Papers, Charles E. Young Research Library, University of California, Los Angeles.
Craik, Dinah Mulock. *A Noble Life.* New York: Harper and Brothers, 1866. Web.
Craik, Dinah Mulock. "To Novelists—and a Novelist." *Macmillan's Magazine* 3 (April 1861): 441–48. Print.
Craik, Dinah Mulock. *Olive.* 1850. Ed. Cora Kaplan. New York: Oxford UP, 1996. Print.
Cruse, Amy. *The Victorians and Their Books.* London: Allen & Unwin, 1935. Print.
Daugherty, Sarah B. *The Literary Criticism of Henry James.* Athens: Ohio UP, 1981. Print.
Davis, Lennard J. *Enforcing Normalcy: Deafness, Disability, and the Body.* New York: Verso, 1995. Print.
Dellamora, Richard. *Friendship's Bonds: Democracy and the Novel in Victorian England.* Philadelphia: U of Pennsylvania P, 2004. Print.
Dennis, Barbara. *Charlotte Yonge (1823–1901), Novelist of the Oxford Movement: A Literature of Victorian Culture and Society.* Lewiston, NY: Mellen, 1992. Print.
Deutsch, Helen. "The Body's Moments: Visible Disability, the Essay, and the Limits of Sympathy." *Prose Studies* 27.1–2 (2005): 11–26. Print.
Dickens, Charles. *David Copperfield.* 1850. Ed. Jeremy Tambling. New York: Penguin, 1996. Print.

Dickens, Charles. *Dombey and Son.* 1848. Ed. Andrew Sanders. New York: Penguin, 2002. Print.
Dickens, Charles. *Great Expectations.* 1861. Ed. Charlotte Mitchell. New York: Penguin, 2003. Print.
Dickens, Charles. *Hard Times.* 1854. Ed. Graham Law. Peterborough, ON: Broadview Press, 1996. Print.
Dickens, Charles. *The Mystery of Edwin Drood.* 1870. Ed. David Paroissien. New York: Penguin, 2002. Print.
Dickens, Charles. *Nicholas Nickleby.* 1839. Ed. Paul Schlicke. New York: Oxford UP, 1998. Print.
Dickens, Charles. *The Old Curiosity Shop.* 1841. Ed. Elizabeth M. Brennan. New York: Oxford UP, 1998. Print.
Dickie, Simon. "Hilarity and Pitilessness in Mid–Eighteenth Century: English Jestbook Humor." *Eighteenth-Century Studies* 37.1 (2003): 1–22. Web.
Diedrick, James. "The 'Grotesque Body': Physiology in *The Mill on the Floss.*" *Mosaic* 21.4 (1998): 27–43. Print.
Digby, Kenelm Henry. *The Broad Stone of Honour; or, Rules for the Gentlemen of England.* 1823. London: C. & J. Rivington, 1846. Print and Web.
Eliot, George. *Adam Bede.* 1859. Ed. Stephen Gill. New York: Penguin, 1985. Print.
Eliot, George. *Daniel Deronda.* 1876. Ed. Graham Handley. New York: Oxford UP, 1998. Print.
Eliot, George. *Felix Holt the Radical.* 1866. Ed. Fred C. Thomson. New York: Oxford UP, 1998. Print.
Eliot, George. *The George Eliot Letters.* Ed. Gordon S. Haight. 9 vols. New Haven, CT: Yale UP, 1954–78. Print.
Eliot, George. *Middlemarch.* 1872. Ed. David Carroll. New York: Oxford UP, 1998. Print.
Eliot, George. *The Mill on the Floss.* 1860. Ed. A. S. Byatt. New York: Penguin, 2003. Print.
Eliot, George. "The Natural History of German Life." In *Selected Essays, Poems, and Other Writings.* Ed. A. S. Byatt and Nicholas Warren. New York: Penguin, 1990. Print.
Eliot, George. "Review of *Westward Ho!*" In *George Eliot: Selected Critical Writings.* Ed. Rosemary Ashton. New York: Oxford UP, 2000. Print.
Eliot, George. *Scenes of Clerical Life.* 1857. Ed. Thomas A. Noble. New York: Oxford UP, 1988. Print.
Eliot, George. *Silas Marner.* 1861. Ed. Q. D. Leavis. New York: Penguin, 1985. Print.
Ellis, Markman. *Race, Gender, and Commerce in the Sentimental Novel.* New York: Cambridge UP, 1996. Print.
Esmail, Jennifer, and Christopher Keep. "Victorian Disability." *Victorian Review* 25.2 (Fall 2009): 45–51. Print.
Farrar, F. W. *Eric; or, Little by Little.* 2nd ed. Edinburgh: Adam and Charles Black, 1858. Web.
Fleming, Gordon H. *George Alfred Lawrence and the Victorian Sensation Novel.* Tucson: U of Arizona P, 1952. Print.
Forgue, E. D. "Le roman de femme en Angleterre." *Revue des deux mondes* 25 (1860): 797–831. Web.
Forster, E. M. *The Longest Journey.* Ed. Elizabeth Heine. 1907. New York: Penguin, 2006. Print.
Frawley, Maria. *Invalidism and Identity in Nineteenth-Century Britain.* Chicago: U of Chicago P, 2004. Print.

Freedgood, Elaine. *The Ideas in Things: Fugitive Meaning in the Victorian Novel.* Chicago: U of Chicago P, 2006. Print.
Freedman, Jonathan. *Professions of Taste: Henry James, British Aestheticism, and Commodity Culture.* Stanford, CA: Stanford UP, 1990. Print.
Gallagher, Catherine. *The Body Economic: Life, Death, and Sensation in Political Economy and the Victorian Novel.* Princeton, NJ: Princeton UP, 2006. Print.
Gallagher, Catherine. *The Industrial Reformation of English Fiction: Social Discourse and Narrative Form, 1832–1867.* Chicago: U of Chicago P, 1985. Print.
Gard, Roger, ed. *Henry James: the Critical Heritage.* London: Routledge and Kegan Paul, 1968. Print.
Garland-Thomson, Rosemarie. *Extraordinary Bodies: Figuring Physical Disability in American Culture and Literature.* New York: Columbia UP, 1997. Print.
Gaskell, Elizabeth. *Mary Barton.* 1848. Ed. MacDonald Daly. New York: Penguin, 1997. Print.
Gilbert, Pamela. *The Citizen's Body: Desire, Health, and the Social in Victorian England.* Columbus: Ohio State UP, 2007. Print.
Gilbert, Sandra, and Susan Gubar. *The Madwoman in the Attic: The Woman Writer and the Nineteenth-Century Literary Imagination.* 1979. 2nd ed. New Haven, CT: Yale UP, 2000. Print.
Gilman, Sander. *Fat Boys: A Slim Book.* Lincoln: U of Nebraska P, 2004. Print.
Gilmour, Robin. "Dickens and the Self-Help Idea." In *The Victorians and Social Protest.* Ed. J. Butt and I. F. Clarke. Newton Abbot: David and Charles, 1973. Print.
Girouard, Mark. *The Return to Camelot: Chivalry and the English Gentleman.* New Haven, CT: Yale UP, 1981. Print.
Goode, Mike. *Sentimental Masculinity and the Rise of History, 1790–1890.* New York: Cambridge UP, 2009. Print.
Gribble, Samuel. *A Treatise on Deportment, &c., Including the Science of Horsemanship.* Derby: William Bemrose and Co, 1829. Print.
Habegger, Alfred. *Henry James and the "Woman Business."* New York: Cambridge UP, 1989. Print.
Haley, Bruce. *The Healthy Body and Victorian Culture.* Cambridge, MA: Harvard UP, 1978. Print.
Haggard, H. Rider. *King Solomon's Mines.* 1885. Ed. Dennis Butts. New York: Oxford UP, 2008. Print.
Haggard, H. Rider. *She.* Leipzig: Tauchnitz, 1887. Print.
Hardy, Barbara. *The Novels of George Eliot: A Study in Form.* London: Athlone Press, 1959. Print.
Hay, William. *Deformity: An Essay. 1754.* Ed. Kathleen James-Cavan. Victoria, BC: U of Victoria, 2004. Print.
Hayter, Alethea. *Charlotte Yonge.* Plymouth, UK: Northcote House, 1996. Print.
Holt, Jenny. *Public School Literature, Civic Education, and the Politics of Male Adolescence.* Burlington, VT: Ashgate, 2008. Print.
Hu, Esther. "Christina Rossetti and the Poetics of Tractarian Suffering." In *Through a Glass Darkly: Suffering, the Sacred, and the Sublime in Literature and Theory.* Waterloo, ON: Wilfred Laurier UP, 2010. Print.
Hughes, Thomas. 1857. *Tom Brown's Schooldays.* Ed. Andrew Sanders. New York: Oxford UP, 1999. Print.
Hughes, Thomas. *Tom Brown at Oxford.* 1861. New York: H. M. Caldwell Co, n.d. Print.
Hutton, R. H. "Novels by the Authoress of 'John Halifax.'" *North British Review* 29 (1858): 466–81. Print.

Hutton, R. H. Review of *The Portrait of a Lady*. *The Spectator* 54 (November 1881): 1504–6. Print.
Huysmans, J. K. *A Rebours*. 1884. Ed. Daniel Grojnowski. Paris: Flammarion, 2004. Print.
Irving, John. *A Prayer for Owen Meany.* New York: Ballantine Books, 1990. Print.
Jacobson, Marcia. *Henry James and the Mass Market*. Tuscaloosa: U of Alabama P, 1983. Print.
Jacobus, Mary. "The Question of Language: Men of Maxims and *The Mill on the Floss*." *Critical Inquiry* 8.2 (Winter 1981): 207–22. Web.
Jaffe, Audrey. *Scenes of Sympathy: Identity and Representation in Victorian Fiction*. Ithaca, NY: Cornell UP, 2000. Print.
James, Henry. *Literary Criticism: Essays on Literature, American Writers, and English Writers*. Vol. 1. Ed. Leon Edel and Mark Wilson. New York: Penguin, 1984. Print.
James, Henry. *The Portrait of a Lady*. 1881. Ed. Nicola Bradbury. New York: Oxford UP, 1998. Print.
James, Henry. *Watch and Ward*. Boston: Houghton, Osgood and Co, 1878. Print.
Jay, Elisabeth. "Charlotte Mary Yonge and Tractarian Aesthetics." *Victorian Poetry* 44.1 (2006): 43–59. Web.
Juckett, Elizabeth C. "Cross-Gendering the Underwoods: Christian Subjugation in Charlotte Yonge's *The Pillars of the House*." In *Antifeminism and the Victorian Novel: Rereading Nineteenth-Century Women Writers*. Ed. Tamara S. Wagner. Amherst, NY: Cambria Press, 2009. Print.
Keble, John. "Morning." In *The Christian Year: Thoughts in Verse for the Sundays and Holydays throughout the Year*. 2nd ed. Oxford: J. Parker, 1827. Web.
Kingsley, Charles. *Health and Education*. London and New York: Macmillan, 1887. Web.
Kingsley, Charles. *Two Years Ago*. 1857. New York: Macmillan, 1885. Print.
Kingsley, Charles. *Westward Ho!* 1855. New York: Macmillan, 1878. Print.
Klages, Mary. *Woeful Afflictions: Disability and Sentimentality in Victorian America*. Philadelphia: U of Pennsylvania P, 1999. Print.
Klaver, J. M. I. *The Apostle of the Flesh: A Critical Life of Charles Kingsley*. Leiden: Brill, 2006. Print.
Klenerman, Leslie. *The Evolution of Orthopaedic Surgery*. London: Royal Society of Medicine, 2002. Print.
Kucich, John. *Imperial Masochism: British Fiction, Fantasy, and Social Class*. Princeton, NJ: Princeton UP, 2007. Print.
Lawrence, George Alfred. *Guy Livingstone; or, "Thorough."* 1857. Leipzig: Tauchnitz, 1860. Print.
Lee, Louise. "Voicing, De-voicing and Self-Silencing: Charles Kingsley's Stuttering Christian Manliness." *Journal of Victorian Culture* 13.1 (Spring 2008): 1–17. Web.
Levine, George. *The Realistic Imagination: English Fiction from Frankenstein to Lady Chatterley*. Chicago: U of Chicago P, 1981. Print.
Lewes, George Henry. George Henry Lewes Journal, Wandsworth, 2 November 1859. In George Eliot, *The George Eliot Letters*. Ed. Gordon S. Haight. 9 vols. New Haven, CT: Yale UP, 1954–78. Print.
Lewes, George Henry. "The Miseries of a Dramatic Author." *Cornhill Magazine* 8 (July–December 1863): 498–512. Web.
Lewes, George Henry. *The Physiology of Common Life*. 1859. 2 vols. Leipzig: Tauchnitz, 1860. Print.

Lewis, Dio. *The New Gymnastics for Men, Women, and Children.* Boston: Ticknor and Fields, 1862. Web.

Linker, Beth. *War's Waste: Rehabilitation in World War I America.* Chicago: U of Chicago P, 2011. Print.

Little, William John. *On the Nature and Treatment of Deformities of the Human Frame.* London: Longman, Brown, Green, and Longmans, 1853. Print.

Lockhart, J. G. *Memoirs of the Life of Sir Walter Scott, Bart.* Edinburgh: Robert Cadell, 1848. Web.

Logan, Peter Melville. *Nerves and Narratives: A Cultural History of Hysteria in Nineteenth-Century British Prose.* Berkeley: U of California P, 1997. Print.

Luciano, Dana. "Invalid Relations: Queer Kinship in Henry James's *The Portrait of a Lady.*" *Henry James Review* 23 (2002): 196–217. Web.

Lund, Roger. "Laughing at Cripples: Ridicule, Deformity, and the Argument from Design." *Eighteenth Century Studies* 39.1 (Fall 2005): 91–114. Web.

Machann, Clinton. *Masculinity in Four Victorian Epics: A Darwinist Reading.* Burlington, VT: Ashgate, 2010. Print.

Mackail, J. W. *The Life of William Morris.* 1899. London: Electric Book Co., 2001. Web.

Mackenzie, Henry. *The Man of Feeling.* 1771. Ed. Maureen Harkin. Peterborough, ON: Broadview Press, 2005. Print.

Malcolm, David. "*The Mill on the Floss* and Contemporary Social Values: Tom Tulliver and Samuel Smiles." *Cahiers Victoriens et Édouardiens* 26 (1987): 37–45. Print.

Mangan, J. A. *Athleticism in the Victorian and Edwardian Public School: The Emergence and Consolidation of an Educational Ideology.* New York: Cambridge UP, 1981. Print.

Markovits, Stefanie. *The Crimean War in the British Imagination.* New York: Cambridge UP, 2009. Print.

Mascarenhas, Kiran. "John Halifax, Gentleman: A Counter Story." In *Antifeminism and the Victorian Novel: Rereading Nineteenth-Century Women Writers.* Ed. Tamara S. Wagner. Amherst, NY: Cambria Press, 2009. Print.

[Massey, Gerald.] "Poetry—the Spasmodists." *North British Review* 28 (February 1858): 125–35. Web.

Maugham, Somerset. *Of Human Bondage.* 1915. New York: Modern Library, 1999. Print.

McCarthy, Justin. *Paul Massie: A Romance.* 1866. New York: Sheldon, n.d. Print.

McClintock, Anne. *Imperial Leather: Race, Gender, and Sexuality in the Colonial Conquest.* New York: Routledge, 1995. Print.

McRuer, Robert. *Crip Theory: Cultural Signs of Queerness and Disability.* New York: New York UP, 2006. Print.

Melda, Ivan. *The Captain of Industry in English Fiction, 1821–1871.* Albuquerque: U of New Mexico P, 1970. Print.

Metzner, Henry. *A Brief History of the North American Gymnastic Union.* Trans. Friedrich Ludwig John. Indianapolis, IN: National Executive Committee of the North American Gymnastic Union, 1911. Web.

Meyers, Jeffrey. *Somerset Maugham: A Life.* New York: Alfred A. Knopf, 2004. Print.

Mitchell, Charlotte, Ellen Jordan, and Helen Schinske, eds. *Letters of Charlotte Mary Yonge*, 13 September 2012, http://yongeletters.com. Web.

Mitchell, David, and Sharon Snyder. *Narrative Prostheses: Disability and the Dependencies of Discourse.* Ann Arbor: U of Michigan P, 2000. Print.

Mitchell, Sally. *Dinah Mulock Craik.* Boston: Twayne Publishers, 1983. Print.

Moore, Thomas. *Letters and Journals of Lord Byron, with Notices of His Life.* London: J. Murray, 1830. Print.

Mossman, Mark. *Disability, Representation, and the Body in Irish Writing, 1800–1922.* New York: Palgrave Macmillan, 2009. Print.

Mossman, Mark, and Martha Stoddard Holmes. "Critical Transformations: Disability and the Body in Nineteenth-Century Britain." *Nineteenth-Century Gender Studies* 4.2 (Summer 2008). Web.

Nelson, Claudia. *Boys Will Be Girls: The Feminine Ethic and British Children's Fiction, 1857–1917.* New Brunswick, NJ : Rutgers UP, 1991. Print.

Newsome, David. *Godliness and Good Learning: Four Studies on a Victorian Ideal.* London: Murray, 1961. Print.

O'Connor, Erin. *Raw Material: Producing Pathology in Victorian Culture.* Durham, NC: Duke UP, 2000. Print.

Oldstone-Moore, Christopher. "The Beard Movement in Victorian Britain." *Victorian Studies* 48.1 (2005): 7–34. Print.

Oliphant, Margaret. *The Victorian Age of English Literature.* Vol. 2. New York: Tait, Sons & Co, 1892. Print.

"On Rowing." In *British Sports and Pastimes.* Ed. Anthony Trollope. London: Virtue & Co, 1868. Web.

Oppenheim, Janet. *"Shattered Nerves": Doctors, Patients, and Depression in Victorian England.* New York: Oxford UP, 1991. Print.

Paxton, Nancy L. *George Eliot and Herbert Spencer: Feminism, Evolutionism, and the Reconstruction of Gender.* Princeton, NJ: Princeton UP, 1991. Print.

Pearsall, Cornelia D. J. *Tennyson's Rapture: Transformation in the Victorian Dramatic Monologue.* New York: Oxford UP, 2008. Print.

Person, Leland S. *Henry James and the Suspense of Masculinity.* Philadelphia: U of Pennsylvania P, 2003. Print.

Philbrick, Rodman. *Freak the Mighty.* 1993. New York: Scholastic, 2001. Print.

Pick, Daniel. *Faces of Degeneration: A European Disorder, c. 1848–c. 1918.* Cambridge: Cambridge UP, 1989.

Poovey, Mary. *Uneven Developments: The Ideological Work of Gender in Mid-Victorian England.* Chicago: U of Chicago P, 1988. Print.

Porter, Carolyn. *Seeing and Being: The Plight of the Participant Observer in Emerson, James, Adams, and Faulkner.* Middletown, CT: Wesleyan UP, 1981. Print.

Puccio, Paul. "At the Heart of *Tom Brown's Schooldays*: Thomas Arnold and Christian Friendship." *Modern Language Studies* 25.4 (Fall 1995): 57–74. Web.

Richards, Jeffrey. "'Passing the Love of Women': Manly Love and Victorian Society." In *Manliness and Morality: Middle-Class Masculinity in Britain and America, 1800–1940.* Ed. J. A. Mangan and James Walvin. Manchester: Manchester UP, 1991. Print.

Rodas, Julia Miele. "Tiny Tim, Blind Bertha, and the Resistance of Miss Mowcher: Charles Dickens and the Uses of Disability." *Dickens Studies Annual* 34 (2004): 51–97. Print.

Rose, Caroline. "Charles Kingsley Speaking in Public: Empowered or at Risk?" *Nineteenth-Century Prose* 29.1 (Spring 2002): 133–50. Web.

Rowling, J. K. *Harry Potter and the Philosopher's Stone.* Vancouver, BC: Rain Coast Books, 2000. Print.

Rowling, J. K. *Harry Potter and the Deathly Hallows.* New York: Arthur A. Levine Books, 2007. Print.

Ruskin, John. "Fiction, Fair and Foul." In *The Works of John Ruskin*. Vol. 37. Ed. Edward Tyas and A Wedderburn Cook. London: George Allen, 1903. Print.
Sanders, Mike. "Manufacturing Accident: Industrialism and the Worker's Body in Early Victorian Fiction." *Victorian Literature and Culture* 28.2 (2000): 313–29. Web.
Schaffer, Talia. "Maiden Pairs: The Sororal Romance in *The Clever Woman of the Family*." In *Antifeminism and the Victorian Novel: Rereading Nineteenth-Century Women Writers*. Ed. Tamara S. Wagner. Amherst, NY: Cambria Press, 2009. Print.
Schaffer, Talia. "*The Mysterious Magnum Bonum*: Fighting to Read Charlotte Yonge." *Nineteenth-Century Literature* 55.2 (2000): 244–75. Web.
Sedgwick, Eve Kosofsky. *Between Men: English Literature and Male Homosocial Desire*. New York: Columbia UP, 1985. Print.
Sedgwick, Eve Kosofsky. *Tendencies*. Durham, NC: Duke UP, 1993. Print.
Showalter, Elaine. "Dinah Mulock Craik and the Tactics of Sentiment: A Case Study in Victorian Female Authorship." *Feminist Studies* 2.3 (1975): 5–23. Print.
Showalter, Elaine. *A Literature of Their Own: British Women Novelists from Brontë to Lessing*. 1977. Princeton, NJ: Princeton UP, 1999. Print.
Shuttleworth, Sally. *George Eliot and Nineteenth-Century Science: The Make-Believe of a Beginning*. New York: Cambridge UP, 1984. Print.
Silverman, Kaja. *Male Subjectivity at the Margins*. New York: Routledge, 1992. Print.
Smiles, Samuel. *Self-Help*. 1859. Ed. Peter W. Sinnema. New York: Oxford UP, 2002. Print.
Snediker, Michael. "Stasis and Verve: Henry James and the Fictions of Patience." *Henry James Review* 27.1 (Winter 2006): 24–41. Web.
Snyder, Katherine V. *Bachelors, Manhood, and the Novel, 1850–1925*. New York: Cambridge UP, 1999. Print.
Snyder Manganelli, Kimberly. "The Tragic Mulatta Plays the Tragic Muse." *Victorian Literature and Culture* 37.2 (2009): 501–22. Web.
Sontag, Susan. *Illness as Metaphor*. New York: Farrar, Straus and Giroux, 1978. Print.
Stanhope, Philip Dormer. *The New Chesterfield: Containing Principles of Politeness*. Ed. the Earl of Car*****. Ed. George Howard. London: Marsh and Miller, 1830. Print.
Stanley, Arthur Penhyrn. *The Life and Correspondence of Thomas Arnold*. 1844. 3rd ed. Boston: Ticknor and Fields, 1870. Print.
Stephen, James Fitzjames. Review of *Guy Livingstone*. *Edinburgh Review* 108 (October 1858): 432–40. Print.
Stephen, Leslie. *George Eliot*. New York: Macmillan, 1902. Web.
Stevenson, Robert Louis. *The Strange Case of Dr. Jekyll and Mr. Hyde*. 1886. Ed. Martin A. Danahay. Peterborough, ON: Broadview Press, 2005. Print.
Sterne, Laurence. *A Sentimental Journey*. 1768. Ed. Tim Parnell and Ian Jack. New York: Oxford UP, 2008.
Stoddard Holmes, Martha. *Fictions of Affliction: Physical Disability in Victorian Culture*. Ann Arbor: U of Michigan P, 2004. Print.
Stoddard Holmes, Martha. "Victorian Fictions of Interdependency: Gaskell, Craik, and Yonge." *Journal of Literary Disability* 1.2 (2007): 29–41. Web.
Sturrock, June. *"Heaven and Home": Charlotte M. Yonge's Domestic Fiction and the Victorian Debate over Women*. Victoria, BC: U of Victoria, 1995. Print.
Sussman, Herbert. *Victorian Masculinities: Manhood and Masculine Poetics in Early Victorian Literature and Art*. New York: Cambridge UP, 1995. Print.
Tamplin, Richard William. *Lectures on the Nature and Treatment of Deformities*. London: Longman, Brown, Green and Longmans, 1846. Print.
Tankard, Alexandra. "Emasculation, Eugenics, and the Consumptive Voyeur in *The

Portrait of a Lady (1881) and *The Story of a Nobody* (1893)." *Critical Survey* 20.3 (2008): 61–78. Print.

Tegg, Thomas. *The Young Man's Own Book. A Manual of Politeness, Intellectual Improvement, and Moral Deportment.* 2nd ed. London: Thomas Tegg and Son, 1834. Print.

Tennyson, Alfred. *The Poems of Tennyson.* Ed. Christopher Ricks. 3 vols. London: Longman, Green and Co., 1969. Print.

Tillotson, Kathleen. "Charlotte Yonge as a Critic of Literature." In *A Chaplet for Charlotte Yonge.* Ed. Georgina Battiscombe and Marghanita Laski. London: Cresset Press, 1965. Print.

Tosh, John. *A Man's Place: Masculinity and the Middle-Class Home in Victorian England.* New Haven, CT: Yale UP, 1999. Print.

Trollope, Anthony. *Doctor Thorne.* 1858. Ed. Ruth Rendell. New York: Penguin, 1991. Print.

Tromp, Marlene, ed. *Victorian Freaks: The Social Context of Freakery in Britain.* Columbus: Ohio State UP, 2008. Print.

Turner, David M. *Disability in Eighteenth-Century England: Imagining Physical Impairment.* New York: Routledge, 2012. Print.

Vance, Norman. *Sinews of the Spirit: The Ideal of Christian Manliness in Victorian Literature and Religious Thought.* New York: Cambridge UP, 1985. Print.

Veeder, William. *Henry James: The Lessons of the Master—Popular Fiction and Personal Style in the Nineteenth Century.* Chicago: U of Chicago P, 1975. Print.

Vidal, Gore. "Maugham's Half & Half." *New York Review of Books* 37.1 (1 February 1990). Web.

von Wilamowitz, Olga. Letter to Charlotte Yonge, 24 January 1866. MS. Morris L. Parrish Collection of Victorian Novelists, Princeton University, Princeton, New Jersey.

Vrettos, Athena. *Somatic Fictions: Imagining Illness in Victorian Culture.* Stanford, CA: Stanford UP, 1995. Print.

Wagner, Tamara S. "'Overpowering Vitality': Nostalgia and Men of Sensibility in the Fiction of Wilkie Collins." *Modern Language Quarterly: A Journal of Literary History* 63.4 (December 2002): 471–500. Web.

Walker, Stanwood S. "'Backwards and Backwards Ever': Charles Kingsley's Racial-Historical Allegory and the Liberal Anglican Revisioning of Britain." *Nineteenth-Century Literature* 62.3 (2007): 339–79. Web.

Walton, Susan. *Imagining Soldiers and Fathers in the Mid-Victorian Era: Charlotte Yonge's Models of Manliness.* Burlington, VT: Ashgate, 2010. Print.

Wendell, Susan. *The Rejected Body: Feminist Philosophical Reflections on Disability.* New York: Routledge, 1996. Print.

Whyte-Melville, G. J. *Riding Recollections.* Leipzig: Tauchnitz, 1879. Print.

Wilde, Oscar. *The Picture of Dorian Gray.* 1890. Ed. Norman Page. Peterborough, ON: Broadview Press, 1998. Print.

Woloch, Alex. *The One vs. the Many: Minor Characters and the Space of the Protagonist in the Novel.* Princeton, NJ: Princeton UP, 2003. Print.

Yonge, Charlotte Mary. *Chantry House.* 1886. London: Macmillan, 1905. Web.

Yonge, Charlotte Mary. *The Clever Woman of the Family.* 1865. Ed. Clare A. Simmons. Peterborough, ON: Broadview Press, 2001. Print.

Yonge, Charlotte Mary. *The Heir of Redclyffe.* 1853. Ed. Barbara Dennis. New York: Oxford UP, 1997. Print.

Yonge, Charlotte Mary. *History of Christian Names.* 2 vols. London: Barker, Son and Bourne, 1863. Print.

Yonge, Charlotte Mary. *The Pillars of the House; or, Under Wode, Under Rode.* New York: Macmillan, 1873. Print.

Young, Arlene. *Culture, Class, and Gender in the Victorian Novel: Gentlemen, Gents, and Working Women.* New York: St. Martin's Press, 1999. Print.

Zola, Irving. "Any Distinguishing Features? The Portrayal of Disability in the Crime-Mystery Genre." *Policy Studies Journal* 15.3 (March 1987): 485–513. Print.

Zwerdling, Alex. *Improvised Europeans: American Literary Expatriates and the Siege of London.* New York: Basic Books, 1998. Print.

Index

Ablow, Rachel, 98
Adams, James Eli, 11, 28–29
Adams, William, 4, 5
alienated American, 104, 108, 152n3
Allen, Dennis W., 80, 149n5
Almond, Hely Hutchinson, 78, 79
Andry, Nicolas
    Orthopaedia, 137n1
Anglican Church, 12, 142n8

Bailey, Philip, 144
Bailin, Miriam, 9, 34
Barker, Charles, 143n17
Beer, Gillian, 150n11
Blackwood, John, 77–78
Blair, Kirstie, 144n21
Blake, Kathleen, 151n12
Bradbury, Nicola, 151n1
Braddon, Mary Elizabeth, 105
Brantlinger, Patrick, 67
Brodie, Benjamin, 36
    Pathological Researches Respecting the Diseases of the Joints, 143
Brontë, Charlotte
    Jane Eyre, 45
Brontë, Emily
    Wuthering Heights, 19

Browning, Elizabeth Barrett, 140n17
    Aurora Leigh, 18, 45
Browning, Robert, 140n17
    "Caliban upon Setebos," 18
Budge, Gavin, 142n9
Burke, Edmund, 138n6
Burns, Robert, 56
Butler, Lady
    The Roll Call, 12
Byrne, Katherine, 114–15, 153n12, 154n13
Byron, Lord, 5, 6, 107, 137n1, 144n21

Carlyle, Thomas, 2, 54, 66
    On Heroes and Hero-Worship, 55, 56–57
    Past and Present, 54–55
Chesterfield, Lord, 87
Christian chivalry, 26–51
    disability and authorship 37–40
    masculine suffering, 30–32
    See also Kingsley, Charles; Young, Charlotte: *The Heir of Redclyffe*
Cleere, Eileen, 70
Clough, Arthur, 140n17
    The Bothie of Tober-na-Vuolich, 18, 80
Colby, Robert, 86, 148
Colella, Silvana, 63, 146n8
Coleridge, John, 39

Collins, Wilkie, 124, 155n1
  Armadale, 125
  The Law and the Lady, 138n5
  Man and Wife, 125–26
    Geoffrey Delamayne, 126, 129
    Sir Patrick Lundie, 126, 155n2
  The Moonstone, 125
    Ezra Jennings, 126–27
    Franklin Blake, 125
    Godfrey Ablewhite, 125
  The Woman in White, 125
    Walter Hartwright, 125
Cotton, G. E. L., 78
Craik, Dinah Mulock, 1, 6, 20, 94, 105, 113, 124, 145nn5–6, 146n12, 147n17
  affective metaphors, 66
  husband, 147n14
  John Halifax, Gentleman, 9, 21, 50, 52–75, 86, 88, 102, 104, 106, 145n3, 145n5, 146n10, 147n16, 148n2, 151n12
    Abel Fletcher, 59, 61, 62, 76
    businessman as hero, 54–56
    Edwin Halifax, 72, 73–74
    extraordinary laconism, 61–63
    grand old name of gentleman, 63–68
    Guy Halifax, 72, 73–74
    John Halifax, 8, 14, 17, 21–22, 23, 52–75, 76, 90, 91, 92, 93, 107, 108, 111, 112, 123, 145n4, 145n7, 146n8, 147n15
    Maud Halifax, 73
    Muriel Halifax, 67, 68
    narrative crotchets, 70–75
    pain and productivity, 68–70
    pairing of disabled narrator and strong man as hero, 56–61
    Phineas Fletcher, 9, 14, 17, 21, 22, 23, 52, 53–54, 55, 57, 58, 59, 60, 61–64, 65, 66–67, 68–76, 86, 88, 90, 104, 107, 111, 123, 145n4, 145n7, 148n8, 147n15
    physical description, 8
    Ursula, 62, 66, 72, 74, 89
  marriage, 147n14
  A Noble Life, 75, 105, 106, 147n17
  Olive, 60
    Olive, 60, 146n9
  self-made man, 90
Craik, George Lillie, 145n5, 147n14
Cruse, Amy, 141n2

Daugherty, Sara B., 152n4
Davis, Lennard, 3, 140n13
  Enforcing Normalcy, 139n12
de Staël, Madame, 95
Dickie, Simon, 10
Dickens, Charles, 18, 54, 64, 65, 96, 146n11, 155n1
  David Copperfield, 19, 20
  Great Expectations, 64
  Hard Times, 160–61
  Nicholas Nickleby, 19
  The Old Curiosity Shop, 138n5
Digby, Kenelm Henry
  The Broad Stone of Honour, 31–32, 142n7
disabling men, 14–19
Dixon, Canon, 141n2
Dobell, Clarence, 59, 145n5
Dobell, Sydney, 144n21, 145n5

Edel, Leon, 153n10
Ellis, Havelock, 24
Ellis, Markman
  Race, Gender, and Commerce in the Sentimental Novel, 138n6
Eliot, George, 1, 2, 19, 20, 105, 113, 123–24, 125, 147n17, 148n4, 150n9, 150n11
  critical of Craik's work, 75
  death, 102
  Daniel Deronda, 5–6, 19, 98, 101, 106–7, 150n11
    Daniel Deronda, 19, 98, 101, 106–7
    Hans Meyrick, 106
    Mirah, 106
    Mordecai, 19, 106
  headaches, 145n3
  The Mill on the Floss, 6–8, 22, 58, 74, 76–102
    Agnes Pembroke, 128
    animal imagery, 151n16
    Bob Jakins, 84, 95
    Emily Failing, 20, 130
    Gerald Dawson, 128–29
    Lucy, 95, 96

Maggie Tulliver, 6–7, 22, 76–77, 79, 84, 85, 86, 88, 89–90, 92, 94–98, 99–102, 129, 150n11, 151n12, 151n16
Mr. Poulter, 88
Mr. Stelling, 22, 87, 88
Mrs. Stelling, 87
Mrs. Tulliver, 86
Philip Wakem, 7, 9, 14, 15, 22, 23, 84–86, 138n3, 150n11, 151n14
schoolboy friendship, 77–79
Stephen Guest, 90–91, 95, 96, 97, 98, 100, 129, 130, 150n11, 151n12
sympathy and the body, 97–102
Tom Tulliver, 8, 9, 22, 23, 84–85, 138n3, 148n2
Tom Tulliver as Self-Made Man, 90–97
Tom Tulliver's laming, 86–90
Uncle Deane, 85, 93, 94, 96, 151n12
Scenes of Clerical Life, 99
shortsighted eyes, 151n15
Esmail, Jennifer, 16

Farrar, F. W.
 Eric, 150n9
Flaubert, Gustave
 Madame Bovary, 137n1
Forster, E. M., 24, 133–34, 155n4
 The Longest Journey, 124, 127–30
 Agnes Pembroke, 128–29
 Gerald Dawson, 128–29
 Rickie, 127, 128–30, 155n4
 Stuart Ansell, 129, 155n4
Frawley, Maria, 10, 57, 91, 118
 Invalidism and Identity in Nineteenth-Century Britain, 138n7
Freedgood, Elaine
 The Ideas in Things, 151n12
Freedman, Jonathan, 118, 152n2
Freudian paradigm, 28
Freudian readings, 143n16

Gallagher, Catherine, 54, 68, 69, 146n11
 The Industrial Reformation of English Fiction, 67

Garland-Thomson, Rosemarie
 Extraordinary Bodies, 139
Gaskell, Elizabeth
 Mary Barton, 11–12, 151n12
Gilbert, Pamela, 139n9
Gilbert, Sandra, 145n3
Gladstone, William, 29, 141n2
Goode, Mike, 138n6
Gribble, Samuel, 87–88
gymnastics, 111–12, 153n11

Haggard, H. Rider, 28, 110, 127
 King Solomon's Mines, 153n9
 She, 127
Haley, Bruce, 12
 The Healthy Body and Victorian Culture, 139n10
Hall, Marshall, 85
Haley, Bruce, 12
Hardy, Barbara, 99
Hardy, Thomas, 134
Hawthorne, Nathaniel
 The Blithedale Romance, 114
Hay, William, 137n2
Herkomer, Hubert von
 The Last Muster, 12
Holt, Jenny, 80
 Public School Literature, Civic Education, and the Politics of Male Adolescence, 148n3
Hu, Esther, 33
Hughes, Thomas, 2, 20, 54, 91, 102, 124, 150n9
 Tom Brown at Oxford, 27, 45, 78, 149n6
 Tom Brown's Schooldays, 9, 22, 58, 77, 78, 79–84, 102, 134, 135, 148n4, 149nn5–6, 150n8
 Dr. Arnold, 83, 149n7
 Job Rudkin, 81, 149n6
 Old Benjy, 80, 81, 149n6
 Diggs "the Mucker," 22, 82
 George Arthur, 22, 77, 80, 83, 123, 125, 131, 135, 150n8
 Jacob Dodson, 22, 80, 81
 Harry Winburn, 81, 149n6
 Madman Martin, 22, 82
 Tom Brown, 22, 58, 59, 77, 78, 79–84, 123, 125, 131, 134, 135, 138n3, 148n4, 149nn5–6, 150n8

Hutton, R. H., 70, 104, 154n16
Huysmans, J. K.
  A Rebours, 23

invalid-observer, 23–24, 104
Irving, John
  A Prayer for Owen Meany, 24, 125, 133–34, 135, 156n9

Jacobson, Marcia, 152n4
Jacobus, Mary, 77
Jaffe, Audrey
  Scenes of Sympathy, 98
James, Henry, 2, 75, 102, 124, 125, 147n17, 152n4, 153nn5–6, 154n15
  British women's fiction, 105–7
  The Portrait of a Lady, 103–22
    American self-made men abroad, 107–14
    Caspar Goodwood, 8, 23, 92, 103, 104, 107, 108, 111–14, 117, 119, 120–22, 123, 153n8, 153n10
    Daniel Touchett, 107–9, 153nn7–8
    Gilbert Osmond, 103, 104, 106, 116, 117, 118, 119, 122, 151n1, 152n4, 153n8, 154n16
    Henrietta Stackpole, 23, 108, 119, 120, 124
    Isabel Archer, 104, 110, 111, 113–16, 117, 118, 119, 120–22, 151n1, 154n14, 154n16
    invalid aesthetes, 117–19
    Lord Warburton, 8, 108, 109–11, 115, 121, 153nn8–9
    Madame, Merle, 116, 117, 153n8
    Mrs. Touchett, 120
    Ned Rosier, 103, 109, 117, 118
    pains and pleasures of observation, 114–17
    Ralph Touchett, 15, 23, 103, 104, 106, 107–11, 114, 115–123, 124, 140n13, 151n1, 152n2, 153n12, 154nn13–14, 154n16
    strong woman, 119–22
  The Watch and the Ward, 106, 152n4
Jay, Elisabeth, 40
Juckett, Elizabeth C., 142n8

Keble, Charlotte, 39
Keble, John, 39
  The Christian Year, 35
Keep, Christopher, 16
Kingsley, Charles, 2, 20, 27, 31, 32, 33, 52, 53, 58, 67, 105, 110, 123, 126, 141n3, 142n7, 145n5, 155n1
  moral suffering, 84
  obituary, 105
  public speaking, 144n20
  reading and disability, 37
  self-made man, 90
  stuttering muscular Christians 46–51
  Two Years Ago, 28
    Elsley Vavasour, 21, 28, 30, 41, 47, 48–50, 51
    Frank Headley, 30, 41, 42–3, 138n3
    Grace Harvey, 29, 41
    John Briggs, 48
    Marie Lavington, 144n18
    Tom Thurnall, 8, 28, 30, 40, 41, 42, 43, 47, 48, 49, 50, 79, 84, 110, 138n3, 155n1
  Westward Ho!, 1, 20, 26, 29, 40–51, 143n15
    dedication, 140n1
    Amyas Leigh, 22, 30, 40, 41, 43–46, 47, 50, 52, 144n19
    Frank Leigh, 9, 30, 41, 44, 47, 49, 50, 138n3, 143n17
Klages, Mary, 67
Kucich, John, 28

Lawrence, G. A., 22, 29, 155n1
  Guy Livingstone, 26, 47, 130–31, 138n3, 148n4
    Frank Hammond, 138n3, 148n4
    Guy Livingstone, 22, 138n3, 148n4
Levine, George, 151n14
Lewes, George Henry, 78, 150n10
Lewis, Dio
  The New Gymnastics for Men, Women, and Children, 112
Little, William John, 4–5, 12, 14, 130, 139n11
Loretto School, 78 Luciano, Dana, 107, 114
Lund, Roger, 10

Machann, Clinton, 19
Mackenzie, Henry, 138n6
Mangan, J. A., 12, 78–79
Manners, John, 141n2
Markovits, Stefanie, 143n15
Mascarenhas, Kiran, 146n8
Massey, Gerald, 144n22
  "Poetry—the Spasmodists," 144n21
Maugham, Somerset, 24, 134, 155n6
  Of Human Bondage, 124, 127–28, 130–33, 138n3
  Harry Griffiths, 155n6
  Mildred Rogers, 132, 155n6
  Philip Carey, 25, 130–33, 138n3, 155n6
  Rose, 131–32
  Sally Athelny, 132–33
McCarthy, Justin
  Paul Massie, 1
McRuer, Robert, 53
Mitchell, David, 15, 18
Mitchell, Sally, 146n12
Morris, William, 29, 141n2
Mossman, Mark
  Disability, Representation, and the Body in Irish Writing, 1800–1922, 139n12
muscular Christianity, 20, 22, 27, 28, 30, 125

names of men, 8
Nelson, Claudia, 80
Newman, John Henry, 26

Oldstone-Moore, Christopher, 139n8
Oliphant, Margaret, 2
Oppenheim, Janet, 11

Paxton, Nancy L. 150n11
Pearsall, Cornelia D. J., 141n6
Philbrick, Rodman
  Freak the Mighty, 133, 134–35, 156n8
physical hygiene and fitness, 139n9
Poovey, Mary, 63
Porter, Carolyn
  Seeing and Being, 154n14
Pusey, Edward Bouverie, 33

Raleigh, Walter, 50
Richards, Jeffrey, 145n7

Rodas, Julia Miele, 140n16
Rossetti, Christina, 33
Rowling, J. K.
  Harry Potter series, 156n7
Royal Orthopaedic Hospital of London, 4
Ruskin, John, 102

Sanders, Mike, 138n7
Schaffer, Talia, 143nn13–14
Scott, Walter, 2, 6, 95
Sedgwick, Eve Kosofsky, 12–13, 53, 89
Sedgwickian rivalry, 77, 88
Selwyn, George Augustus, 140n1
shortsighted eyes, 151n15
Showalter, Elaine, 76, 146n12, 151n14
silence, 23, 46, 47, 50, 55, 56, 57, 61, 62, 64, 94, 110, 114, 129
Silverman, Kaja, 30, 143n16
Smedley, Frank, 147n17
Smiles, Samuel, 65–66, 94
  Self-Help, 146n10
Snyder, Katherine, 114, 145n2, 146n13
Snyder, Sharon, 15, 18, 114
Spenser, Edmund, 49, 50
Stephen, James Fitzjames, 47–48
Sterne, Laurence, 138n6
Stevenson, Robert Louis, 28
  The Strange Case of Dr. Jekyll and Mr. Hyde, 126
Stoddard Holmes, Martha
  Fictions of Affliction, 3–4, 15, 16, 17, 19, 139n12
strong man, 6–14, 17, 18, 19, 23, 47, 89, 104, 106, 119, 120, 130, 15n6; anti-, 55; become weak, 108; consciousness, 20; homoerotic friendship, 52, 64, 101; conventional, 109; moral progress, 44; muscular upper body, 58; normalcy, 126; pairing with weak man, 3, 20, 21, 24, 28, 40, 41, 42, 51, 52, 57, 75, 77, 88, 96, 97, 102, 103, 107, 109, 110–11, 121, 122, 123, 124–25, 127, 128, 129, 133, 134, 136, 143n13; pain in the moral development, 32; praising, 56; restraint, 24; self-mastery, 46; silent, 2; taciturn, 24, 54

Sturrock, June, 142n10
suffering, 4, 8, 12, 13, 29, 35, 38, 39, 55, 89, 136, 137n2, 143n16
  Christian, 43
  lingering, 37
  long, 135
  masculine, 20, 21, 23, 26–27, 28, 29, 30–32, 36, 43, 51, 97, 104, 142n10
  mental, 3, 5, 25
  moral, 46, 84
  for others, 26
  physical, 30, 33, 34, 45, 46, 50, 51, 54, 69, 142n8
  psychological, 6
  silent, 22
Sussman, Herbert, 11, 92
Sydney, Philip, 50

Tamplin, R. W.
  Lectures on the Nature and Treatment of Deformities, 4
Tegg, Thomas, 65, 94
Tennyson, Alfred, 29, 63–64, 140n17
  Enoch Arden, 13
  Idylls of the King, 18
  The Princess, 18
  Spasmodic, 144n21
  "St. Simeon Stylites," 18, 30–31
  "Tithonous" 18
  "Ulysses,"
theories of emotion and disability in literature and medicine, 3–6
Tosh, John, 28, 93–94, 148n1
Trollope, Anthony, 54
  Doctor Thorne, 71
Turner, David M., 10

Wagner, Tamara S., 125–26, 155n2
weak man: pairing with strong man, 3, 20, 21, 24, 28, 40, 41, 42, 51, 52, 57, 75, 77, 88, 96, 97, 102, 103, 107, 109, 110–11, 121, 122, 123, 124–25, 127, 128, 129, 133, 134, 136, 143n13
Wendell, Susan, 140n13
Whyte-Melville, G. J., 87
Wilde, Oscar
  The Picture of Dorian Grey, 126
Wizard of Oz, 135
Woloch, Alex, 18

Yonge, Charlotte, 1, 6, 28, 30, 31, 41, 43, 44, 46, 47, 50–52, 53, 67, 69, 84, 105, 123, 131, 141n2, 142n7
  Anglican Church, 142n8
  Chantry House, 74, 147n16
  characters find their duties and fulfill them, 142n9
  The Clever Woman of the Family, 38, 143n13
  The Heir of Redclyffe, 20–21, 27, 29, 32–40, 105, 140n1, 141n4
    Amy, 34, 35, 36, 39
    Charles Edmonstone, 21, 27, 29, 33–40, 46, 51, 53, 57, 69, 104, 107
    disability and authorship, 37–40
    domestic vision, 142n10
    Guy Morville, 26, 29, 33, 34–35, 36, 37, 38–39, 41, 44, 52, 138n3, 141n2, 142n10
    Laura Edmonstone, 38–39
    Mrs. Edmonstone, 36, 37, 39
    Philip Morville, 29, 34, 35–36, 37, 38–39, 40
    third-person narrator is not omniscient, 142n9
  History of Christian Names, 8
  letters, 143n12
  Oxford movement, 142n9
  raise dissidence to tame it, 143n14
Yonge, Julian, 39, 141n4

Zwerdling, Alex, 153n8